T0121155

Praise for

Joker One

"The arrangement known as 'embedding'—the almost complete immersion in the movements and life of a military unit . . . is seldom available to nonjournalists. But [*Joker One*] is its literary equivalent. . . . [This story] is a cross between the Battle of Agincourt as seen from the French side and the opening scenes of *Saving Private Ryan*, with no one to save."
—James Glanz, *The New York Times Book Review*

"[A] beautiful and harrowing debut . . . Campbell unspools blow-by-blow accounts of his unit's patrols from street level. The fuzzy radio transmissions, the roadside bombs laid by faceless enemies, the dust-filled, hand-trembling confusion —it all comes dizzyingly alive. . . . By the time the platoon finally returns home, exhausted, scarred, and with fewer men than they set out with, Campbell's admiration for his men has become contagious. It's only then that you realize that *Joker One* isn't as much a story of war as it is a story of love. [Grade:] A"
—*Entertainment Weekly*

"An extraordinary book . . . [*Joker One* is] a moving narrative that brings a complicated and often messy war down to an extraordinarily personal level."
—*The Boston Globe*

"[Campbell] recounts his unit's seven-and-a-half-month tour in powerful, exacting detail . . . [and] he tells it all with lyrical grace. . . . The swiftest current through Campbell's book is the love these Marines shared for one another."   — *The Dallas Morning News*

"Nobody but a soldier knows what war is really like, but the next best thing may be reading Donovan Campbell's *Joker One*."
                                                    — *Fort Worth Star-Telegram*

"Donovan Campbell, first as a Marine and then as a writer, shows us that the dominant emotion in war isn't hatred or anger or fear. It's love. His story stands as a poignant tribute to his men — their courage, their dedication, their skill, and their love for one another, even unto death. This is a deeply moving book."   — NATHANIEL FICK, author of *One Bullet Away*

"*Joker One* is the real goods, the classic military story: one platoon leader, the men of his platoon, and the impossibility and urgency of the assignment. The book will sharply take its place in ranks beside *Blackhawk Down* and *Jarhead*. If you want to know what American fighting will look like in this century, you need to read Campbell. Like the best stories, military and nonmilitary, it's a story about love, community, and a brotherhood."
  — DAVID LIPSKY, author of *Absolutely American: Four Years at West Point*

"*Joker One* is the finest small-unit description of a platoon at war in Iraq. Hang on and cheer them on."
                                    — BING WEST, author of *The Strongest Tribe*

"Donovan Campbell was a platoon commander in the 2nd Battalion, 4th Marine Regiment in Al Anbar in 2004 — the unit that had my flank. In *Joker One*, he tells the story of that hard fight from the ground level better than I thought possible. This is what it is like to lead men in battle. Read this book if you are going to war, or if you have gone to war, or if you want to know what war is."
                    — LIEUTENANT COLONEL JOHN A. NAGL (ret.), "Centurion 3,"
                                    author of *Learning to Eat Soup with a Knife*

Donovan Campbell

JOKER ONE

A MARINE PLATOON'S STORY OF
COURAGE, LEADERSHIP, AND BROTHERHOOD

RANDOM HOUSE TRADE PAPERBACKS

NEW YORK

2010 Random House Trade Paperback Edition

Published in the United States by Random House Trade Paperbacks, an imprint of The Random House Publishing Group, a division of Random House, Inc., New York.

RANDOM HOUSE TRADE PAPERBACKS and colophon are trademarks of Random House, Inc.

Originally published in hardcover in slightly different form in the United States by Random House, an imprint of The Random House Publishing Group, a division of Random House, Inc., in 2009.

LIBRARY OF CONGRESS CATALOGING-IN-PUBLICATION DATA
Campbell, Donovan.
  Joker One: a Marine platoon's story of courage, leadership, and brotherhood / Donovan Campbell.
    p.   cm.
  ISBN 978-0-8129-7956-5
  eBook ISBN 978-1-58836-778-5
  1. Iraq War, 2003—Campaigns—Iraq—Ramadi. 2. Iraq War, 2003—Personal narratives, American. 3. Campbell, Donovan. I. Title.
  DS79.76.C355 2009   956.7044'345—dc22   2008023896

www.atrandom.com

Book design by Casey Hampton

147028622

This book is dedicated to the men of Joker One and to the parents, spouses, and fiancées of the fighters overseas. Those who wait at home have the hardest job in the military.

*Then the Lord answered Job out of the whirlwind,
and said: "Who is this who darkens counsel by
words without knowledge? Now brace yourself like
a man; I will question you, and you shall answer
me. Where were you when I laid the foundations
of the earth?"*

—JOB 38:1–4

*And now abide faith, hope, love, these three; but
the greatest of these is love.*

—1 CORINTHIANS 13:13

MAIN CHARACTERS

Sergeant Mariano Noriel—Joker One's first-squad leader, a twenty-five-year-old Filipino immigrant with a feisty personality and can-do attitude. The unofficial second-in-command of the platoon.

Sergeant Danny Leza—Joker One's second-squad leader, a twenty-three-year-old Latino fluent in both English and Spanish. A quiet intellectual and one of Joker One's ablest tacticians.

Corporal Chris Bowen—Joker One's third-squad leader, a twenty-year-old New Hampshire native and one of the best all-around Marines in the platoon. Three years younger than his squad leader peers because of numerous merit-based promotions.

Corporal Brian Teague—Joker One's first fire team leader, first squad, a twenty-one-year-old native of the backwoods of Tennessee. The platoon's best shot and one of its most skilled Marines.

Lance Corporal William Feldmeir—Member, first fire team, first squad, a twenty-year-old refugee from a series of foster homes. A narcoleptic whom Teague constantly supervised.

Lance Corporal Todd Bolding—Member, second fire team, first squad. The twenty-three-year-old leader of Joker One's mortar team, and the only African American in the platoon. Nicknamed "Black Man."

Lance Corporal Joe Mahardy—Radio operator, first squad. Twenty-year-old Mahardy had achieved academic honors at Syracuse University. Intelligent, tough, and talkative in equal measures.

Private First Class Gabriel Henderson—Member, second fire team, first squad. Nineteen-year-old Henderson persevered through unexplained chest pains early on to become one of the most cheerful, well-loved members of the platoon. Nicknamed "Hendersizzle."

Lance Corporal Nick Carson—Third fire team leader, second squad. The biggest Marine in the platoon at six foot three and well over two hundred pounds. Twenty years old, he was strong, unselfish, and inhumanly tough.

Private Josh Guzon—Member, second fire team, second squad. The shortest, stockiest Marine in the platoon at five foot four and one hundred and sixty pounds. Nicknamed "Gooch."

Private First Class Ramses Yebra—Radio operator, second squad. Twenty years old and the fastest Marine in the platoon, running three miles in under sixteen minutes. Tough, calm, and quiet, he was saddled with the radio shortly after joining Joker One.

Gunnery Sergeant Winston Jaugan—Company gunnery sergeant, Golf Company. Known simply as "The Gunny" and responsible for the 180-man company's logistics and training. A forty-something Filipino immigrant, the Gunny was the heart and soul of Golf Company.

Captain Chris Bronzi—Commanding officer, Golf Company. Called "the CO" for short, the thirty-something Bronzi was responsible for everything Golf Company did or failed to do. The 2004 deployment to Ramadi was his first combat deployment.

The Ox—Executive officer, Golf Company. The CO's right-hand man. Worked with the Gunny on Golf Company's training and logistics issues. With twenty-two months commanding an infantry platoon, the twenty-five-year-old Ox was the most experienced lieutenant in the company.

Staff Sergeant—Platoon sergeant, first platoon, Golf Company. Joker One's formal second-in-command, the twenty-nine-year-old Staff Sergeant theoretically worked hand in hand with the platoon commander to take care of the Joker One Marines.

This list of characters features some of the main personalities from my platoon's time in Ramadi, Iraq, throughout the spring and summer of 2004. Written from my limited perspective as a Marine lieutenant and a platoon commander, this book can pay only small tribute to so many, named and unnamed, who acted heroically overseas. During the writing, I consulted my patrol logs, my men, and my memory to help tell our story as accurately as possible. Any mistakes that have been made are unintentional and the inevitable by-products of the all-pervasive fog of war.

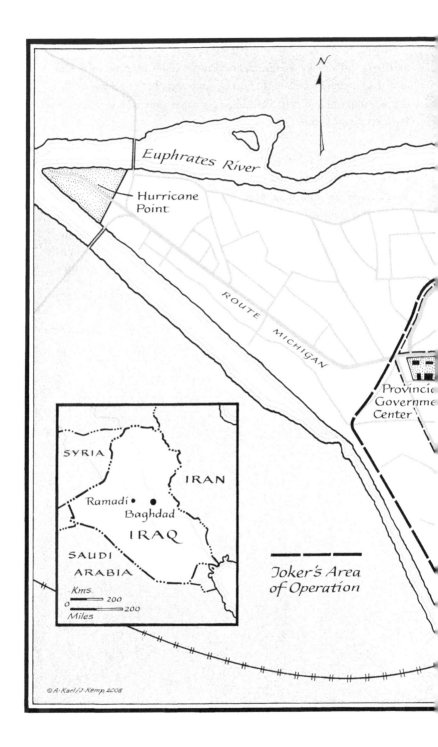

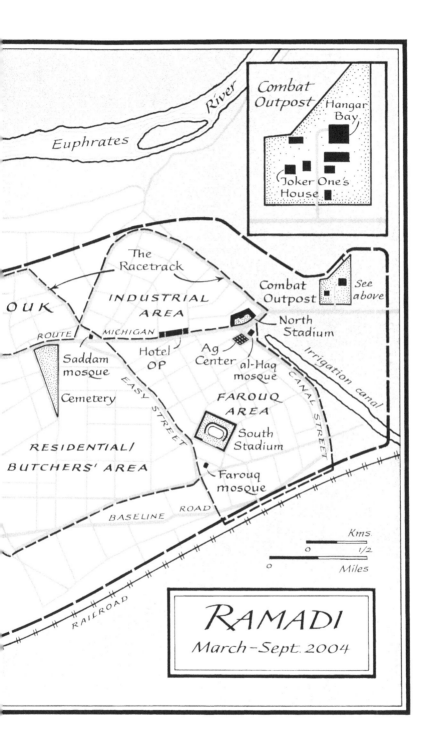

Combat
Outpost

Hangar
Bay

Joker One's
House

River

Euphrates

The
Racetrack

INDUSTRIAL
AREA

Combat
Outpost

See
above

OUK

ROUTE   MICHIGAN

North
Stadium

Saddam
mosque

Hotel
OP

Ag
Center

al-Haq
mosque

Irrigation canal

Cemetery

EASY STREET

FAROUQ
AREA

CANAL STREET

RESIDENTIAL/

South
Stadium

BUTCHERS' AREA

Farouq
mosque

BASELINE   ROAD

Kms.

0   1/2

0

Miles

RAILROAD

RAMADI

March–Sept. 2004

Part 1

EAGER

ONE

found myself fascinated by the interesting geometric designs of the twisted iron rebar in front of me. For a time, my eyes traced each of the dark, thumb-thick strands where they spewed out of the cinder-block walls like the frozen tentacles of some monster from the myths of antiquity. I have no idea how long I spent engrossed in contemplation, because time in and around firefights is somewhat fluid, but eventually I tore myself away from profound admiration of the destruction in front of my eyes. It was difficult, this return to a reality that sometimes seemed more like a myth — or maybe a nightmare — but it was necessary, because the problem immediately at hand was all too real. If I ignored it for too long, I might get everyone around me killed.

So I stepped back from the abandoned building's wall and surveyed the floor around me. Somewhere in the various piles of newly created rubble scattered about the floor were pieces of the rockets that had just ripped through two feet of cinder block to explode inside my observation post (OP). I needed to find at least one of these pieces, preferably the base of the warhead, because this was the first time that my unit had been hit by rockets capable of doing this much damage. If I could find a piece, then we could figure out what kind of rockets these were, estimate what it would take to launch them, and predict how they would be used in the future. We could then effectively plan to thwart them and potentially save several lives, which was important to me because my job description was twofold: 1) save lives and 2) take lives. Not necessarily in that order.

With these considerations in mind, I sifted diligently through the rubble until I found what I was looking for: a smooth black object, just a little larger than a hockey puck, with a half dozen or so holes drilled through it. Though the little puck looked fairly innocuous, I knew from hard-won experience that it was actually a thing of great pain; it was the base of one of the rockets that had just struck us. Without stopping to think, I grabbed the thick circular object as firmly as I could, shrieked manfully, and then dropped it as quickly as I could. Even ten minutes after its firing, this part of the explosive warhead was still hot enough to sear my palm. Important safety lesson: When picking up a newly fired enemy rocket warhead base, allow proper time for cooling *or* handle it with gloves. I filed that one away with other lessons learned the hard way, right after "RPGs (rocket propelled grenades) that you need to worry about always make two booms" and "No one here is your friend." We now lived in a bizarre world where explosions were so commonplace that we had ways of distinguishing the more from the less harmful and where little tips and tricks about proper expended rocket handling made perfect sense to collate, absorb, and pass on. The absurd had become our baseline.

Ten minutes ago, though, the world was very simple, for it consisted solely of something that seemed like one gigantic explosion. Actually, it was three separate large explosions within half seconds of one another, but it's fairly difficult to make the distinction when you're lying on your back with your ears ringing. However, it's fairly easy to think rapidly and incoherently, which was exactly what I was doing as I lay on my back, wondering whether my hearing would return this time, and, incidentally, what in the hell had just happened to me and my men.

Time, I already knew, would answer the former question without any help from me, but as the lieutenant and the unit leader, it was my job to answer the latter one, and time in this case was working against me. If you're a

Marine lieutenant in a firefight, a situation that's probably as good a proxy as any for hell, then it's your job to figure out at least 50 to 70 percent of what is going on around you so that you can make intelligent decisions, which translate into good orders, which lead to focused, effective, and decisive action. This whole process needs to be rapid to be relevant, but if you're too hasty, then you can lead your men to their deaths, all the while believing that you're leading them to safety. It's not an easy tension to manage on an ongoing basis.

However, it can be done, and to do it well you must have absolutely no concern for your own safety. You can't think of home, you can't miss your wife, and you can't wonder how it would feel to take a round through the neck. You can only pretend that you're already dead and thus free yourself up to focus on three things: 1) finding and killing the enemy, 2) communicating the situation and resulting actions to adjacent units and higher headquarters, and 3) triaging and treating your wounded. If you love your men, you naturally think about number three first, but if you do you're wrong. The grim logic of combat dictates that numbers one and two take precedence.

After the explosions, I rose, ears still ringing, and grabbed for the radio handset. Once the black handset was pressed firmly against my ear, I pushed the button with my thumb and, as calmly as I could manage, informed headquarters that my eleven men and I had just been hit by several large rockets. There were probably multiple casualties, I said, and maybe some of us were dead, but I didn't know just yet. I'd call back. Headquarters squawked something in return, but, with my hearing still questionable and one of our machine guns firing full bore inside the all-concrete building, I couldn't understand a word, so I told HQ I'd be back in touch when I could hear again. Then I put the handset down and resolutely ignored it until I could sort out what was going on inside the old abandoned hotel that my eleven-man squad and I were using as an observation position.

After five minutes of running helter-skelter through the thick dust that the rockets had kicked up, I found Sergeant Leza, my squad leader, and we conferred. Slowly the pieces of the attack came together to form a coherent picture: The massive explosion, which we assumed to be the rockets, had kicked off the insurgent assault. Seconds after their impact, one enemy from our southwest had fired an RPG at us but had missed, probably because one of my men had shot the insurgent as he took aim.

Simultaneously, several enemies off our southeast flank had sprayed the building with AK-47 fire, and the two Marines covering that sector had returned fire with their M-16s. They were unable to tell whether they had killed anyone. We had also taken some fire from our direct north and south, and the Marines in those positions, including my medium machine gunner, had reciprocated in spades. They, too, were unable to tell whether their return fire had had any effect. For the most part it was all pretty routine, with only two small deviations.

First off, directly across the street from our hotel, a car blazed furiously in an alleyway. I had seen burning cars before, but they were usually the result of either nearby bomb detonations or steady machine gun fire during particularly fierce combat. I had yet to see a burning car accompanied by a simultaneous rocket attack. I pushed the incongruity aside—the more important question was how the enemy had managed to attack us with such powerful rockets, which were almost certainly antitank weapons and definitely not man-portable. Ten minutes later, my first squad, patrolling in from the north, called in with an answer: The backseat of the burning car bore the clear remains of a homemade-rocket launcher, still smoldering inside. Our attackers had simply parked the vehicle in an inconspicuous place next to the gates of a house, hoping that we would lose track of the nondescript vehicle amid the hustle and bustle of the thriving marketplace area below us. When the rest of the assault was ready, a spotter within the crowd had launched the rockets with a cellphone call.

The second small plot twist, however, was that no United States Marines were wounded or killed in this story, a very unusual thing for a Ramadi day in August 2004. In spite of their clever plan and their disciplined execution, our enemies had failed—we hadn't stopped our mission for even a second. Indeed, we had probably winged at least one of our attackers, although it's sometimes difficult to tell because most people don't go down when you shoot them with our little .223 bullets. So on that day, I believed that God had been watching over us. Up to that point, even with the horrors I had witnessed, I retained my faith, if only barely. Every time events made me ready to throw in the towel, a small miracle happened—like antitank rockets missing our floor — or I saw something supernaturally beautiful in the actions of one of my Marines, and for one more day, it was enough to keep faith and hope alive.

Now, nearly three years after that August day, those Marines and I have long since parted ways. Our time together in Iraq seems like someone else's story, for there's nothing in America even remotely similar to what we experienced overseas, nothing that reminds us of what we suffered and achieved together. And none of us have really been able to tell that story, not fully, not even to our families, because each small telling takes a personal toll. No one wants to suffer the pain of trying to explain the unexplainable to those who rarely have either the time or the desire to comprehend. So, many of us have simply packed our war away and tried hard to fit into normalcy by ignoring that time in our lives.

But our story is an important one, and I believe that it's worth telling truthfully and completely no matter what the cost. For seven and a half months, from March to September 2004, my company of 120 Marines battled day in and day out against thousands of enemy fighters in a city that eventually earned the title of Iraq's most dangerous place, a city called Ramadi. Our story has been largely overshadowed by the two battles of Fallujah that bookended our deployment, battles in which the U.S. Marine Corps (USMC) brought the full weight of its combat power — jets, tanks, artillery, and so on — to bear on a city populated almost entirely by insurgent fighters. Fallujah I and II have probably been the closest thing to conventional fighting since Baghdad fell, and they're a gripping story: intense, house-to-house combat between clearly defined foes — the Marines on one side, the jihadists on the other — with a negligible civilian population muddying the battlefield.

We, by contrast, fought a much blurrier battle, a classic urban counterinsurgency, a never-ending series of engagements throughout the heart of a teeming city where our faceless enemies blended seamlessly into a surrounding populace of nearly 350,000 civilians. These civilians severely limited the assets we could bring to the fight, negating entirely the artillery and air power that American forces invariably rely upon to win pitched battles.

Thus my men and I usually fought on foot, street by street and house by house, using only what we could carry on our backs. Outnumbered and out-gunned in nearly every battle, we walked the streets of Ramadi endlessly, waiting, tensely, for another enemy ambush to kick off. For us there was no end to the mission, no respite from the daily violence—for seven straight months we patrolled without ever having a single day off.

Indeed, we never experienced anything even remotely resembling a nor-mal day, and as I searched my memory and my diary for one to bring the reader into our world, the brief August rocket attack was the best I could come up with—nothing too terrible, just a standard day with a few little twists that made it slightly memorable.

During our entire deployment, I prayed for something other than this standard day, for a respite from the unrelenting pace of combat, but a break never came. Instead, we fought and fought and fought until, on our return, one out of every two of us had been wounded—a casualty rate that, we were told, exceeded that of any other Marine or Army combat unit since Viet-nam.

However, our perseverance and our sacrifices paid off. Despite the de-termined attacks of the insurgents, Ramadi never fell entirely into their hands as had its sister city Fallujah, and we retained control of the key thor-oughfares and all the institutions of government until we were relieved by other Marines. Three weeks thereafter, Central Command doubled the U.S. forces in Ramadi, then tripled them. In early 2005, the Marine Corps formally honored our efforts by giving the Leftwich award to my company commander (CO), Captain Chris Bronzi. With this award, the USMC offi-cially stated that it considered Captain Bronzi its best combat company commander (and our company as its best combat company) for all of 2004, a year that included both Fallujah invasions.

Throughout all the fighting, I led a forty-man infantry platoon—one-quarter of our company—under the CO's command. Day after unrelenting day bound our platoon tightly together, eventually creating a whole much greater than the sum of its parts, and we grew to love one another fiercely. I knew these men better than my best friends; better, in some ways, than my wife. For what they did and what they suffered, my men deserve to have their story told.

But it's so hard to tell the truth, because the telling means dragging up painful memories, opening doors that you thought you had closed, and re-visiting a past you hoped you had put behind you. However, I think that someone needs to do it, and I was the leader, so the responsibility falls to me.

I was neither born into the military nor bred for it—aside from a two-year stint my grandfather did as an Air Force doctor, no one in my family had ever served in the armed forces. Indeed, the thought of joining the service never really occurred to me until my junior year at college, when I decided that the Marine Corps Officer Candidate School (OCS), the ten-week se-lection process that qualifies university students for an officer's commission, would look good on my résumé.

With this less-than-altruistic motivation to spur me on, I headed down to Quantico, Virginia, to take in the ten weeks of uninterrupted screaming that constitutes OCS. Unsurprisingly, I hated the experience, and on the day I completed the course, I swore internally never, ever to join the Marine Corps. I hadn't done ROTC, and I hadn't accepted a dime from any of the services to help pay for college, so I didn't owe the military a thing. I in-tended for it to stay that way.

Over the course of my senior year, though, something shifted. Some-how, the Fortune 500 recruiters and the postgraduation salaries lost their luster, and, somewhat to my surprise, I soon found myself casting about for a pursuit that would force me to assume responsibility for something greater than myself, something that would force me to give back, to serve others. Try as I might to avoid them, I kept coming back to the United States Marines. I knew from OCS that if I could make it to the Marine infantry, then I could be a platoon commander and have forty men whose lives would be entirely my responsibility. I also knew that in the infantry I'd be in a place where I could no longer hide behind potential, a place where past academic achievements and family connections were irrelevant, a place where people demanded daily excellence in action because lives hung in the balance. As my final semester of school wound down, I thought of the words one of my sergeant instructors had screamed at me over the summer: "Candidate, the currency in which we trade is human lives. Do you think you can handle that responsibility?"

I didn't know if I could, but I did know that I wanted to try, and I knew that I wanted to learn to lead, which, I soon discovered, simply meant serving others to an increasingly great degree. Surprising everyone in my family (my mother called me crazy), I joined the Corps after graduation, and I foundered at first in the training, but eventually I righted and eventually I got my wish—I made it to an infantry platoon.

So, that's me: an ordinary young man who once made the choice to serve. I wish I could present someone greater to the reader, someone whose exploits and whose fame could automatically make people sit up and pay attention to the story of my men, but I can't, because I'm not that someone. However, to this day I love my Marines with all that I'm capable of, and in spite of my shortcomings I want to do my utmost to help tell their tale. Though I can't offer myself to the reader, I can offer my men, and I can tell a true story with love and heartfelt emotion from the inside out. And I hope and I pray that whoever reads this story will know my men as I do, and that knowing them, they too might come to love them.

TWO

fter joining the Corps, the road to my platoon was anything other than smooth and short. In fact, it took a year and a half of intense training, one combat deployment, and some significant complaining on my part before I could get there. The complaining occurred mainly because I was promised one thing and given another. After toiling away on staff intelligence work in Iraq throughout the summer and fall of 2003, which essentially involved reading human source reports, writing the 1st Marine Division's daily intelligence summary, and briefing the division commander, General Jim Mattis, I returned to the United States with a promise that I would be given command of a scout-sniper platoon with the 2d Battalion, 4th Marine Regiment (spelled 2/4 and pronounced "Two-Four"). And I wanted that sniper platoon, in part because my training had sent me through a cut-down version of Marine sniper school and in part because I wanted to tell people that I commanded snipers. However, when I reported for duty to the battalion's executive officer ("XO") at Camp Pendleton, California, he cheerfully informed me that although 2/4 already had a sniper platoon commander, it just so happened to be in desperate need of an experienced intelligence officer.

The XO thought that I would fill the bill nicely. Aside from the brand-new battalion commander, Lieutenant Colonel Paul Kennedy, I was, at the time, the only Marine in 2/4 who had actually been to Iraq—the battalion had spent the entire 2003 invasion, and the whole last year, deployed to Okinawa. Furthermore, my time overseas had given me extensive real-world intelligence experience but zero real-world infantry experience, making me very valuable as a staff officer but possibly even worse than worthless as a line platoon commander.

This news came as a crushing disappointment, and it even managed to sap some of the joy out of my reunion with my wife, Christy. I had left Camp Pendleton for my first deployment to Iraq three days before our one-year wedding anniversary, and the four months of deployment that followed had given me a vivid reminder of how much I needed and depended on my wife. It's strange how so often we don't truly appreciate our blessings until they're taken from us. It's equally strange how quickly we adapt back to a new normal and lapse into our old assumptions and our old foibles. Throughout the second week following my return (I took only four days off after my arrival in the States, so eager was I to get down to an actual infantry battalion), I stewed about my new assignment, focusing on the disappointment of unmet expectations to the exclusion of the reunion with my better half.

I hadn't joined the Marines to make PowerPoint presentations and to debrief those who had just come back to the base from patrols. I had joined the Corps to lead those patrols, to take care of my men, to test and stretch myself in every way possible. Even though four months spent working fourteen-hour, seven-days-a-week shifts, hot, sweaty, dirty in the desert had sucked most of the glamour out of war and all of the exotic appeal out of Iraq, I still wanted to at least put myself in a position to lead Marines on the ground. The prospects of a USMC return to Iraq seemed fairly remote in October 2003—after all, major combat operations had been declared over, and the insurgency was still simmering out of sight—but, if by some miracle it did occur, then I wanted to be on the front lines with my men, not in an air-conditioned headquarters building safely removed from the action.

So I did one of the only things that an officer can do when given a set of orders that he or she doesn't want to execute: I complained (some might say whined) mightily and incessantly to my superiors. After about two weeks of moaning, and at about the same time that a higher-ranking, more experienced intelligence officer joined 2/4, Colonel Kennedy took pity on me and assigned me to infantry company G, known simply as Golf Company. I wouldn't get the promised sniper platoon, he told me. In his opinion, I would get something far better—a basic, straight-leg infantry platoon. "If it's leadership you want," Colonel Kennedy told me, "then there's nothing better than taking a bolt-plate, nineteen-year-old lance corporal straight out of school and making him the best young man, and the best Marine, he can possibly be." At the time I was a bit disappointed; "infantry" didn't sound as sexy and elite as did "scout-sniper." In retrospect, though, Colonel Kennedy was absolutely right, and not getting my first choice of platoons was one of the best things that ever happened to me.

On October 15, I checked into the Golf Company office, a tiny room on one end of the red-roofed, whitewashed cinder-block building that was the battalion's headquarters. In typical military fashion, four desks were crammed inside the office. Only two were occupied. Sitting at one was the company clerk, a young enlisted Marine named Corporal Mangio, who signed my check-in sheet and then turned back to his computer. Not really knowing what else to do, I took a seat at one of the unoccupied desks and thought about what I should do during my first day on the job.

I didn't have any grandiose ambitions, nor did I really expect to accomplish all that much. During my training, my infantry instructors had gone to great lengths to tell me all kinds of things that eager, insecure lieutenants had tried to do on day one with their new platoons to establish power and authority, from assembling all their Marines and then running them until they puked to telling recent returnees from the Persian Gulf War, "It's not like you just got back from the fucking island-hopping campaign. You've still got a lot of fucking training to do. Now let's get to it." Some lieutenants, chomping at the bit to make their mark, had even changed all of their platoon's way of doing things simply because the new leader hadn't thought of these things himself.

None of those hard entrances had worked out well for the young and the eager, so I decided that the first thing I would do was meet my noncommissioned officers (NCOs)—the sergeants and corporals with between three and six years of infantry experience apiece and whom, in spite of my relative lack of experience, I would lead. I didn't expect to make grand speeches and

I had no plans to immediately reinvent the wheel, but I did want to meet those who would form the backbone of my platoon, so I asked Mangio where I could find my platoon's squad and team leaders. Each infantry platoon comprises three thirteen-man squads usually led by a sergeant, and each squad comprises three four-man teams usually led by a corporal. Together these squad and team leaders form the leadership backbone of every infantry platoon, and I wanted to get to know mine right away. However, they weren't available because, according to the twenty-year-old Golf Company clerk teaching the new lieutenant the ropes, they were out doing their jobs somewhere on the base. I couldn't come up with anything else to do, so I found myself fidgeting nervously in the office for about half an hour, trying to look like I was doing something useful as I mulled over what I was going to say when I introduced myself to my team.

Sitting at my metal desk in that cramped company office, I was painfully aware of the fact that I had no idea what to do and no idea how to go about figuring it out. Suddenly I became aware that someone was staring at me. My evident cluelessness had caught the eye of someone I would come to know as the Ox, who at the time was sitting at the desk directly across from me, and he decided then and there to take me under his wing whether I liked it or not. As I sat staring at the ground, muttering to myself, the Ox rose, lumbered over, and proceeded to greet me in standard Marine fashion by shaking my hand as hard as he possibly could, and then asking if I wanted to go work out with him. As my digits were slowly crushed in the Ox's death grip, I took stock of the sturdy twenty-something lieutenant planted in front of me. He stood about five foot ten and must have weighed just over two hundred pounds, and given the way his chest and shoulders strained his camouflage blouse and the painful screaming in my knuckles, most of that bulk was muscle. A close-cropped sandy blond flattop sat spiked into crispy gel-laden perfection on the top of the Ox's round head, and a pair of sharp blue eyes bore into mine, insistently demanding an immediate answer to the crucial workout question. Slightly intimidated and growing desperate to extricate my now-nerveless fingers, I quickly agreed to the Ox's proposal.

Initially I was happy to have a comrade. For reasons unclear to me then, the Ox was the only other lieutenant present in Golf Company, which was strange, as there are normally five lieutenants in each infantry company. As the Ox clapped plate after plate onto the weight bar and then, later, cranked up the treadmill to six-minute miles, I realized that my initial assessment of his bulk had been correct—he was very fit, very strong, and very fast. Over the course of the morning, I found out why: The Ox had been a star football player at his small college, and for a few years before joining the Corps he had actually played semipro football in various leagues across America. After joining, he had spent nearly two years leading an infantry platoon for 2/4, and Captain Bronzi, the brand-new Golf Company CO, had just moved him out of that role and made him the company's weapons platoon commander.

Every Marine battalion is comprised of five companies: three infantry companies, also called "line" companies, one weapons company, which contains the battalion's heavy weapons—82mm mortars, .50-caliber machine guns, Mark 19 automatic grenade launchers—and one headquarters and service company, which contains the mechanics, the truck drivers, and the administrative and logistical personnel necessary to keep the battalion running smoothly. Occasionally the sniper platoon falls under weapons company, but more often it is its own stand-alone entity, and it reports directly to the battalion commander.

Each infantry company, in turn, comprises four platoons, usually three infantry platoons and one weapons platoon. The infantry platoons, around forty men apiece, are the company commander's units to maneuver against the enemy, and in order to remain foot-mobile, the Marines in them carry fairly light weapons—M-16 rifles, some with attached M-203 grenade launchers, M-249 squad automatic weapon (SAW) light machine guns, and, sometimes, little green baseball-shaped hand grenades. The weapons platoon contains the company's heavier (but still man-portable) weaponry—medium machine guns, 60mm mortars, and the shoulder-launched multipurpose assualt weapon (SMAW) rocket launchers—and the crews trained to use them. Usually, the most experienced lieutenant in an infantry company commands the weapons platoon, so, even though he hadn't deployed to a combat zone yet, I figured that the Ox would have a lot of good platoon commander advice to give me. I was glad he had taken me under his wing.

As the day drew to a close, though, I started reconsidering that feeling. After our workout, the Ox and I spent the rest of the afternoon together, and during that time, he had somehow managed to tell me his entire life story from about twelve years old on—how he had grown up working in his father's steel company, how he had met and married his wife, and, most recently, how miserable his year with 2/4 Okinawa had been. Apparently, while he was there all the other platoon commanders had stopped inviting the Ox to their social functions because, according to the Ox, his impeccably upright and virtuous behavior had put a damper on his fellow officers' well-thought-out plans for riotous fornication. The Ox further claimed that, fortunately for him, the enlisted Marines were his good friends, so he had spent his free time hanging out with them instead of with his fellow officers. But since there were only twenty-four enlisted men in his platoon (not the standard forty-two—the Ox informed me that his Marines had kept inexplicably getting hurt shortly before their deployment), and because they had been stuck on an island together, even the Marines had gotten pretty old for him. I was brand-new to the whole platoon commander thing, but something about the Ox's description of his deployment didn't ring true. As the day started winding down, and the Ox continued to talk at full speed, with no signs of slowing, I began to appreciate what it must have been like to be stuck on an island with this man.

Just as I was beginning to wonder whether I would ever have the chance to meet my NCOs, a young Marine strode into the office. Physically nondescript, he seemed an average, five-foot-ten, one-hundred-and-sixty pound, early-twenties kid. The new arrival looked around the small room until his eyes settled on the camouflage name tape over my right breast pocket. Locking on, he marched over, squared himself off in front of me, struck the position of attention, and announced crisply:

"Corporal Bowen reporting as ordered, sir."

Somewhat startled, I gave the Marine a more careful once-over and immediately upgraded my impression. Even in his cammies, Bowen suddenly looked like he could have stepped out of a recruiting poster. With neat creases in his pants and blouse, black hair shaved up high on the sides of his head, a ramrod-straight body, and a fixed, unwavering stare, this young man was the picture of a squared-away NCO. Perhaps equally important, Bowen's forceful entry had managed to get the Ox to stop talking, which even then I recognized as a moderately heroic feat. Whether he meant to or not, Bowen had just started what would soon become a regular practice—recognizing when his lieutenant was in a jam and then taking whatever action was necessary to extricate him.

In fact, I was so impressed and grateful that I just sort of stared at Bowen for about a minute or so, wondering why he wasn't speaking to me. Then I realized that I had completely forgotten to release him from the position of attention (Marines generally don't talk when locked rigidly into this position). The Ox cleared his throat.

"At ease, Corporal. What can I do for you?" I said.

When put at ease, most people relax into a natural standing posture. The hands unclench and move away from the sides. The feet spread or start shuffling around. The spine slackens. Not so with Bowen. His only concessions to "at ease" were moving his hands to take notes, moving his mouth to speak, and maybe moving his feet two to three inches apart from each other. Aside from that, nothing changed.

"Sir, I hear that you're my new platoon commander. Since the platoon sergeant's out right now, I just wanted to introduce myself. I'm your third-squad leader. Now, I also wanted to let you know what the platoon did today and what the schedule is for tomorrow. We need your input on a few things, sir."

This terse introduction finished, Bowen had begun succinctly listing the day's training highlights when the Ox interrupted.

"Corporal Bowen, I hear that you're the Marine who's running the remedial PT session today." (Remedial PT, physical training, is extra exercise that is assigned to all Marines deemed too out of shape or too fat by their command. Each remedial session is supervised by an NCO and takes place after the regular training day has ended.)

"Yes, sir. That's correct, sir."

"You know, of course, that the PT is supposed to be difficult, right, Corporal?"

"Yes, sir. I've got a pretty good program today. We're going to—"

"We'll see," the Ox said, smiling. "I want you to make the Marines exercise aerobically in addition to just lifting weights. So many of you guys think that remedial PT is just a chance to get another lift in and sculpt your beach muscles."

"Yes, sir. I'm actually planning—"

"Why do you think that the Marines need aerobic exercise, Corporal?"

And so it went for about five minutes, with the Ox smiling broadly and asking, with the calmly reasonable tone of voice of the know-it-all, a series of demeaning questions, all of which seemed designed to reinforce that he, the Ox, knew all things workout-related. Unfazed, Bowen responded to every question as if it were the most serious in the world, worthy of a well-thought-out, dignified reply. Not even his body language changed—he looked as engaged and attentive during this strange Socratic session as he did while re-counting the day's training highlights. It was an impressive display of professional bearing and dignity. I had expected to find professional, poised, and knowledgeable officers supervising young Marines in need of a bit of guidance. Instead, I had found exactly the opposite.

THREE

nother week passed, and I still hadn't met most of my men. The time-consuming check-in process (draw gear from this person, update your medical records with that one, get sized for a gas mask, and so on) that every officer has to complete when he joins a new unit had kept me very busy getting lost as I tried to find offices in a part of the base where all the buildings looked exactly the same. My interactions with my new platoon had been confined mainly to end-of-the-day briefs from Bowen on what the men had done that day. Frustrated, I began planning a group training run so that I could forget the administrative headaches for a while and do something physical with my men, most of whom I still didn't know by name. However, the CO preempted me by suddenly announcing he had planned an event of his own, and, hearing of it, I was happy. The CO was taking his "company" hiking.

The quotes exist because, at the time of the CO's announcement, Golf was a far cry from the standard four-platoon, 180-man-strong Marine infantry company that doctrine stipulated. In fact, Golf Company consisted of only two platoons—my infantry platoon and the Ox's weapons platoon—both of which were operating at about three-quarters strength. By now, I had discovered why the Ox and I were the only two lieutenants in Golf Company: 2/4 as a whole was operating with a skeleton crew.

After sitting out the 2003 ground invasion of Iraq because of the yearlong Okinawa deployment, the battalion had returned to the States and hemorrhaged bitter, dissatisfied Marines. Most felt the Marines of 2/4 had missed the only shot at combat that they would ever have, forever dooming them to unwanted stepchild status in a tight brotherhood of battle-hardened warriors. Most of those who had enough seniority to request a transfer or enough time in to leave the Corps altogether did so, and those who remained were, by and large, very new and very green. Thus, companies functioned at half strength while the Marines inside them, me included, yearned for combat and a chance to redeem ourselves, a chance to join the elite circle of combat-blooded infantrymen.

Captain Bronzi had missed both the Oki deployment and the war in Iraq—he had joined 2/4 only about a month before I—but he had determined that, no matter how remote the likelihood of combat and no matter how depleted the ranks of his company, he would train his men as if they were heading to Iraq within the month. Thus when the CO hiked, he hiked all-out. The infantryman's job, after all, is to load up with as much gear and ammo as he can carry and then to hump that gear along until told to stop, typically fifteen to twenty miles over any and all terrain, with enough energy left in reserve to fight fiercely if called upon. Nothing—not running, not weight lifting, not swimming—can prepare you for this essential task better than simply doing it again, and again, and again.

So, in what I would soon learn was his standard practice, the CO hiked us that day in every bit of gear that we might possibly carry overseas, including flak jackets (flaks), Kevlar helmets (Kevlars), mortars, and machine guns. A lot of company commanders shy away from making their Marines carry more than packs, rifles, and their load-bearing vests because of the injuries that hours of hiking carrying sixty to a hundred pounds can cause (blisters, turned ankles, stress fractures, and so on), but not ours. If we stood a chance of carrying it in combat, then we'd practice carrying it before we got there.

Hearing of the CO's plans from the Ox that morning, I had instructed Bowen to reserve one of the medium machine guns, the M-240G, for me to carry along with the standard gear load. I needed to start building credibility with my men, and one of the easiest ways to do that was to demonstrate toughness and physical fitness. Carrying a medium machine gun on a hike isn't the worst of things, but it isn't a cakewalk, either, and I wanted my Marines to know that I would, and could, do anything I asked them to do. Also, I figured that if I hiked with this awkward, twenty-five-pound hunk of metal, then I could ensure that another Marine didn't have to. Thus if I carried a 240 throughout the movement, I could kill two birds with one stone: I could serve at least one Marine and simultaneously prove that I had some intestinal fortitude. Best of all, this way no one else had to look bad for me to look good—ideally we would all make it through the hike and look good together.

Of course, any time you take on extra gear, you risk failing to complete the hike—"falling out"—which is the worst possible thing for a young leader. No matter how smart, composed, or strong he may be, if a lieutenant cannot complete an event that most of his men can, he immediately digs a credibility hole that is very difficult, if not impossible, to climb out of. However, I was in good shape and confident that the machine gun and I would make it through just fine.

The morning of the hike, then, found me at the head of my platoon with a machine gun slung across both shoulders behind my neck, resting on my traps and balanced with alternating hands. My heavy pack rested on my back, with its straps cutting into my shoulders and occasionally cutting off circulation to my hands. A nonbreathing Kevlar vest covering my entire torso completed the painful ensemble. As soon as I had everything reasonably situated on my body, I looked back behind me. My Marines, nearly all of whom were shorter and smaller than I, were bowed under the weight of all the gear, and my platoon was strung out in two long, parallel lines behind me. At the head of Golf Company, the CO suddenly began walking. The hike was on.

Though we normally try to keep the basic two-line formation during hikes, it inevitably breaks down at some point—usually just after particularly difficult hills. Here the Marines sort themselves into different types: the physically fit, gung-ho ones who lead the way, seemingly effortlessly; the less fit but mentally tough ones who hurt but keep going anyway; the unfit and less tough ones who begin lagging as soon as they begin hurting; and those from the first group who consciously drop back to encourage the stragglers.

As I slogged through the hike with the 240G on my back, I periodically looked back and checked on my Marines to see who was struggling, who was straggling, and who was encouraging the stragglers.

It was during one of the check-back moments that I first noticed Lance Corporal Carson. The CO had just stormed his way up a steep hill, and I was clambering along behind. When I got to the top, legitimately winded, sweating rivers down my back and breathing hard, I looked down to see how the Marines were faring, because a solid hill combined with sixty pounds of gear is a good gauge of physical mettle and mental toughness. Everyone was more or less bent double, strung out like a line of carpenter ants, but on closer inspection one of these ants looked a little different from the rest. Carson, as it turned out, was carrying not one but two packs on his back while simultaneously pushing, with both of his arms, another Marine up the hill and shouting at him not to fall out. I marveled as I watched this twenty-year-old corn-fed kid from Idaho in action; I had never seen anything quite like it. He was about six foot two and weighed in at about 210 pounds of which about 40 percent was sheer heart and guts. Carson, I would soon learn, was that rare combination of physical gifts, mental toughness, and relentless discipline. When he got to the top, Carson didn't even pause to catch his breath. Carrying his two packs, he passed by me, nodded and said "Sir," and then kept on walking. At the time, Carson wasn't one of my team leaders, but I determined on the spot that I would make him one at the first opportunity. With less than a year in the Corps he didn't yet have the knowledge, experience, or formal training of a more senior Marine, but you can't teach the kind of heart and selflessness that Carson showed on the hike that day.

Over the next two weeks, I slowly got to know a few of my NCOs, the enlisted men who would become my squad and team leaders. Each of those men has his own little moment enshrined in my memory, that one time when he did or said something that gave me my first glimpse of his true core. Sergeant Leza, the man who eventually became my second-squad leader, completely underwhelmed me during that first hike. A short, round, twenty-three-year-old Marine whose dark features reflected his Hispanic background, Leza looked slightly like a pudgy cinder block even in his formfitting Marine cammies. With all of his gear on for the hike, he looked almost fat. Though Leza didn't fall out during that first hike, he didn't particularly distinguish himself, either—he simply walked steadily, never pulling ahead and never falling back until the hike was completed. I immediately concluded that my sergeant probably couldn't run quickly to save his life.

Furthermore, though Leza had been born and raised in El Paso, English clearly wasn't his first language. In fact, after my third time tasking him with something, I walked away convinced that the only two American words in Leza's vocabulary were "Check" and "Sir." Perturbed by his reticence to speak, I dug a bit deeper into his background and experience and learned that he had been promoted to sergeant just a few weeks prior to our first meeting. He had never led a squad before in his life. Terrific, I thought. A round, out-of-shape sergeant with no experience who can barely speak English. But Leza would soon make me realize that this early impression was wrong. The day after I concluded that I would have my work cut out for me with him, Leza walked into my office.

"Hey sir, I figure that since we'll probably be fighting insurgencies no matter where we go, you might want to read this," he said.

I picked it up. It was Che Guevara's *Guerrilla Warfare*. Multiple pages were dog-eared, so I opened up the book and scanned them. Paragraphs were underlined and notes had been written in the margins—notes in both English and Spanish.

"Is this yours, Leza?" I was dumbfounded.

"Yes, sir. It is. But you can keep that copy, sir. I prefer the one in the original Spanish. I think there's some valuable stuff in there, sir. You can read the whole thing if you want to, but I've dog-eared the best pages for you." Leza, as it turned out, was as close to an intellectual as you can find in a Marine infantry squad leader, and his knowledge of guerrilla warfare and tactics more generally would prove extremely useful. And it turned out that he wasn't so out of shape: A few days later he ran three miles in under twenty-one minutes, which wasn't bad for anyone, let alone someone as sturdy as he.

A week later, it was 1 AM, and I was lying facedown on the cold ground, my right leg interlocked at the knee with the leg of another Marine. The platoon was out in the field for a couple of days learning ambushes, and I had decided to tag along with my first squad as they did their own squad-level training. Corporal Teague, who at the time was my first-squad leader, was taking advantage of some spare time after dark to teach his squad how to communicate silently with one another in an ambush position. If anyone was qualified to teach this kind of stuff, it was Teague. Growing up in Tennessee's backwoods, he was the embodiment of the laconic, field-smart southerner, and his natural gifts had been honed through some of the best training and experience the U.S. armed forces has to offer, that of the Army Rangers. At twenty-one years old, Teague was probably our best shot and almost certainly our best navigator, and, since he spent most of his free time rock climbing and hiking, he was in terrific shape. Teague was also a bit taller than average, standing right at about six feet, and had the wiry climber's build—all broad shoulders and spare, lean muscles wound tightly around a long-limbed frame.

That night Teague was showing everyone, his lieutenant included, how one Marine could signal that the enemy was approaching by shaking his leg. With all of our legs intertwined, the shaking continued down the squad until the last Marine, me in this case, had been alerted and primed for action, so that not a sound had to be made until the first shot was fired. Later that night, the entire platoon had a competition to see who could reload an M-16 the fastest, and it came down to Teague and me. As we started the final round, and he quickly outpaced me, I realized that Teague would be an invaluable resource—not only a great leader and teacher but also one of our strongest individual contributors. I was glad that he had my first squad.

Those moments of quick clarity kept coming, and I soon determined that though my platoon was understrength, it had at least a few strong leaders or potential leaders. Most, including Bowen, who continued to impress me with his competence and unflinching professionalism, and Leza, had been newly promoted, and they now were leading a squad or a team for the first time in their lives. Others, like Carson, showed signs of having the kind of heart and selflessness that couldn't be taught and that was rarely learned from experience. NCOs have been called the "backbone of the Marine Corps," and I was beginning to see signs that my platoon's skeleton would be strong. Eventually we would start hanging fresh meat on the bones and find out whether my initial assessment was correct.

FOUR

October and November were a blur of routine physical activity for Golf Company. As we hiked the hilly terrain around the base, ran muddy trails through the various training areas, and conducted patrolling exercises through the Southern California scrub brush, the NCOs and I did our best to prepare our understrength platoon in the absence of a specific mission. For the Army soldiers in Iraq, however, it was a completely different story. By November 2003, it became apparent that the ever-widening violence in the country was not, in fact, the spastic death throes of the former regime. In some places, the fighting between U.S. forces and their attackers had grown quite fierce, and a strapped Army had its hands full trying to rebuild the major and minor civil institutions of Iraq while simultaneously trying to contain a slowly coalescing insurgency.

Though occupation, with its emphasis on reconstruction, infrastructure, and noncombat operations is not the specialty of the Marine Corps, dismounted (that is, on foot) light infantry is, and as the fighting spread so did rumors that the Marines would eventually be needed in Iraq to help shoulder the military's load. In 2/4, none of us knew exactly what would happen, but speculation was rampant that the battalion might just get its shot at combat after all. One afternoon in early December, Colonel Kennedy called for his battalion to assemble on the basketball courts. Such gatherings happened only rarely, and they were generally convened only for announcements of the greatest importance. As we made our way toward the courts, tense with anticipation, it occurred to me that I might be spending my second anniversary in the same place as I had spent the first, Iraq, though likely in less comfortable circumstances. If this battalion formation was just a ploy to announce another in a series of asinine and restrictive base policies purportedly designed to make us safer, then I was going to be severely disappointed.

For about twenty minutes, Marines poured toward the assembly. NCOs in all platoons barked orders, and slowly several hundred camouflage suits shuffled into the shape of a horseshoe. Once the maneuver was complete and all Marines had been accounted for, Colonel Kennedy took his place at the middle of the horseshoe. As he began to speak, I could see the battalion leaning forward in anticipation.

"The Marines," Colonel Kennedy announced, "are going back to war." He paused, then added what everyone so hoped to hear. "And we're going with them."

Grunts and cheers erupted, and Kennedy waited for them to die down before continuing. The Army, he explained, had screwed everything up in Iraq by being too hard on the civilians, and now, typically, the Marines had been called in to clean up the mess. In all likelihood, Kennedy's statement reflected the fine tradition of interservice competition as much as it did his belief in the Army's Iraq mismanagement. Hearing this, most of us smiled; I know I certainly did. It felt good to be needed. The colonel continued: Running true to form, the Corps had volunteered to assume control of one the most violent pieces of Iraq—the volatile Sunni-dominated Anbar province—not the relatively quiescent Shiite south that the Marines had occupied before their recent withdrawal. As one of only a handful of infantry battalions in the Corps that had not yet been to Iraq, 2/4 had been selected by higher headquarters to be in the first wave of Marine returnees (or, in our case, first-time visitors). Make no mistake about it, Colonel Kennedy told us. You are going to be in combat soon enough.

However, no one knew our departure date or our final destination just yet. The colonel told us that we would definitely assume control of an important area, likely a town called Habbaniyah, and that we would probably leave sometime in the late spring or early fall of 2004. However, he took pains to emphasize that nothing was certain—higher headquarters was still hashing everything out. One thing, though, was quite clear: We could not go back at half strength, and the battalion was more likely to leave sooner rather than later. Prepare yourselves, Colonel Kennedy said. We're going to get a whole host of new Marines, and from now until we leave, things are going to go very quickly.

few days after the announcement, Golf Company received the first of the promised new arrivals: two new second lieutenants who would lead the second and third platoons. Eric Quist and Jonathan Hesener ("Hes") both came straight from Infantry Officer Course, the Marine infantry officers' finishing school. Hes was a U.S. Naval Academy grad and a leukemia survivor—he had contracted the disease during his first year of college, had a complete bone marrow transplant during his second year, and somehow managed to complete the rigorous program three years later. Standing five foot ten with sandy brown hair, light eyes, pale skin, and a long, thoughtful face, Hes struck me as smart but completely physically nondescript, at least until he raised his shirt to reveal the Lord's Prayer tattooed in Aramaic across his ribcage. Quist came from a Marine family (his father was a colonel in the Corps) and he looked exactly how he acted: slightly pinched and nervous and extremely smart. With graying hair, steel-rimmed glasses, and wrinkles already starting to appear at the corners of his constantly squinted eyes, the six-foot-tall Quist had taken a roundabout way into the Corps: He had sold commercial off-the-shelf software for about five years before deciding to follow in his father's footsteps.

Not long after their arrival, Golf got a fourth lieutenant, Craig Flowers, who rejoined the company after a six-week absence occasioned by a winter survival course in Alaska. After a few days, we found out that Flowers had graduated from West Point and then, improbably, had managed an interservice transfer to the Marine Corps, something quite rare.

Happy as I was to have three compatriots, there was a problem with their arrival: The company still had only two understrength platoons, mine and the Ox's weapons platoon, so the new lieutenants and Flowers were platoon commanders with nothing to command. Once Hes and Quist had finished checking in, though, the CO remedied the situation by splitting my platoon into three pieces. I kept Bowen and most of his twelve-man squad, along with Teague, Leza, and Carson. Quist got my second squad, which was now renamed second platoon, and Hes got my third, becoming, in turn, third platoon. Flowers took over Weapons, and the Ox moved to the position of executive officer (XO), a move that made him the CO's right-hand man and put him one bullet away from controlling our lives. Thus, by mid-November, Golf Company had the standard four platoons, each manned by roughly one-third of its usual strength. When the rest of the promised Marines arrived, the men in these platoons, most of whom currently served as basic riflemen, would, ready or not, all become team and squad leaders.

The Corps has specific courses to help Marines make this transition from follower to leader, but we didn't have the time to send anyone to them, because less than a week after its reorganization, Golf Company received its first wave of new-enlisted Marines, and that wave was huge. To fill the skeleton-like 2/4 to full fighting capacity, Marine finishing schools started shunting graduates to our battalion as quickly as possible. Instead of the normal batch of roughly a dozen new Marines that an infantry company gets at each school graduation, Golf received nearly fifty during the third week in November. It was a substantial administrative and logistical nightmare to swallow such a huge chunk of new joins all at once, and our difficulties were compounded by the fact that among this wave of new Marines, there was not a single one with any previous experience in the operating forces. They were all fresh out of infantry school, and my NCOs called them "boot drops."

The term "boot" is one of the most derogatory in the Corps. In a Marine's mind, if someone is a boot, then that someone is essentially raw, untrained, and unfit for whatever position they find themselves in. A huge amount of time and effort needs to be poured in as quickly as possible to ready the new one for even the most mundane tasks of the infantry, let alone for combat. By that definition, then, first platoon doubled in size, from thirteen to roughly twenty-five, with nothing but straight-up boots.

As I met our new arrivals, there were a couple of things that they all had in common aside from their lack of any worthwhile combat training. First, they were all short and skinny. In sharp contrast to most members of the existing group, not a single one of my new Marines stood over six feet tall or weighed over two hundred pounds. Second, they had baby faces, every single one of them, and if I had had to guess their ages individually, without knowing that they were Marines, I might have put each of them at around fifteen to seventeen (their actual ages were between eighteen and twenty-one). Third, they were all very nervous. The new Marines spent a lot of time stuttering, snapping to attention randomly and unnecessarily, and throwing frantic salutes while addressing everyone in sight as "Sir."

As the boot drops poured in, we got to work straightaway, following the time-honored leadership principle that states that if our Marines fail, it won't be because they were poor raw material, but because we were poor teachers. My first order of business was to assign all the new men to one of my three squads so that first platoon could begin drilling with the standard three subunits. Within a few days, we had done so, and Teague took over first squad, Leza, second, and Bowen, third. As the squad leaders took command of their brand-new, slightly understrength squads, we kept an eye out for a suitable radio operator (RO) among the new Marines, because in the infantry the only thing more important than having men who can shoot straight and walk fast is having at least one who can talk well.

Enter Private First Class (PFC) Yebra, a first-generation Colombian American who came to us fresh from his immigrant parents' dairy farm in Wisconsin. He did not immediately impress me. Standing a wiry five seven, with black hair and nearly black eyes, Yebra spoke so softly that I had to strain to hear him the first time he snapped to attention. He was so gentle and un-Marine-like that I wondered how the little PFC had made it through basic training. However, a few days later, as Yebra proceeded to run three miles in under fifteen minutes, handily beating everyone in the platoon, I realized that this Marine would lead by example. I watched, stunned, as he cruised through the finish line running at a pace that would have been an all-out sprint for me. As it turned out, before joining the Corps, Yebra had been a high school cross-country star, even receiving a few college scholarship offers. In addition to being a physical prodigy, Yebra soon proved calm, cool, and deliberate (all necessary qualities for a Marine RO), so the squad leaders and I decided to reward Yebra's physical ability and mental presence by making him carry thirty extra pounds—the radio and its spare batteries—every time we trained.

With our maneuver units set and our primary communicator identified, first platoon headed out to its maiden platoon training event, one planned by our new XO and training officer extraordinaire, the Ox. Even though his recent appointment had made him a staff officer with no platoons or squads to command, the Ox hated to let his status as Captain Bronzi's subordinate stand in the way of his deserved supreme command authority. Thus he tried his utmost to control every aspect of the company's training day, from when we worked out to how we patrolled to which sorts of classes the platoon commanders taught their men. Unsurprisingly, soon after Golf's four new platoons had sorted themselves into maneuverable units, the Ox announced one afternoon in late November that he had generously reserved a specific fortified hillside for all of us to attack with our respective platoons the next day.

Hearing the news, Flowers shook his head and sighed. Less familiar with the Ox than he, the rest of us didn't fully understand the horror that this dictate implied, so we were cautiously enthusiastic about the exercise—after all, it would be our first real test drive with our new Marines, and the training seemed straightforward enough. Armed with weapons and firing blanks, one platoon would man the trenches cut into the side of the hill while another assaulted the position as it saw fit. Leading up to the hillside was a broad, flat plain covered with a fairly complex system of obstacles, the heart of which was three rows of double-stranded concertina wire, the military version of barbed wire in which the barbs are replaced with double-sided straight razors. It's nasty stuff that rips up anyone who tries to move through it. Were the training a real-life assault, that wire meant that anyone conducting a frontal attack on the hillside without serious artillery/air support and a heavy smoke screen would have been cut to ribbons by the defenders. Of course, the wooded hills of California were nothing like the urban jungles of Iraq's cities or the desolate moonscapes of Iraq's deserts, so conformity to real life didn't have a high priority in the Ox's training scenario.

My platoon had gotten to the training area first, so we were allowed to conduct the first attack. I had no desire to shred my Marines in uselessly breaching row after row of wire, so, rather than assaulting frontally, we moved through the thick forest bordering the plain, breached a single strand of wire using an entrenching tool and some rope, and assaulted the trench line from its side, running quickly down its length while pretending to throw grenades and saying hello to our third-platoon friends who were playing the bad guys. When our "attack" finished, we took third platoon's places in the trench line.

Up on the hill, I thought that the exercise had gone reasonably well, but down at its base, the Ox was livid. He had wanted all platoons to attack the way he would have done it, which would have been an all-out frontal assault through the wire. Furthermore, he wanted everyone to practice breaching concertina wire again and again, never mind the fact that none of us had breach kits, ladders, or even sheets of plywood to lay on top of the razors. Without those, the quickest way to cross the wire is to have one Marine who is geared up in his Kevlar vest and helmet take a running leap and launch himself on top of the razors in a technique known as "the Flying Squirrel." The rest of his platoon would then run across his back, using the Marine as a bridge over the wire and lacerating his legs in the process. The delightful prospect of multiple Flying Squirrels greatly excited the Ox, and first platoon had disappointed him.

So an enraged Ox commanded Hes, Quist, and Flowers to assault the obstacles frontally. Being new, Hes and Quist complied, and my men and I watched in astonishment as Marine after Marine performed the Flying Squirrel and then limped painfully off the mock battlefield once the rest of their platoon had laid railroad tracks across their backs. The new Marines were wide-eyed; for all they knew this kind of absurdity was standard. Carrying the radio for me, Yebra leaned over and asked, even more softly than usual, "Sir, why are they doing that? We would have just shot them all in the first minute anyway, sir."

"Yebra, I have no idea, but I'm sure there's a reason that second and third are assaulting frontally. If nothing else, it's good obstacle-breaching practice," I replied somewhat lamely.

My RO didn't say anything else after that.

Fortunately for his men, Flowers flatly refused a head-on assault, and the afternoon concluded much more pleasantly. The exercise highlighted the Ox's greatest strength—his unthinking, unhesitating aggressiveness—and his greatest weakness—his unthinking, unhesitating aggressiveness. When the situation called for a frontal assault on a well-fortified enemy position, the Ox would attack fiercely. Similarly, when the situation called for diplomacy or the restrained use of force, he would attack fiercely. And when the situation called for patience or for a measured retreat, never fear, he would attack fiercely. Like Hes, Quist, and Flowers, I treated the Ox's lack of tactical sense mostly as a joking matter; a few days after the training event, we first reversed the letters of his XO title, giving him the sobriquet by which he would be known from that day forward.

Even in those earliest days, though, platoon leadership wasn't all tactics and training and "follow-me-let's-get-'em"-type exercises in the hills and forests of Camp Pendleton. Good leadership, it seemed, entailed spending quite a bit of time on administrative details that I never dreamed would have been the responsibility of an infantry platoon commander. Teague, Bowen, Leza, and I spent countless hours determining the shoe and trouser sizes of each new man, taking counts of how many pairs of military-issue glasses we needed to order (it could take up to two months to get them from the procurement system), making certain that everyone's pay was going to the proper bank accounts, scanning personnel files to see who had what relatives, and doing various and sundry other nontactical things to ensure that our new men were being taken care of off the battlefield as well as on it. Most of this work, though, was simple diligence and detail, and it wasn't until a week after the hillside assault that our first major leadership headache cropped up. One of my brand-new Marines, Lance Corporal Mahardy, was accused of underage drinking.

Any offense involving the use of alcohol is considered a deadly and often unforgivable sin in the American military—the peacetime, zero-defects leaders of the 1990s entirely eliminated the drinking culture that has been a proud part of military heritage worldwide since the days of Herodotus. Having grown up in the '90s military, Colonel Kennedy and Captain Bronzi were both determined to make examples out of alcohol offenders, and they planned on throwing the book at Mahardy. As he was ultimately my responsibility, I decided to call my Marine into the company office to hear his account firsthand before I took the official logbook's word for it. So, late one afternoon, a relatively tall (six-foot), extremely skinny (160-pound), twenty-year-old Marine with pale skin, sandy-blond hair, and light freckles across his cheeks and arms stood at parade rest and explained his side of the story to me. He had been on his way to do his laundry and had stopped by another Marine's room to say hello. He found a group of Marines passing around a case of beer, but he hadn't actually drunk any of it. After hearing Mahardy's explanation, and observing his demeanor as he gave it, I believed that my man was guilty of nothing more than wandering into the wrong room. I didn't believe that he deserved harsh punishment, or any punishment at all, for that matter. But by the rules of the Corps, which prohibited his very presence in a barracks room containing alcohol, he was guilty as charged.

As I pondered what to do about Mahardy, I ran into another of the constant tensions faced by young officers: the tension between justice and mercy, and, to some extent, between respect and love. Respect from your Marines is founded on a number of different leadership traits, but foremost among them are competence and justice, and justice hinges on leadership applying an even, consistent system of punishments and rewards. A uniform set of standards across the Marine Corps outlines the criteria for both, and the Marines can always reference those standards if they have any questions surrounding what they can reasonably expect to result from their actions or the lack thereof. They anticipate, then, rewards for outstanding achievement, and they justifiably fear reprisals, often severe, for misdeeds or laziness.

To my surprise, I later found out that my Marines could accept even the harshest punishment with equanimity provided that 1) they understood the rules well in advance of the infringement, 2) they felt that the mandated sentence was appropriate for the misdeed, and 3) they were confident that you, as the punishment's administrator, would have doled out the same penalty to anyone else in their situation. The Marines should absolutely fear what their lieutenant, company commander, or NCOs can do to them, but they should never, ever believe that those appointed over them either apply punishment out of a rush of emotion or occasionally suspend deserved sentences for reasons unknown. Failing to administer justice, or at least to push for justice to be done, is one of the absolute best ways of cutting your legs out from under yourself as a young leader.

My first thought, then, was simply to let the CO determine the correct punishment. This would have been the easiest course of action, and nobody, including Mahardy, would have held it against me, but it didn't sit well with me because I believed that Mahardy hadn't been drinking. Fur-

thermore, even in my inexperience, I had some intimation that in spite of
the need for consistency, there are moments when simply following the letter of the law is a cop-out, and ultimately hinders your efforts to pull the best
out of your men. In my opinion, the latter requires a love founded on hu-
mility, self-sacrifice, and, in some cases, mercy. Sometimes a punishment
may be warranted because the letter of the law was violated, but you believe
that the sentence should be suspended because of mitigating circumstances
surrounding that violation. Or you might believe that the offender rates by
law a specific punishment but that the offense was committed out of igno-
rance rather than malice. Maybe your Marine is a good kid who has potential that would be crushed by such treatment, or maybe they, in your best
judgment, simply deserve a second chance.

I wasn't sure exactly which of these situations applied to Mahardy's case,
but I believed that at least one or two of them did. If I abided solely by the
letter of the law, I worried that I might come across as an automaton in my
men's eyes. But it was important not to signal a willingness to defer justice
on a regular basis; though this might make the Marines like me more, I
needed to be their leader, not their friend, and maintaining this boundary at
all times is crucial. What, then, should a young officer do to navigate the
delicate tension between justice and fear, between mercy and love?

I certainly don't have all the answers to this age-old question, but I have
found one way that a lieutenant can resolve this tension, and I applied it as
best I could to Mahardy's case. This thing can't be done every time that you
might like to, and even when you can do it, it is often extremely personally
unpleasant. The way to satisfy both justice and mercy is, quite simply, to
take the hit for your men, to divert whatever punishment they may rate onto
your own head if you believe that mercy is warranted. This trade-off is just
because as the lieutenant, you are held accountable for everything that your
men achieve or fail to achieve, for everything that they do or that is done to
them. While you may not be directly responsible for the deeds and misdeeds
of your men, you are certainly qualified to interpose yourself between them
and justice, should you so choose.

This concept of an acceptable proxy goes much further than merely the
dispensation of justice and mercy—ultimately it translates into the lieutenant's greatest and sometimes final responsibility: to lay down his life for
his Marines in combat, if such an action is necessitated by circumstances.

The idea is very, very simple and clear. If you wear the bars on your shoulders, then it is your job to consistently practice the greater-love principle. If you didn't want that job, then you shouldn't have accepted the commission.

In this case I couldn't directly take the hit for Mahardy, so I tried the next best thing: I stuck my neck out for him with the CO. After sending Mahardy away and mulling over our conversation, I went into the CO's office, where I related to him the story as Mahardy had related it to me. The CO looked extremely skeptical throughout. When I tentatively broached the idea of deferring punishment, the CO cut me off and proceeded to explain to me that I was young and didn't realize yet that enlisted Marines often couldn't be trusted. Marines in general, he explained, were extremely "fucking sneaky," and they often relied upon the naïveté and bad judgment of inexperienced lieutenants to get away with heinous crimes. That wasn't going to happen on his watch, he told me.

We held the formal punishment ceremony a few days later. Colonel Kennedy sat at a desk, while those accused and their leaders stood at attention off to the side. When Mahardy's time came, I publicly stood at attention and voiced my opinion that my lance corporal should be spared. He wasn't, but he was given a lighter punishment than the CO had originally threatened, and a few hours later I pulled Mahardy aside to talk to him, to explain that he had a choice to make going forward. He could either sulk at the injustice and retreat within himself, which, since we were going to war, would probably only get people killed, or he could work doubly hard going forward to prove everyone wrong, to prove that he wasn't the Marine they had judged him to be.

Standing at parade rest, with his hands behind his back and his blue-gray eyes locked on mine, Mahardy nodded throughout my short pep talk, and when I finished, he responded simply, "Sir, don't you worry. I know what I've got to do. I'm gonna prove to you and everyone that I belong here in the infantry. Don't worry, sir."

Mahardy would not be my only leadership challenge in those early days. One day after training, Leza approached me and told me that one of our new Marines, a lance corporal by the name of Feldmeir, had been falling asleep everywhere he went, and at all times. It seemed that we had a genuine narcoleptic in our ranks. Unfortunately, Feldmeir didn't offset this weakness with other strengths. He wasn't big or particularly fit; in fact, Feldmeir was on the smaller side of the curve, standing a wiry five feet, eight inches tall. With a completely shaved head and ears that stuck out at an almost perfectly perpendicular angle from his scalp, Feldmeir looked like the children's book character Curious George. It wasn't exactly an image guaranteed to strike fear into the hearts of enemies. His shooting was average, his hiking was average, and his reaction time to most stimuli was slightly slower than average. I have no idea how Feldmeir made it through basic and infantry training, but make it he did, and it quickly became apparent that if the narcolepsy didn't improve, he might jeopardize the safety of his fellow Marines on the battlefield.

In talking with Feldmeir about the situation, I learned that there might have been some explanation outside of genetics for his condition: Feldmeir had been raised in a series of foster homes and adoptive households ever since he had stopped living with his mom at the age of ten. The narcolepsy was one of his ways of dealing with the resulting trauma. A few days after the problem was brought to our attention, the squad leaders and I decided that Feldmeir would need huge amounts of special attention, so we assigned him to Corporal Teague, who had continued to distinguish himself as one of the best and fittest of our squad leaders. We would have preferred to reassign him to another unit, but we couldn't afford to. We were going to combat very soon and, understrength as we were, we could ill afford to lose another man.

Fortunately, Feldmeir proved the exception rather than the rule, and as November ticked by in a blurry haze of paperwork, patrolling, and endless lines of shots and gear draw, I continued to learn the ins and outs of my new men. Many, like my radio operator, Yebra, had either disenrolled from college or turned down college scholarships after 9/11 to serve in the armed forces. Others wanted to carry on a family's military tradition, or sought adventure and camaraderie. Though the individual reasons for joining varied, nearly all of my men were with us because they very much wanted to be with us. Indeed, when I asked each of my Marines why they had joined the Corps, during the one-on-one interviews that I scheduled with all of them, nearly to a man they gave me a variation of the same answer: *Sir, I love this country and I wanted to serve and I wanted to be the best, so I joined the Marine infantry, sir.*

In fact, several of my men were so motivated to be Marine riflemen that they had surmounted serious physical difficulties to make it through boot camp. PFC Henderson was one of these. Not long after he joined, we sent him for a medical screening because he mentioned in passing that he was having fairly intense chest pains following each run (additionally, Henderson looked roughly fifteen years old—he had an amazing baby face—so it couldn't hurt to get a doctor's second opinion regarding our man's true age, or so Leza told me with a wink). A series of tests indicated some cardiovascular abnormality, but the doctors couldn't identify the condition and they couldn't determine whether the unknown was serious. Predictably, they erred on the side of caution and forbade Henderson from any and all strenuous training, so we stuck him in the company office and gave him a desk job. He hated it, but he worked hard anyway.

I was disappointed—Henderson was a genuinely sweet kid who had tried hard to help everywhere he was placed, and staffed as we were at just over 50 percent of our standard fighting capacity, first platoon could not afford to lose one man so soon after gaining him. However, less than a week later my spirits perked up, because Golf received a much-needed addition: a company gunnery sergeant. Alongside every officer chain of command is an enlisted one, and the company gunnery sergeant ("gunny" for short) is the enlisted counterpart to the company XO. Together they are responsible for all the administrative and logistical groundwork that keeps a company fed, equipped, trained, and fighting. Without a gunny, the day-to-day operations of the infantry would likely grind to a halt. As our old gunny was about to retire—he had one foot out the door already—things were bound to improve. And indeed, while I didn't know it at the time, that day in late November when the new gunny joined Golf Company was one of the best days of my life.

The man's full name and title were Gunnery Sergeant Winston C. Jaugan, but I will always remember him as simply the Gunny because, as far as I'm concerned, there's only one gunny that matters—Golf Company's Gunny, the best in the Corps. The Gunny was born in the Philippines and retained the distinctive dialect of the Tagalog people, the Philippines' second-largest ethnic group, making for bizarre English syntax in general and exceptionally amusing swearing when the Gunny got worked up. He had come to us straight from an assignment as a drill sergeant, so, aside from the weathered, cragged face that had clearly seen its share of lessons learned the hard way, the Gunny looked as if he had just stepped out of a shrink-wrapped box. His wide shoulders and thick chest tapered down to a narrow waist, and the forearms that protruded from his perfectly rolled sleeves were cabled with muscle.

And the Gunny didn't walk; he stalked. Everywhere he went, his head and shoulders were thrust aggressively forward as he swiveled his eyes this way and that, searching for the lost in need of instruction. Within a day of his arrival, Golf Company started functioning with noticeably more efficiency. Even better, the Gunny took all of the young lieutenants under his wing because he was a true professional, and he realized we needed it. The best senior enlisted NCOs usually take it upon themselves to teach and mentor the younger officers, and the task requires a deft hand, because every officer, no matter how young or inexperienced, outranks every enlisted man. Within a week of his arrival, the Gunny was already teaching me, helping me to better understand both my men and myself. When he found me deeply engrossed filling sandbags with a few of my men, for example, the Gunny waited until I was alone and then gently suggested that since I was a lieutenant and my time was limited, I might want to focus on planning and coordination and let the men deal with the details.

I was grateful for the help, and soon enough I began to rely on the Gunny for more than just straightforward leadership advice and general company efficiency. You see, not long after the Gunny's arrival, I received my own enlisted counterpart—my platoon sergeant. If the gunnery sergeant is the enlisted equivalent of the company executive officer, the platoon sergeant is the enlisted equivalent of the platoon commander. In theory, an infantry platoon sergeant should be a lieutenant's right-hand man, seeing to logistical and administrative tasks so the commander can focus his attention solely on tactics, on finding and defeating the enemy and accomplishing the mission. With at least ten years in the Corps under his belt, a platoon sergeant should also serve as the enlisted leader of the Marines, a trusted voice of experience who anticipates their needs because, as a young Marine, he once had those very same needs. He should be a careful mentor to the young lieutenant, protecting the inexperienced officer from himself, and with time a platoon sergeant should become the lieutenant's best and closest confidant. In theory, the two should function as two halves of a whole unit dedicated wholeheartedly to taking care of the men in their charge.

Unfortunately, with my platoon sergeant, whom we'll call simply Staff Sergeant, reality diverged wildly from theory. Even though he had served in the Corps for a little more than eleven years by the time he got to us, Staff Sergeant had spent at least half that time in nonleadership roles, and he hadn't been in the infantry for the past six years. The time off showed in his physique—tall, skinny, and flabby all at the same time. Staff Sergeant stood nearly six feet, three inches, with long, gangly arms and legs that connected to a hunched torso and a slightly concave chest. With his cammies on, Staff Sergeant looked almost skinny, but when his top came off it became apparent that most of the weight he carried wasn't muscle. And though he was only twenty-nine years old, Staff Sergeant's pitted, lined face made me initially put him at closer to forty than thirty.

Most recently, my platoon sergeant had toured with the Marine Corps Rifle Team, a select group of the Corps's best shooters, who tour the country and represent the Marines at various shooting competitions. He had considered the job his own personal heaven. Within a week of his arrival, Staff Sergeant began to share this view with my Marines by complaining vocally about his pitiful new lot in life in the infantry, and I had to pull the man aside and tactfully remind him that, as a leader, he no longer had the luxury of complaining down.

His response did not fill me with hope.

"Sir, I have no idea how to be a platoon sergeant."

I was at a complete loss as to how to respond. Fortunately, the Gunny saw my dilemma, and when he wasn't mentoring officers or smoothly running the company, Gunny Jaugan took it upon himself to "supervise" my platoon's latest addition. After two weeks of the Gunny's tender care, Staff Sergeant literally cowered at the sight of the fiery Filipino. Consummate professional that he was, the Gunny never let me see his sessions with my platoon sergeant. All I knew was that occasionally the Gunny would roar "Staff Sergeant" and my platoon sergeant would drop whatever he was doing and start running.

In truth, I was somewhat ambivalent about having an effective staff sergeant anyway. Over the past two months I had become quite jealous of my status as the sole authority for my men, and I feared and distrusted anyone who threatened to diminish it. I, in my inexperience, was unwilling to admit that when it came to leading a platoon, there was more than enough responsibility for two.

So, by December 2003, an inexperienced platoon sergeant and a jealous lieutenant had been paired together to lead a whole clutch of boot Marines into a combat deployment. Fortunately, I had three excellent squad leaders in Teague, Leza, and Bowen, terrific younger Marines like Carson and Yebra, and solid compatriots in Hes, Quist, and Flowers. As for Staff Sergeant, Henderson, Mahardy, and Feldmeir, only time would tell how they would work out, but we had time enough before we deployed, I believed.

FIVE

t turned out I was wrong. In mid-December, word came down that we wouldn't be leaving in April, May, or June as we had planned. It would be more like early February. We'd be heading to a still-undetermined location somewhere in the heart of the volatile Anbar province. To make matters worse, our standard two weeks off at Christmas would count as our predeployment leave (the two- to three-week vacation that every Marine unit gets immediately before it heads overseas), and all of our gear would have to be packed and in boxes by the first week of February.

As if this wasn't bad enough, we had just received our second huge wave of boot drops, roughly fifteen new Marines, every bit as green as the last bunch, who filled us to nearly 100 percent fighting capacity. The standard period for a new Marine before deployment is six months; we'd been hoping for at least half of that. The new timetable handed to us allowed Golf a little less than two months to get the first wave of new joins ready for combat, and the second would have only four weeks to integrate, train, and settle all of their domestic affairs before shipping off.

As the new Marines poured in, we tried our utmost to process them as quickly as possible. NCOs stormed about all through the barracks, measuring pants, assigning men to squads, and shepherding their new Marines to dozens of different administrative appointments. Every morning, long lines formed outside the medical offices as hundreds of boot drops waited for their anthrax and smallpox inoculations, and our Navy dental officers had their hands full trying to clean and repair hundreds and hundreds of teeth. Every afternoon, Marines queued up outside the armory or the supply shack, waiting to draw the equipment and weaponry they'd be using in training and in combat. Meanwhile, the platoon leaders, Hes, Quist, Flowers, and I, spent hours assigning and reassigning weapons, night vision equipment, and all the other specialized gear specific to each Marine. We debated responses to different types of enemy attacks in an attempt to come up with a platoonwide set of standard operating procedures, and we studied, as best we could, the reports coming out of Habbaniyah so that we would have some idea of what to expect when we got there.

By the time Christmas break rolled around in late December, Golf Company had completed almost all the administrative groundwork necessary to enable us to focus entirely on training when all our Marines returned from the two weeks off. Personally, I was looking forward to the break, because my hectic schedule and Christy's work as a night shift nurse in a pediatric hospital had allowed us very little time together over the past two months. Indeed, we had, on occasion, passed each other going opposite ways on Interstate 5—she headed to work, and I returning from it. Even when I wasn't in the field overnight, it was fairly common for my wife and I to go for four days without seeing each other. We communicated via notes left on the kitchen counter and hurried phone calls snatched during quick breaks. It wasn't ideal, but it was all we had, and I was eager for more time to pour into our barely year-old marriage.

However, only a few days into the Christmas break, I realized it was impossible to try to treat this as just another relaxing vacation. All I thought about was how I'd be leaving again in under two months and that my newly formed platoon had, at best, six or seven weeks to prepare ourselves for combat. It didn't help that Christy was working twelve-hour night shifts, meaning that during those two weeks our time together was sporadic and disjointed at best. Indeed, my wife had to work on Christmas and New Year's Eve, so I volunteered as the battalion's officer of the day on both those days. As the rest of California opened presents and counted the seconds until

2004, Christy put IVs into dangerously sick children, and I walked the empty barracks and continued to diagram responses to enemy IED ambushes.

When everyone returned to work in the first week of January, I was almost relieved that the charade of time off had ended and that real life had begun again. Finally at full strength, Golf Company ramped up the training as rapidly as possible, focusing initially on all of the standard combat techniques common to the Marine Corps infantry. We did mock all-out urban assaults in a bizarre five-block "city" in the middle of Camp Pendleton. Several-day events, these exercises taught house-clearing techniques, city-patrolling procedures, crowd control, and other things specific to operating in an urban environment. We practiced combat shooting and reloading on the ranges available to us during the day and night to get our new recruits comfortable moving with and using loaded weapons under all conditions. Ranges and urban assaults take a lot of lead time and logistical support to set up, so when those weren't available, Hes, Quist, Flowers, and I grabbed our platoons and patrolled through the surrounding woods and through the barracks, working on tactical movement across danger areas like road intersections and endlessly reviewing 360-degree coverage of the patrol formation so that no one could attack us unawares.

When we weren't patrolling, I gave class after class on topics ranging from how to paint your face for maximum concealment to why we put our dog tags in our left boots (no matter how severe the explosion, usually the boots survive) and our first-aid kits on our left sides (you can't waste time hunting for a Marine's tourniquet when he's spurting blood out of a severed artery). Where I left off, Teague, Leza, and Bowen began, teaching their new men the basics of life in an infantry battalion. Long after the training day had ended and I had returned home for the evening, the three squad leaders remained in the barracks with their teenage Marines, teaching them things like how to pay their bills while overseas, how to balance their checkbooks, and how to lay down ferocious covering fire in response to an enemy ambush. Leza had a pregnant wife and one small boy, so eventually he too would leave the barracks for the comforts of home, but Teague and Bowen were single, and they stayed available to their men literally all night long. As NCOs, both could have moved to more comfortable apartments off the base—as many of their friends had done—but they didn't. Instead, they chose to stay in the barracks with their new men because, as Bowen put it, "Sir, we've got little enough time as it is, and my Marines need all of mine if we're gonna be ready. I just want to be there for my Marines in case they need me, sir."

Even Staff Sergeant pitched in, trying to teach the men how they too could shoot like the USMC Rifle Team, until I caught him and focused his efforts on more relevant matters. I didn't mind these off-topic discourses too much, though, because at least Staff Sergeant was making an effort to teach the only thing he really knew. If my platoon sergeant had to instruct (and he did if he wanted any credibility with the Marines), I preferred him erring on the side of sticking with what he knew to pretending to know what he didn't, because the Marines immediately sniff out this kind of deception and never fully trust you afterward.

Above all else, though, the squad leaders and I tried desperately to instill in our Marines the proper combat mentality. Throughout my training, my instructors had hammered home the idea that the most deadly weapon on the modern battlefield is not a tank, a jet, or any other exceptionally high-tech combat system; rather, it's a sharp and flexible mind combined with a decisive and creative mind-set. "War is inherently chaos," our instructors had told us. "You, young lieutenants, must embrace this concept and pre-pare yourselves to think creatively and independently, because, more often than not, conditions on the ground will change so rapidly that original or-ders and well-thought-out plans become irrelevant. If you can't manage chaos and uncertainty, if you can't bias yourself for action and if you wait around for someone else to tell you what to do, then the enemy will make your decisions for you and your Marines will die." Ultimately, then, the best way to keep men alive on the battlefield is to instill in every Marine a deci-sive mind that can quickly separate the crucial from the irrelevant, synthe-size the output, and use this intelligence to create little bubbles of order in the all-out chaos that is war.

Bowen, Leza, and Teague understood this concept intuitively—perhaps they had picked it up from their years spent as riflemen in 2/4, or perhaps they were just that good—and throughout the month of January, the four of us set out to teach this combat mentality to our new joins. Simultaneously, we tried to convince them that they now had great worth in our eyes, that their input was always necessary and important, and that everyone in their chain of command respected them enough to take their thoughts seriously. After all, when you're fighting an enemy that uses the civilian population as just another piece of terrain (as we knew the insurgents did), quick input from the most junior Marines can save many lives, but they'll give you that input only if you take the time to convince them that you'll use it. And our new joins were still so robotic, so scared of taking any action without instruction, that we worried they'd completely freeze up under fire or be incapable of independent action if anything happened to their team leaders.

As January and our training days slipped by all too quickly, I continued to learn everything from the mundane to the profound about both my NCOs and my new Marines. Nothing about them was too small to be overlooked and filed away for future reference. In addition to his previously demonstrated leadership, and not to mention the ability to carry two backpacks up a hill while pushing another Marine, Carson could instantaneously put an M-203 grenade anywhere you wanted him to without using his sights. Not only that, but his wife's name was Sarah, and he had a huge tattoo that read "one shot, one kill" across both shoulder blades. Carson's highest ambition apparently was to become a Marine sniper. Bowen, the picture of the professional Marine NCO, moonlighted as a licensed tattoo artist who practiced his craft on himself. When I saw my third-squad leader in his Marine-issued, tight green PT hot pants for the first time, I nearly fell over: Crazy designs spilled out of Bowen's sleeves down to his forearms and out of his pants down to his calves. The one I remember most vividly was the many-eyeballed, screaming, writhing skull that wrapped around Bowen's right forearm. Teague caught me staring and said simply: "Oh yeah, sir, Bowen's crazy. Don't worry about it." Clearly, there was always more to my men than met the eye.

During our urban assaults, Corporal Raymond, a new team leader in Leza's squad, told me, "Sir, if you can't be smart, you've gotta be strong," shortly before turning himself into a human cannonball as he used his entire body to smash through a barrier that I had previously considered impenetrable. Mahardy, who had kept on the straight and narrow since being accused of underage drinking, had a gift for talking incessantly and loudly, but he was also extremely intelligent (1370 on his SAT and a dean's list student at Syracuse University before the Corps) with a knack for thinking one step ahead of his orders and asking insightful (and sometimes sarcastic) questions thereof. In a clever move, Teague combined this love of the spoken word with twenty extra pounds and made Mahardy our backup radio operator. By contrast, our primary operator, Yebra, still rarely spoke, but he had wholeheartedly dedicated himself to his machine and had turned himself into a technical wizard capable of teaching others the radio's most esoteric inner workings.

Feldmeir, alas, could fall asleep walking. I had never seen anything like it. One moment he would be patrolling, and the next he would be sprawled over on his side, fast asleep with arms and gear akimbo. However, Feldmeir tried so hard to be a good Marine and to be accepted by the squad that watching his painful eagerness, particularly since his squad mates remained standoffish toward him at best, hurt sometimes. After all, the platoon was probably the first real home he had ever had. Teague spent hours working with Feldmeir, desperately trying to get him ready to save and protect lives in combat, but nothing seemed to work. For a time, I debated whether to try and pawn our narcoleptic off on the Ox and his small company headquarters staff, but eventually I decided against it. Feldmeir had been given to me, and he was, therefore, my responsibility to develop. Besides, we were going into combat slightly shorthanded as it was. We were going to need all the trigger pullers we could get, even if they were narcoleptic. Like Feldmeir, but for different reasons, Staff Sergeant also had trouble walking; he demonstrated this shortcoming very visibly to the Marines by falling to the back of the company on his first hike out with us. But he never quit, and I began to realize that he was fiercely loyal to me — never once did he contradict my orders in front of the men, and whenever the Ox questioned my actions, my platoon sergeant was the first to leap to my defense. By now, Staff Sergeant's initial fear of the Gunny had developed into full-blown terror, for the Gunny continued to ride my platoon sergeant mercilessly.

Meanwhile, the tattooed Bowen got better and better with every passing day. As each training event followed hard on the heels of its predecessor, I became overwhelmed with the responsibility of it all. Bowen somehow managed to pick up on this, and would devise ways to help shoulder my load, usually without me knowing. When I had to assign and reassign weapons, Bowen would do it for me. When it came to after-hours PT sessions for our laggards, he would take them on himself. When any discipline issues cropped up with his men, he would handle them well before they reached me. If I ever needed anything, no matter how Herculean or how last-minute, I could ask Bowen for it, and somehow he would have the job done two hours quicker and three times better than I imagined—my squad leader had that rare gift of fulfilling not only the task that I had actually assigned him but also the task that I *should* have assigned him. His men clearly responded to his unswerving dedication and he quickly became one of the best leaders in the platoon, myself included. So, as per the Corps's propensity to punish its most competent performers, in mid-January I separated Bowen from his squad and packed him off to an Arabic immersion course.

This brand-new course was part of a larger 1st Marine Division program to prepare 2/4 for a mission that none of the platoon commanders had ever heard of before: SASO, short for Stability and Support Operations. The acronym's relative obscurity had a simple explanation—it was an Army term coined to describe the duties of foreign occupation. Ironically, at the same time that the Marines chose to adopt the Army's terminology for our future mission, my division was busily engaged disparaging the Army's performance in its current one. "The Army is all screwed up," we were told in a speech by Colonel Kennedy. "They're too hard on the Iraqi people—it's no wonder that they're having problems." Our division commander, General Mattis, clarified this point in a number of different newspaper articles, the gist of which was the following: "The Army is always bringing down the iron hammer on a timid and abused populace, but the Marines will be different. We're going to extend the people the velvet glove. We're going to make the Iraqis our friends. We're going to be nice to them and win hearts and minds."

If there were still any questions outstanding about how we were going to differentiate ourselves from the Army, General Mattis laid them to rest when he told his officers that when the Marines returned to Iraq, "One civilian death equals mission failure." The division motto had even been changed to: "First Do No Harm—No Better Friend, No Worse Enemy." It was somewhat strange to see a line from the Hippocratic Oath adapted to fit our line of work, and we knew even then that the general had set a nearly impossibly high standard, but we believed in all of it wholeheartedly. After all, most insurgencies desperately need the support of at least some portion of the indigenous population, and if we could drive a wedge between the

Iraqi people and the enemy fighters, we could cut our foes off from their lifeblood. The general knew bone deep that in any counterinsurgency the people are the prize, and he took every step necessary to instill this strange population-centric mind-set into a force oriented toward high-intensity combat against a well-defined enemy.

So, two weeks into January we shifted much of our time and effort away from proficiency in traditional missions and toward a new goal: learning how to avoid offending the Iraqis. My Marines, 50 percent of whom previously probably could not have named Islam as a major world religion, now learned the intricacies of the historical and doctrinal conflicts between the Sunni and Shiite Islamic sects. We crammed Iraqi cultural nuances down their throats as fast as they could swallow them. Showing the bottom of your shoes is a horrible offense, we told our new men, and touching people with your left hand is even worse. Don't stare at the women and talk only to the men. Be polite and smile a lot. Wave when you patrol and don't paint your faces in urban areas. After all, the Iraqis' lives are scary and miserable enough; we certainly don't want to make them worse. We are the friendly Marines, here to help.

The rationale underpinning this new training emphasis was well in line with our population-centric approach, but it was also very risky, because Marines always have default settings that inform their actions in those precious first moments of a firefight. By training as we did, we flipped our Marines' default switches from "be fierce" to "be nice"; we told them to hesitate, to ask questions before shooting, and to assume greater personal risk to better protect the civilians. It was a calculated risk, and one that we suspected might cause us to take higher casualties in the short run in pursuit of longer-term aims.

But 2/4 hadn't seen combat yet, so friendly wounds weren't real to us in January 2004; we couldn't truly feel yet what the words "higher casualties" meant. Besides, none of Golf Company's leadership could disagree with the idea of trying to protect the innocent at our own expense. After all, it was why most of us had joined, only, in this case, the innocent were not our fellow countrymen; rather, they were citizens of a strange land, and they spoke a strange language and kept strange customs. In keeping with this sentiment, my CO made a bold decision to eliminate his weapons platoon altogether, a move that ran counter to at least twenty years of past standard organization but that made a lot of practical sense for our future success. We would almost certainly be deployed to an urban environment, and, given the counterinsurgency nature of our mission (and general morality), our company was highly unlikely to be firing mortars and rockets regularly into a densely populated city. So, with a little horse trading, the CO transformed Golf Company from three rifle platoons and one weapons platoon to four straight-up rifle platoons. We kept the mortars and the rockets, though, and if things got really bad we could always re-form the teams to use them.

It was a brilliant if unorthodox call, and it would make our company significantly more flexible in combat than the others. However, the decision came with a very personal cost: Corporal Teague, whom I had come to depend upon as one of my best young leaders and as one of my most competent individual Marines in general, would be replaced as our first-squad leader by a new sergeant from Flowers's platoon whom nobody, including Flowers, knew. I had told the CO that I preferred to keep Teague, but I was overruled, so I had to break the bad news to my now-former first-squad leader. Fearing the conversation and tempted to postpone it, I managed to force myself to pull Teague aside fairly soon. When I told him that we were getting a new sergeant, and that my request to send the man somewhere else had been overruled, he nodded, then told me simply, "Sir, even if I ain't called a squad leader, I'm never gonna stop acting like one. You need anything, sir, you can count on me. I'll be there for you and the new guy."

Whoever this new sergeant was, he had better be damn good.

If you had told me when I was a young undergraduate that, for the rest of my life, I would owe a deep debt of gratitude to a tattoo of a naked she-devil, I would probably have laughed in your face. It goes to show how much I knew as a college student, because I am, as it turns out, eternally grateful for one of the most tasteless tattoos I've ever seen in my life, for that tattoo combined with the CO's organization decision to give me Sergeant Mariano O. Noriel, the man who would become my first-squad leader and the closest thing that I had to a confidant and friend.

Noriel was our mystery sergeant, and the reason that no one knew him was that until very recently, he had been stationed at a recruiting office somewhere near San Diego. With six years in the infantry and one straight year in Okinawa, Noriel had earned himself a break from the action for a while, and recruiting was supposed to have been it. However, shortly after starting his cushy new desk job, the good sergeant had to have all his tattoos photographed (the Marines have strict guidelines limiting the number and type of tattoos on a potential recruit, and they expect their recruiters to adhere to the same guidelines). When my future first-squad leader removed his shirt for the photos, his then-bosses were horrified to find that pasted across Noriel's entire right shoulder was a tattoo of a squatting naked devil woman, complete with horns, tail, and all the other pieces that make for an anatomically correct female devil. Immediately thereafter, Noriel's commanding officer pulled the new sergeant into his office to explain how such a tattoo might cause some to feel uncomfortable in a mixed-sex work environment. The senior officer ended the conversation by asking Noriel how he thought his female colleagues would view the reprehensible shoulder art. Noriel pondered the question for a bit, then shrugged and in the typical infantry fashion, said, "Sir, to be perfectly honest, I don't much give a damn what in the hells anyone thinks of my tattoos."

A screaming master sergeant immediately yanked Noriel out of the room, and within a week my future squad leader found himself kicked out of the recruiting office and sent back to Golf Company.

The only way that I can describe this utterly unique character is as a five-foot, ten-inch, 180-pound Filipino ball of fire with a perfectly shaved head and not a single ounce of fear in his body. Noriel had immigrated to the States at the age of fourteen, so his English was even more idiosyncratic than the Gunny's in normal conversation—he assigned personal pronouns to all inanimate objects, for example—and usually completely unintelligible when he got worked up. More than once I watched first squad stare blankly at Noriel while he shouted a set of orders in a weird English-Tagalog amalgamation that only a cryptologist could understand; then, when no one responded, he screamed, "Well, what the fuck is wrong with you alls? The orders was simplified, so get him done!" It usually fell to Teague to tell him that no one was being disrespectful—they just couldn't understand a word of what their squad leader had just said. The two of them made a terrific team, with Teague as the patient, laid-back tactical expert and Noriel as the motivated, can-do sergeant. As it was with Bowen, if I needed anything done, I could ask Noriel and it would happen, maybe not as cleanly or elegantly as Bowen would have done it, but it would most undoubtedly happen and happen quickly. Best of all, Noriel never hesitated to tell me or anyone else that what we were asking was all screwed up and that he had a few better ideas. He was fiercely protective of his Marines, and he defended their well-being against all comers, officer and enlisted alike.

By late January, our team was set, or so I thought. Then the division, in our first hint of things to come, sent my company ten naval corpsmen ("docs"), and I got two of them. This was a somewhat strange and disconcerting development because a Marine company normally rates only one doc, and all the platoons share him. If major combat operations were truly over, then why were we multiplying the standard medical capacity tenfold?

I pushed the incongruity and my own questions aside for the time because I was happy to have our naval brethren. The senior corpsman, Doc Aaron Smith, was a scruffy white kid who always needed a shave and who could barely run three miles. He could walk all day, though, and eight months previously he had been assigned to a rifle platoon in the drive up to Baghdad, which made him, ironically enough, the most experienced combat veteran in my platoon, myself included. I assigned Smith to second squad and made him teach everyone classes about physiological responses in combat. We all paid rapt attention, and it became pretty clear that this flabby naval corpsman with questionable personal hygiene was very good at what he did and that what he did was save Marine lives in combat.

The junior corpsman, Doc Geovanni Camacho-Galvan, could not have been more different. A week prior to arriving, Camacho didn't even know where our Marine base was, let alone what a Marine infantry unit was like, let alone what he had to do to save lives in combat. For the entirety of his two-year Navy career, Doc Camacho had been taking care of newborn babies in a neonatal ward at a naval base in Balboa, California, and he was shocked when he was assigned to the infantry with absolutely no warning. Indeed, I was shocked when he joined us, because Doc Camacho was even smaller than the smallest of my new Marines—he stood about five feet, four inches tall and weighed perhaps 110 pounds soaking wet. He spoke Spanish as his first language and English rapidly and nervously in quick little bullets of tightly compacted words. Doc Camacho shivered a lot, and he constantly worried that his complete lack of training would fail him, that he would let the Marines down when they needed him the most. I shared this nervousness, but we needed the medical expertise, so I assigned Doc Camacho to Sergeant Noriel with the idea that if anyone could get the neonatal baby tender ready in time, it was Noriel.

Unfortunately, the only training that the young corpsman would get with the platoon was 2/4's capstone exercise at March Air Reserve Base over the last week of January. As this was scheduled to be the battalion's be-all, end-all culminating event before shipping out, each company was given a call sign by the battalion CO that would serve as its primary identifier from here on out. In a standard call-sign selection process, the company commanders usually pick the most manly, fearsome name they can think of, like "Warhammer" or "Reaper," and then submit it up the chain for approval. If it succeeds, all the better, and if not then they move on to their slightly less alpha-male backups, for example, "Apache" or "Cold Steel." Colonel Kennedy, however, had a solid sense of humor and other plans for his subordinates. The colonel had designed his own name-assignment process, one that hinged on first identifying an eccentricity particular to each company commander and then encapsulating that eccentricity in a single word. My CO, for example, had a laugh like a donkey's braying, and when he was amused the entire battalion command post knew. Thus, our company's call sign became "Joker." It could have been worse—our sister company, Echo, earned the moniker "Porcupine," abbreviated "Porky."

My Marines and I were all Jokers now, and each platoon and its commander got their own company subidentifier. My platoon became Joker One, the same name that I took on when I represented my Marines corporately, which was more or less all the time. I became differentiated only when someone needed to talk just to me over the radio, at which point I became Joker One–Actual (usually abbreviated "One-Actual"). This simple renaming process expresses far more eloquently the relationship between a lieutenant and his Marines than anything that I could write. Quist, Hes, and Flowers became Jokers Two, Three, and Four respectively. The CO became Joker Six, and the Gunny became Joker Eight. Officially the Ox was given the title of Joker Five, but to all the platoon commanders he remained, as ever, the Ox.

With platoon and company call signs identified appropriately, the other Jokers and I trooped off to March Air Reserve Base to earn the official deployment stamp of approval from the 1st Marine Division. Even though the exercise took place in a condemned and abandoned base housing area, it was still the best, most realistic training that we had been through to date. However, the training had its limitations. No existing American housing complex could properly simulate the tightly packed streets and the long, walled city blocks of a densely populated Iraqi city. Also, when all is said and done, a nineteen-year-old Marine lance corporal from Idaho with a bed-sheet over his head has only limited success simulating a Sunni Arab woman, no matter how hard he tries. Some things we would simply have to learn on the fly.

The March Air Reserve Base exercise concluded successfully in early February, so we returned to our homes, packed up our gear, and waited for our turn as guinea pigs for the division's new hearts-and-minds campaign. While we were waiting, I turned twenty-four, and two days after my birthday I got a present: The medical doctors cleared Henderson for full-time duty (and certified that he was indeed nineteen years old), and our man came back to the platoon. The only downside to the return was that Henderson hadn't completed a single major training event with Joker One, but the Marines accepted him back with open arms nonetheless. After all, they certainly weren't ones to throw stones. Fully one-third of our men hadn't even been with the platoon for a full month.

n the days leading up to our mid-February flight, the stress of the imminent deployment started to take a toll, and Marines across the battalion
began behaving strangely. Fortunately, my problems were confined to
only two men, PFC Joshua Guzon and Lance Corporal Todd Bolding.
Shortly before our departure, nineteen-year-old Guzon decided that he
didn't want to come back to Camp Pendleton after a three-day weekend
with his fiancée. Somehow, Staff Sergeant tracked him down and convinced him to return, and once he did so we demoted him to a buck private.
It didn't matter—Guzon did the exact same thing the very next weekend,
just two days before we were scheduled to depart. This time, Staff Sergeant
had to call Guzon's future father-in-law—a former military man himself
who understood well the severely negative implications of desertion before
a combat deployment—to get him to send our private back to us.

With only two days to go until deployment, we weren't taking any
chances, and as soon as Staff Sergeant had corralled the now Private Guzon,
he put the reluctant Marine under the 24/7 care of Corporal Teague, who
would confide to me that he had serious concerns about Guzon's mental

stability. Staff Sergeant had also begun to worry that Guzon would shoot him in the back the first time he had access to live ammunition.

Staff Sergeant's nerves gave me pause, but after thinking it over I decided that Guzon was just a nineteen-year-old kid who had made a very stupid short-term choice without considering the long-term consequences of his actions. I believed that he would behave normally once we got him out of the States.

Guzon never got away again—the rest of my Marines saw to that. Sometime later, I asked Teague how they had managed to corral our slippery little private. "You don't wanna know, sir, trust me," came the reply, but I did, in fact, want to know, so I pressed until the full story came out. It was about what I expected: As soon as Guzon returned, Teague and a few others had zip-tied him to a heavy chair and taken turns standing guard until it was time to depart.

Lance Corporal Bolding was much more subtle about his unauthorized departures. Sometime over the winter, the twenty-three-year-old Bolding, one of our team leaders, had married his longtime girlfriend, and the endless training days were taking their toll on the new couple. So, when Joker One wasn't staying overnight in the field, Bolding would leave the base at random, unauthorized times—usually a few hours before the rest of the Marines were let go—to spend time at his new off-base home with his new wife. We finally caught him when we had to draw equipment—more helmets and flak jackets—early one morning, and Bolding never showed up. Away from my wife more often than not myself, I sympathized with the new husband's plight, but it didn't matter. We couldn't rely on Bolding to complete even the most basic assignments if they fell either at a day's beginning or its end, so shortly before we left for Iraq, I relieved Bolding as a team leader and gave his two men to another lance corporal. Bolding took it well, saying that he understood, that he'd work hard to make up for his shortcomings, and that he'd respect whoever his new team leader happened to be. When our conversation ended, Bolding walked away with a big grin spread widely across his face. It was his default expression, his trademark, and I hoped that it meant the demotion hadn't embittered him.

However, no matter how challenging these problems seemed to me, others had it far worse. One morning shortly after Guzon's first unauthorized absence, Flowers was standing watch as 2/4's officer of the day (OOD) when he received a frantic call from the barracks that one of the Marines from Echo Company, our first unit scheduled to fly out, had hurt himself somehow. Rushing to the scene, Flowers found the Marine lying in a pool of his own blood—he had tried to commit suicide by stabbing himself with his Ka-Bar fighting knife. Flowers called an ambulance and immediately administered first aid. Thanks to his and others' quick thinking, the Marine lived through the suicide attempt, but that incident was our first taste of the unsparing mental strain that the anticipation of war places on its participants, and from then on out the platoon commanders were on high alert for any signs of instability in their men.

In the midst of all this tension, we got one piece of good news. Instead of Habbaniyah, 2/4 would be going to Ramadi, a city that seemed relatively stable and that, we were told, had well-developed U.S. bases with at least a few of the comforts of home, such as running water and intermittent electricity. Hearing our destination, I searched all the recent news articles I could find for mentions of the city, but there were very few, a good sign in and of itself, for less news generally (but not always) meant less violence. The articles that did include Ramadi usually did so only in passing—the city was primarily referred to as the capital of the "volatile" Anbar province in articles that focused on Fallujah, a wild no-man's-land even in the winter of 2004. Indeed, the longest quote I could find in reference to our future home came from one of its American overseers, who declared in an interview that Ramadi was "on the glide path to success." As long as U.S. forces didn't screw things up, the city, it seemed, was fixing itself.

Our battalion intelligence officer did his homework as well, compiling a list of all the hostile incidents that had occurred in the city over the past several months. The most serious of these was a single RPG attack on an Army vehicle-mounted patrol, and the attacker was so incompetent and the Army patrol so responsive that they had run down the would-be insurgent and sent him off to prison for quite some time. We also noticed that occasionally weeks had gone by without any enemy contact at all.

On February 15, the night before Golf Company flew to Kuwait, I held Christy tightly and assured her that Ramadi wouldn't be that bad, that nothing of significance had happened in the place for the past few months, and that we as Marines would certainly make it even better. It made some difference, I suppose, but not much. After all, I'd only been home for four months, and by the time I returned from this new deployment, if I ever did, I would have spent as much of our marriage in Iraq as I had at home, and Christy knew it. I didn't know how to explain to her how conflicted I felt about leaving; on the one hand, I was really excited about leading an infantry platoon overseas, but on the other, I loved my wife deeply and hated to be away from her again, and so soon. Somewhere, a part of me also questioned myself for being so happy and excited about a job that would put her through the horrible experience of waiting for that dreaded knock on the door that every military wife fears more than almost anything else in the world. So I just held my wife, and together we prayed and cried throughout the night.

The fateful next morning came far too quickly. At about 8 AM, Christy and I once again loaded up my backpack and canvas duffel bag into our Jeep and drove out to the parade deck, a large, flat, asphalt-covered square where all the departing Marines and their families assembled before loading the buses and heading out. The poignant, heartbreaking scene is one known by every American who has gone into combat. In the center of the parade deck, nervous young Marines staged their gear in neat, well-aligned rows under the watchful eyes of their platoon sergeants. Wives, children, and parents, some crying and some not, stood on the periphery, waiting for the work to be done so that, one last time, they could say goodbye to the men they loved, the men whom they couldn't be sure that they would ever see again.

When the staging was finished, we let the Marines wander off to wherever they wanted. Those that had families went to them. Staff Sergeant's three children clustered around his legs, tugging on his pants, asking him why he had to go and when he was coming back. He had to go to work, he said, and he didn't know when he'd be coming back. Hopefully soon. The CO's two kids, Cactus Jack and Caroline, were asking the same questions. Captain Bronzi promised the Cactus that he'd bring him back a desert rock. He told them that he'd think of them every day. Caroline was inconsolable— "I'll miss you, Daddy" was all she said, over and over again, as the CO's wife, Amy, tried hard to shush her and be strong for her husband. Sergeant Noriel held his two-year-old daughter, Brianna, with one arm and his tearful wife,

Nicky, with another and alternated kissing the two of them. Sergeant Leza put his hand on his pregnant wife Martha's stomach. Be strong, he said. I'm coming back to be a daddy to the little one. I promise. The Ox held his newborn daughter tightly and asked his wife, Melissa, to please, please, send him videotapes of her first birthday party.

Those Marines without family present, which was most of them, milled about nervously in the middle of their respective platoon's staging areas. Most were smoking. Characteristically, Bowen, who had returned just one week ago from the Arabic immersion course, was there with his squad, walking around and reassuring them with a quiet word of kindness here, a brief pat on the shoulder there, giving them all a final once-over before departure. The platoon commanders' wives all clustered together until their husbands were done with their work. From time to time, I glanced over at their little huddle to see how things were going. Christy, Lyndsey (Hes's wife), and Lisa (Quist's wife) seemed to be holding up well enough. They were chatting with one another animatedly, and every now and again a small smile even shone out. Relieved each time, I would turn my attention back to the Marines.

Finally, all the gear was staged and all the Marines were squared away, so the other platoon commanders and I walked over and held our wives one last time. I don't know how long that bittersweet moment lasted, but it certainly wasn't long enough. Then, like thousands of Marines before and after us, we said goodbye, grabbed our gear, and boarded the buses. As they pulled away, I stood up and stared out the back window at our wives for as long as I could. As soon as they thought we weren't looking, their brave faces crumbled. Christy had her arms wrapped around herself, and silent tears streamed down her cheeks. Lisa looked much the same, but Lyndsey was the worst. All the blood had drained from her face, and she suddenly looked as if she no longer knew who or where she was. She was just standing there forlornly, rocking back and forth, hands hanging limply by her sides.

Five hours later, we boarded a chartered 747 and strapped ourselves into our seats and into a completely alien life. As the plane winged its way over the dark ocean, for the first time in several months I had a few free hours to reflect. I hoped that I had done enough, that I had worked hard enough both apart from and together with my Marines to make myself into the leader they deserved, but I wasn't certain that I had or that I was. I hoped that the short time my platoon had had together in the States had been enough to at least assimilate all of our new Marines, but I wasn't sure. I hoped that Henderson's heart wouldn't stop in the middle of a mission, that Doc Camacho wouldn't curl up into a little ball the first time he heard gunfire, that Guzon wouldn't shoot Staff Sergeant in the back after all, and that somehow Feldmeir would be miraculously cured of his narcolepsy, because I had no idea how to fix him. All this and more I pondered and hoped as the hours ticked slowly by.

But hope is not a course of action, and, ready or not, Joker One was headed straight into the capital city of Iraq's most violent province.

Part 2

NEW

SEVEN

stepped out of the plane and onto a jetway in the middle of the barren Kuwaiti desert. After thirty-six hours tucked away in a dark passenger cabin, the sun and the sand blasted my eyes, and I flinched. I fumbled for my sunglasses, stowed somewhere in one of my many pockets, and inhaled a lungful of the sandy air. I coughed. Kuwait was still the bleak, windswept moonscape I remembered from my flight out just four months previously.

Cautiously, I descended the stairs. With my long M-16 slung across my body, my pistol strapped to my right leg, and other bits of gear weighing me awkwardly down, I didn't want to take a tumble in front of my men. Once I hit the sticky asphalt-and-concrete tarmac, I hustled over to our assembly area, designated as such by a shouting transportation NCO. Behind me, Noriel, Leza, and Bowen went into action, chivying their men off the plane, marshaling their squads, and checking that all the important gear was still with the Marines.

It was, so Joker One hustled off the tarmac and into the plywood-and-canvas structure that was the designated Kuwait reception area. Quickly and efficiently, my three squad leaders streamed their men onto the benches inside as I stood and watched, observing my platoon on its very first day in-country. Bolding, as usual, was smiling and joking with the men around him. He didn't betray even a hint of nervousness. Mahardy wasn't talking at all, which was highly unusual—perhaps he understood better than most the enormity of the task in front of him, or perhaps he was just tired. Carson stood a full head taller than the rest of his team as he stolidly herded them into place. Feldmeir fell asleep nearly as soon as he hit the bench. Without breaking stride—and without even needing to look at his Marine—Teague quickly slapped Feldmeir across the back of the head as he walked past the snoozing kid. The slap had apparently become the standard Feldmeir main-tenance procedure, and my narcoleptic Marine sat up so quickly that he very nearly fell off the bench. It was hard to tell how Noriel, Bowen, and Leza were doing. They were too busy and too focused on their men and their tasks to have any time to reflect on their own feelings. After the entire platoon settled into their places on the benches, I took my seat behind them.

The standard "Welcome to Iraq" briefings began. I tuned them out. I'd heard it all before and didn't need to be reminded to take my antimalaria pills or to refrain from drinking the local water. Instead, I thought about my men and what we had to do together. I was nervous but cautiously excited. For the first time since joining the Corps nearly two and a half years ago, I had my own platoon, and we were about to start doing our jobs for real. In spite of our short time together, I trusted my squad and team leaders be-cause I knew that they were strong, and that strength gave me hope for the job to come. Besides, the Iraq to which we were headed in early 2004 didn't seem all that dangerous. Though U.S. newspapers had raised the specter of a nascent insurgency, many people, including us, debated whether it even existed. The city of Ramadi had been quiet recently, so I expected to do far more school building than street fighting. I looked forward to establishing a rapport with the locals, to learning the Iraqi culture and working together to improve their lives and their country.

And this time around, unlike the last, I knew my exact position and the people with whom I'd be working. I was terrifically nervous about how I'd do as a leader, about whether I had whatever it took to properly take care of my men, but looking around at Joker One, I was comforted. The thirty-seven Marines who sat there were mine, and leaving home as part of a defined unit was much less lonely than deploying as an isolated individual had been.

When the series of briefings ended, Joker One and I rose and made our way out of the darkened tent and back into the blinding sunlight. We quickly wound our way through clumps of Marines and soldiers scattered haphazardly throughout the small cluster of reception tents. My squad leaders moved all along their men, hustling them through the crowds like nervous shepherds. All around us stood thousands of other people with the exact same haircuts and the exact same clothes as we. After all, Golf Company and 2/4 had arrived in Kuwait as part of America's largest rotation of troops and equipment since World War II, and hundreds of different units were simultaneously flowing into and out of the small desert kingdom. After an hour of looking, we found the vehicles that would take us to our new temporary home, a desert camp about fifty miles away, still well inside the Kuwait border. Twenty hours after we arrived in the country, an exhausted, bedraggled Golf Company made it into Camp Commando.

It was no different from the several other staging camps I had been to. Row after row of giant white tents sprouted out of a desert plain, housing thousands of troops headed the two days' journey north into Iraq. Artillery pieces, tanks, armored fighting vehicles, and other assorted troop carriers staged in one huge, flat corner of the camp, away from the living areas to minimize the chances of accidentally crushing someone to death. Bisecting this small city in the desert ran a large, crushed gravel road, and surrounding the whole thing was a gigantic dirt mound, about fifteen feet high, with guard towers placed every hundred meters or so.

The desert sand was ubiquitous. It was different from what I was used to on American beaches; it had a powdery rather than granular consistency, much like flour, and it got into everything—weapons, living areas, boots, underwear, toothbrushes. Whenever the wind kicked up, which was often, visibility dropped to less than a hundred feet. We covered our mouths and noses in handkerchiefs or scarves in vain attempts to keep the sand at bay. Within about a week, most of us had developed some version of a hacking cough as the fine particles rasped at our lungs. When I sneezed, sand came out.

Sandstorms couldn't stop us from training, though, which was a good thing, because our still-green company desperately needed all the practice we could get. We would be in the camp for about two weeks before heading north in early March, and Hes, Quist, Flowers, and I planned detailed training schedules for our platoons each day. By now, the four platoon commanders had developed a smooth and amicable working relationship. We weren't especially close—the short time together and the intense training schedule hadn't allowed us too much interaction outside of work—but we respected one another as professionals, and at least three of us had easygoing personalities that made the inevitable give-and-take relatively painless.

Our first morning we set a routine we would follow for the rest of our time there, beginning at around 5 AM with a run through Camp Commando. Hearing the chants of the men and their forced bravado in the face of the sand and the heat, I was reminded of my first run with Joker One, one that I had taken back in Camp Pendleton just a few days after coming to the platoon.

After assembling on our basketball courts, we had begun a series of quick stretches together. When we took off running down the soggy dirt paths through the woods of base, I heard the following chant:

> Loooowww right, your low right leh-oh . . .
> Looww right right, your low right leh-oh . . .
> When I get to heaven . . .
> Saint Peter's gonna say-ay . . .
> How'd you make your living boy, how'd you earn your pay-ay . . .
> Iiiiiii'll reply with my kni-ife . . .
> SHUT UP, BITCH, I'M GONNA TAKE YOUR LI-IFE!!

I had loved the fact that a group of teenage kids had felt cocky enough to threaten Saint Peter with a knife (never mind referring to him as a bitch) and, later on in the chant, to put Satan himself on notice. Their attitude had seemed amusing, foreign, and attractive all at once. I had never developed the chutzpah to talk about the sacred so casually, and some part of me envied my Marines their bravado.

ow, standing in the desert of Kuwait for the third time with the harsh reality of deployment all around me, I heard the same chants as I had that
day in Pendleton, and I remembered that just a few short months before
joining Joker One, I had been just like my Marines. I also had thought that
scars were cool and that getting wounded doing heroic, leadership-type
things wouldn't necessarily be all that bad. In the Corps, we're thoroughly
trained on stories of its magnificent battle history, a history writ strong by
people like Gunny Basilone in World War II, and, more recently, Captain
Chontosh in Operation Iraqi Freedom I—both of whom single-handedly
destroyed fiercely defended, numerically superior enemy strongpoints and
saved lots of Marine lives in the process. Officer and enlisted alike pray that
that kind of fortitude combines with that kind of opportunity to produce that
kind of glory.

As I stood there in the desert sand, stretching and cooling down and re-
flecting on all these things, I hadn't yet been shot at or returned fire, but I
had been in a combat zone, and I had met plenty of blooded infantrymen.
All the good ones had more or less carried themselves the same way, and the
chest-beating machismo embodied in our chants was nowhere to be seen.
The only words I can find that might come close to suggesting what had replaced that false bravado are "grim determination." Nothing else can really
explain that battle-hardened air, but you know it when you see it.

I had also seen a few of the lightly wounded brought back to my base;
heard firsthand about the Marine who shot his friend in the face to prove
that his weapon was unloaded; and stood and watched the flies congregate
on the congealed blood outside the port-a-john where some nameless major
had put his pistol in his mouth and pulled the trigger. My stupid, young
machismo had been largely burned out of me. Death was no longer an altogether complete stranger. Glancing around at the high walls of the desert
berms around us, it hit me more than ever that Joker One was headed north
soon, headed into an area officially designated a war zone. I didn't think that
the fighting would be all that fierce, but I suspected that at least some would
occur, and I suspected that someone, somewhere might get hurt.

And what you don't hear about in training is the anonymous officer who
was crushed to death because one night he slept too close to the amtracs, or
the PFC who got shot through the lower spine on his first week in country

and who will now never walk again, let alone perform heroic feats in combat. And what you can't see—and what no one can teach you and what you can't really even envision until you get into it—are the wounds. Before they heal, most look more or less the same (if you can even see them through all the blood): like raw, red meat. Afterward they sort of differentiate themselves, but I have yet to encounter any combat scar that looked cool in any form or fashion. Mostly they look pink and jagged and discolored and puffy—accurate reflections of the trauma that cause them. Bullet entry wounds are often puckered and the exit wounds, if you're unlucky, are swollen and deformed where the flesh has been blown out. Shrapnel wounds almost always look like someone took a jagged shovel and dug a chunk of flesh out of the body, then filled it in awkwardly with hairless, discolored skin that shouldn't belong on a human being. Burn wounds are smoothly hideous, like the skin was turned into peanut butter and then spread in stretched, uneven dollops on the body. Or maybe you come back missing a finger or your face, or the whole or parts of your limbs. Maybe your eyes are gone. However, it's hard to try to explain random, mundane death and wounding to unblooded college-age Marines, because—like having a child—some things you just have to experience to fully understand. Few people, especially at that age, truly comprehend the idea that tomorrow is by no means certain—they usually have to see a few tomorrows forcefully and tragically taken away before they understand the gift of time. And the Corps as a whole focuses on its heroes and on its magnificent battle history, partly to instill a strong service culture in its new recruits, partly to instill the values necessary to do the job, and partly to teach all Marines that they have the potential to achieve something beyond themselves. After all, young Marines can understand and aspire to valor and greatness; death and defeat they cannot.

It's left to the small unit leaders, to the corporals, the sergeants, and the lieutenants, to gently tone down as much of the bravado as possible, to transform the lust for glory and the desire to be a hero into the deep need simply to take care of your buddy and to serve your team, squad, and platoon. With a partial understanding of combat already underneath my belt, I realized as we prepared for our trip north that I would have to slowly do my part to ready my Marines to assume the grim determination that would carry them through combat once harsh reality had ripped its way into their dreams. So, gently, Noriel, Leza, Bowen, and I toned down the screaming and the shouting during the training. "Dial back the volume, turn up the effort, and don't focus on making yourself look tough and hard," we said. "Don't worry about how you appear, just do your jobs and take care of each other. That should take everything you've got and then some."

After each morning's run, we ate breakfast and then trained for every conceivable combat scenario, with a heavy emphasis on casualty evacuation (casevac) procedures during each. A Marine lying laughingly on the desert sand after he's just been unexpectedly "wounded" isn't the same as one screaming in the city streets with no hand and blood everywhere, but it was as close as we could get for now. We also cross-trained ourselves on our own equipment to emphasize forcibly that we might lose one of our rocket, machine gun, or mortar specialists.

One week into this training, Division sent Golf Company a lawyer who tried to explain to our Marines exactly when they could and could not shoot. We had just finished a patrolling exercise, so 120 dirty, sweat-soaked infantry Marines sat in a rough horseshoe in the desert sand with their weapons sticking up from between their legs as the slight lawyer in pristine cammies began his lecture. According to this lawyer, we had to be absolutely certain that our prospective target demonstrated one of two things: a hostile act or a hostile intent. Hostile acts were usually fairly easy to identify because they almost always involved a potential target either aiming or firing a weapon at us, the lawyer said. Hostile intent was a bit trickier, and the lawyer couldn't give us an actionable definition of the term. Apparently, the concept allowed a lot of room for individual interpretation.

The lawyer also touched on what happened after the firing started. Apparently, our decision to *stop* shooting also hinged on establishing one of two things: whether the enemy was "still in the fight" or "out of the fight." An enemy "still in the fight" was one who, despite wounds or suppressing fire, continued to demonstrate an active intent to kill Marines. Think of the insurgent who's been shot but is crawling toward his weapon, the lawyer said. These people are fair game. By contrast, "out of the fight" referred to an enemy who no longer tried to kill you, whether through loss of will or loss of practical ability. To help clarify, the lawyer gave us the example of the insurgent who's been shot and whose RPG launcher is lying twenty feet away, or the insurgent who drops his weapon and flees the fight. In both of those cases, we were legally obligated to stop firing.

The problem with the lawyer's earnest talk was that, while it sounded good in theory, it was almost impossible to execute with any precision. Generally, when you most need to act on the specified legal conditions, you are least likely to be able to verify unquestionably whether they have been met. How do you tell if an enemy is crawling toward or away from his weapon when he's two hundred meters away, your eyes are stinging with sweat, and the insurgent is surrounded by the thick cloud of dirt that always kicks up when an RPG-7 fires? How do you determine whether someone calling on his cellphone in the middle of a crowd of two hundred people is preparing to detonate an IED or talking to his mother? Maybe these questions were obvious to the lawyer, and maybe they weren't. After all, the zero-defects mentality of the 1990s peacetime military hadn't been fully jettisoned by the realities of our current war.

The lawyer's precise, bloodless presentation managed to confuse a lot of the Marines—after all, training had taught us that theory and reality often wildly diverged. So the CO instructed the platoon commanders to simplify it. Since hostile intent was so hard to verify, we would keep all decisions surrounding that issue firmly in the hands of the platoon commanders. Better to take risks ourselves than to kill innocent civilians, the CO said, and we agreed. Once the firing started and once the targets had been positively identified, though, the in/out of the fight concept would get tossed out the window. Instead, we would stop our shooting according to the dictate of the Pine Box Rule: If there's any question about whether it's you or the bad guy who is going home in a pine box, you make damn certain that it's the bad guy. Of course we wanted to avoid as many innocent victims as possible, but if someone had already tried to kill us, there was no way we would risk our own lives simply to meet a vague legal condition of extremely dubious validity.

With this issue clarified as well as it could be, and with most of the basics of foot patrolling well covered, in the second week of our stay in Kuwait we shifted our training to emphasize convoy operations. Golf Company's first mission into Iraq was a three-day road trip north to Ramadi, and we wanted to be as prepared as possible. So each day I made Joker One practice jumping into and out of stationary Humvees and seven-ton trucks, the huge, fifteen-foot-high troop carriers that would be our primary people movers during the northbound convoy. To a casual observer, the sight of thirty-seven fully loaded Marines bouncing all around unmoving vehicles for hours in the desert heat might have seemed ridiculous at best and sadistic at worst. However, I knew that the little things we learned during this endless repetition might very well make the difference between life and death.

In our world, basic tasks have to be repeatedly rehearsed in conditions mimicking predicted combat scenarios as faithfully as possible. For example, you can never be sure which small detail might mean the difference between exiting a vehicle caught in an enemy ambush kill zone in two seconds or in ten. That kind of time differential can be fatal. Where is the door handle on the seven-ton truck? Do you have to pull it up or down to get out? How far is the drop out of the truck bed, and where exactly do you need to put your feet before you hurl yourself out the door? Once all the little questions have been answered, those answers must be practiced again and again until they become muscle memory. The Marines didn't like the mind-numbingly repetitive nature of such drills, and they didn't exactly love the squad leaders and me for putting them through the endless rehearsals, but every time we did something tedious and painful, we tried to lay out the reason behind the drills to everyone. I became amazed at how much my men would tolerate if someone just took the time to explain the why of it all to them.

To make things even more realistic, one day the Ox managed to scavenge enough vehicles from the battalion to mount up all four Joker platoons. Our company drove around in three-block squares inside the Kuwaiti camp for hours, rehearsing different enemy contact scenarios late into the evening. For lap after dull lap, we practiced responses to small IED ambushes, to civilian traffic jams, to herds of goats crossing the road, and to friendly vehicle breakdowns.

After two hours of pretending, I felt that we had exhausted the repertoire of likely scenarios and useful responses. The platoons were making one final circuit, and I was mentally preparing myself to head to bed, when the Ox got on the hook and announced a typical Ox scenario:

"All Jokers, be advised, this is Joker Five. We have an enemy platoon dug in, in the defense two hundred meters off our right flank. We need to fucking assault those bastards. Dismount the company and kick their asses. Over."

I rolled my eyes. It was typical of the Ox to dream up the most hard-core scenario possible, regardless of whether his fantasy bore even a remote resemblance to anticipated reality. Unenthusiastically, Jokers One through Four ordered our men to dismount and execute the tedious assault. When the evening's convoy operations were finally finished, each exhausted platoon commander took turns bashing the Ox. Flowers started off: "Did you hear what that dumb Ox was saying? What does he think we're going to be fighting? The damn Red Hordes pouring into Eastern Europe?"

Quist, Hes, and I all chimed in with our own insults. Then, tired and filthy and muttering angrily to ourselves, we trudged back to our tent to try to get some sleep.

EIGHT

His affinity for sadistic training regimens aside, the Ox had learned a thing or two about infantry leadership from his nearly two years as a platoon commander. One event, in particular, made me realize that he was wiser than I thought. Because Camp Commando was full far beyond its capacity with troops ready to head into Iraq, time at its few phone banks and e-mail systems was difficult to come by. However, our company had two satellite cellphones that would allow us to call back home whenever we liked. The company officers and staff NCOs retained one of these phones for their own use, and the other was put in the hands of the platoon sergeants and rotated through each platoon. As there were only twelve officers and enlisted men on the company staff and just over 140 Marines in the company, the platoon commanders could call home much more frequently. And we did, often talking to our wives as much as once a day. The Ox, however, noticeably refrained from using the phone. Watching us so casually chat with our families, he cautioned all the platoon commanders to keep a close eye on how often our Marines were able to reach home before we burned up the airwaves ourselves. We ignored his advice and blithely continued our calling.

About three days before we headed into Iraq, Carson lumbered up to me.

"Sir, I've got, ahhh, something I need to say, sir," he said, shuffling his feet and alternately looking down at the ground and at me.

I looked up at him. "Yeah, Carson, go ahead."

"Sir, with all due respect, and it's no huge deal, sir, but we kind of notice that you're using the cellphone a lot to call home. Sir, none of us have really been able to use it, and the phone banks are always jammed, so we haven't been able to call home like you, sir. Maybe you could, you know, like, give us the phone every now and again? It's no big deal, though, sir."

"Has Staff Sergeant not gotten you guys the phone yet?"

"No, sir. Third and fourth platoon have gotten to call home, though."

Hearing that, I felt all of about three feet tall, and I found myself humbly apologizing to my team leader. I knew better than to take care of my needs before taking care of my men, but knowing and doing are unfortunately two different things. I had thought that the key to earning my men's respect was to demonstrate excellent tactical judgment in combat, a strong set of individual skills (fitness, good shooting and navigating, and so on) and a general willingness to make large, spectacular sacrifices—in short, most things that I thought it took to be a war hero.

I could not have been more wrong. Being a good leader and being a hero, I was beginning to realize, were not at all the same thing. For the young lieutenant, much more difficult than thirty-second acts of courage, and ultimately much more telling, are the small, quiet, almost unnoticeable acts of service that he must perform day in and day out if he wants to appropriately ensure the welfare of his men. I was determined that I would never make the same mistake again. It would mean talking to Christy much less—rarely more than once a month—but it was necessary. Besides, the intensity of combat leadership was beginning to wholly consume me. As Iraq got closer and closer, home grew farther and farther away. Thoughts of my wife and an American reality that no longer existed for me got neatly compartmented and tucked away.

The next day found the diminutive Yebra and I marching in endless squares around the various gravel roads running through the camp. To rehearse the battalion's impending convoy north, every officer had been paired up with his radio operator and told to simulate a vehicle. Thirty of these "vehicles" were now slowly trundling around Camp Commando under the blazing noonday sun. The night previously, the CO had designated me as the company's navigator, so Yebra and I were the second vehicle in the long, snaking line of officers and radiomen (the first vehicle would be an armored Humvee with a .50-caliber machine gun to guard us as we moved). I was the only one in the company who had actually led a convoy in Iraq before, so the assignment hadn't come as a surprise. Still, staring back at all the men behind me, realizing that they were only a tenth of those whom I'd lead into Iraq, the enormity of the responsibility started to sink in. It was my job to get some thirty vehicles and 180 people safely to their destination, and if I screwed anything up, all of their lives would be put at risk unnecessarily.

Once the exercise finished, Yebra and I trudged over to the two seven-ton trucks that had been assigned to carry Joker One. The cab of each truck held only two people—myself and a driver from the truck company in the first and the platoon sergeant and another assigned driver in the second. The rest of Joker One had to sit in the truck beds. Unfortunately, the seven-tons were still configured for movements back in the United States, where carrying capacity took precedence over personnel protection or fighting capability. As a result, a thin canvas covering was the only thing between the Marines and the open road. Furthermore, the benches in the back sat along the sides of the truck, forcing the Marines either to sit with their backs to the road or to twist painfully around for hours at a time, trying to scan their surroundings as their backs screamed at the unceasing torque. It had taken only a few rehearsals to convince us that this setup was impossible to handle for even an hour, let alone for a three-days-straight convoy into the heart of Iraq.

To help improve our protection, we lined the truck beds with as many sandbags as each vehicle could safely carry. They wouldn't cover people above their waists, but the bags were certainly better than nothing. The entire company scavenged Camp Commando for benches that we could put into two lines down the center of the seven-tons so that Marines could sit back-to-back, facing outward without having to twist themselves for hours. We had no luck, so the CO instructed each platoon to come up with two designs apiece for centerline benches using only what we could carry with us: boxes of MREs, crates of water, and our own duffel bags. The best design would be standardized and used throughout the entire company.

Hes, Quist, and Flowers—the engineer—had each come up with his own design, and they put their platoons to work constructing what they had planned. I hadn't been able to think of anything particularly clever, or different, so I called Noriel, Leza, and Bowen together and explained what the CO wanted and why he wanted it. They all nodded as I went along. Many painful hours spent twisted in the back of the seven-tons had convinced my squad leaders of the absolute imperative for the centerline benches. Once finished, I turned them over to their squads. Noriel and Leza got to work on one truck, and Bowen and his men took another.

As much as I wanted to direct their efforts, to appear the in-charge leader who knew exactly how things should turn out, two minutes of observation convinced me that my men working together would create something far better than I would working on my own. Bowen had his guys huddled around him, and was explaining to them what I had explained to him, and design suggestions flew back and forth. Noriel and Leza were doing the same thing with the same results. After five minutes, the squads had broken up, and the seven-tons swarmed with Joker One Marines. Bowen took position at the head of the truck bed, standing atop two huge green duffel bags as he directed his men's efforts, blouse off and tattoos straining as he lifted here, pointed there. Noriel did the same thing in his truck while Leza moved about on the ground, shunting men from one vehicle to another depending on the manpower needed for each.

Fully involved in the process, the Marines worked with a vengeance. The stocky, muscular Guzon shunted back and forth tirelessly, usually with at least two huge packs slung across his shoulders. Henderson, as it turned out, was a car wizard, and many of the best suggestions for load configuration came straight from him. Ideas were tested and discarded, gear was arranged and rearranged, and slowly but surely, two centerline benches began taking shape in each vehicle. Nearly every one of my men had a suggestion for how to do something better, and sometimes the smallest ideas—such as interweaving the handles of the duffel bags for greater stability—made the biggest difference. Standing on the side, carrying the occasional bag or case of water, I looked for opportunities to give direction, but they didn't need it. Nearly an hour later, Noriel and Bowen pulled me up into their trucks to show off their handiwork. Both designs were good, but Bowen's was best; it would become the company standard.

Two days later, Golf Company readied itself to head north. March 1, 2004, was our last night in Camp Commando, and I spent it checking and rechecking my crude map consisting solely of several eight-by-eleven print-outs that I had taped together to form one continuous strip. I also had a GPS, and should that fail, I wore an electronic compass on my wrist and a magnetic compass on my flak jacket. Of course, inside a gigantic ferrous metal truck cab, these instruments can only be trusted to tell the most basic cardinal directions, but they were better than nothing. This redundancy may seem like overkill, but I was all too aware that if I missed a checkpoint or made a wrong turn somewhere, a thirty-vehicle convoy spread over two miles would somehow have to make a U-turn on a two-lane highway with no shoulder to speak of and treacherous, slippery sand on each side. Further complicating this difficult movement would be the fact that any road we were on would likely be jammed solidly with U.S. vehicles heading into and out of Iraq. Road signs were limited and printed mainly in Arabic, and we had no translators. Looming large over all these concerns, though, were the faceless insurgents who even in early 2004 had demonstrated the capability to attack a lost convoy made vulnerable during a missed turn or a complicated circling maneuver. The best way to ensure the safety of my company was to never make a navigation mistake. I was terribly worried that I would.

I spent the late evening hours of March 1 trying to sleep but failing miserably. I thought back to all the land navigation exercises I had done at my Basic School. I had failed the first one miserably and then spent every single Saturday morning working to improve in remedial sessions. I wondered if it had been enough, or if I would fail under the pressure. The weight of two hundred or so lives was heavier than I expected. So I prayed a simple prayer over and over:

"Dear God, please don't let me screw up and get everybody killed."

NINE

On the evening of March 3, I surveyed my Marines for the last time before crossing into Iraq. I had been leading the company's convoy north through Kuwait for the past two days, and Golf was now staged just south of the Iraqi border inside yet another U.S. camp. Hundreds of other vehicles waited alongside our convoy, lined up in dozens of long canvas-and-steel rows in a huge gravel parking lot. Slowly, I walked down our row, checking to see what my Marines were doing before I tried for a few hours of sleep.

Noriel, Leza, and Bowen were doing much the same thing: giving their men one last look-over, walking around the vehicles, checking on the gear. They appeared busy and focused. Teague, Carson, and the other team leaders were hanging out with their men. Most were laughing with one another, or reading. Some wrote letters in the day's last light while others did what Marines do best—they slept, bedded down in sleeping bags next to the trucks. None looked too nervous. Walking back to my truck, it suddenly hit me: These kids laughing and writing and sleeping and talking, they were mine. They made up Joker One, and I was their leader, about to take them into a country designated a combat zone. I felt nervous and proud and slightly unready all at the same time. But, ready or not, the next morning was coming and Iraq was coming with it. I pulled out my sleeping mat and bedded down in the gravel, trying to grab a couple of hours of shut-eye before a very early morning.

At 2 AM on March 4, Joker One woke up, packed up, and boarded our two trucks. I climbed up into the cab of mine and began checking the radio, talking to the other platoon commanders as my Marines settled into the bed behind me. The canvas sides that covered the top half of the truck beds had been rolled up, so I could see the silhouettes of my men clambering about underneath the stars. After determining that my radio worked, I put down my handset and used a small flashlight to review my crude map. I wasn't tired in the least. My body had pumped what felt like a quart of adrenaline into my bloodstream, and, for the moment, my heart was pounding rapidly. I felt hyperalert. The tiredness, I knew from experience, would set in later, so I had collected five or so packets of instant coffee to help keep me sharp when the adrenaline wore off.

For two hours, Golf Company waited, vehicles running, for units ahead of us to clear the border checkpoint. Hundreds of convoys were traveling into and out of Iraq during the rotation from Operation Iraqi Freedom I to II, and traffic marshals had been set up along the border to help control their movements. We couldn't proceed north until the marshals told us to. During the delay, each platoon commander periodically talked with his counterparts to make certain that everyone's communication gear was still working. Inch by inch, our lightless convoy slowly crept forward until we nearly bumped up against the base gates, lit up like day under the sterile white glare of two giant arc lights.

Finally, at 4 AM, we received permission from the checkpoint controller to leave Kuwait. The giant traffic light set up on the left-hand side of the gates turned from red to green, and Captain Bronzi ordered the convoy forward. As the huge steel gate rolled slowly to one side, I gave my first combat order over the PRR, the small intraplatoon radio whose headset was fastened firmly to my right ear and throat.

"Squad leaders, have your men make Condition One."

Behind me, thirty-seven snick-snacks rang out almost in unison as my men pulled their M-16 bolts to the rear and then let them slam forward, chambering a round. There's nothing else on earth that makes that sound.

Joker One was locked and loaded. I racked my own bolt back and felt some-what satisfied as it slammed home. Then I ordered my vehicle forward, and the Jokers rolled out, weapons ready, adrenaline blasting, minds amped for any and every possible scenario. We were finally doing it for real.

My seven-ton made it all of two hundred meters into Iraq before grind-ing to a halt. The road ahead of our convoy was packed with military vehi-cles stacked end to end, all waiting to go around a single-lane cloverleaf that would dump us onto a highway heading north. As there are only a few of these northbound highways in Iraq, huge numbers of coalition vehicles in-termixed with the normal local traffic clogged each one. Our thirty-vehicle convoy was just a small part of an unbroken line stretching for as far as my eyes could see. At nearly the exact same time that our convoy halted, my radio went dead, and I lost all communication with the rest of the convoy. Still, the Jokers weren't going anywhere anytime soon, so I took my atten-tion off the road and pulled out the radio to sort out what had happened.

Thirty seconds later, a rapid, frantic banging on my truck door jolted me out of my technical inspection. I pulled up on the latch and leaned out to find an agitated, wide-eyed Captain Bronzi hopping from foot to foot and shouting rapid-fire sentences at me.

"Joker One, my radio's gone completely out, I can't talk to anyone, the convoy's stopped moving. We are sitting ducks out here, man. And I can't talk to anyone. We are sitting ducks out here! We've got to do something. We've got to get these vehicles moving. We are sitting ducks out here!"

I restrained the impulse to point out that we were a mere two hundred meters north of the Kuwaiti border and that about two-thirds of the convoy was still safely inside the base. I also decided not to mention that the like-lihood of an attack this close to the heavily armed border watchtowers seemed fairly remote. I did, however, point out that if we were indeed sitting ducks, then at least we were in good company—those several hundred other military vehicles stacked along the highway to our north. Looking for the first time at the massive logjam in front of us, the CO regained his compo-sure and headed off to try to fix the communication problem.

Two minutes later, the radios began working again, and the traffic ahead of us began to move and we entered the highway. But as our vehicles stretched, I started losing Flowers, the platoon commander responsible for keeping track of the convoy's rear third. Our capricious long-range radios would work only sporadically for the remainder of the trip, so I relied heavily on my little intrasquad PRR to communicate with Quist, the platoon commander closest to me. I would pass him a message, he would pass it back to the next vehicle equipped with a PRR, they would pass that backward, and so on in a long game of high-speed telephone. Messages traveling from the convoy's back to its front reached me the same way. Compounding our difficulties, vehicles at random points along the convoy broke down every so often. We could ill afford to be separated from them. With thousands of same-color, same-model military vehicles on the same road at the same time, it would have been easy for a few of our separated members to latch on to the wrong convoy and end up hundreds of miles from our final destination.

Fortunately, our rehearsals in Kuwait paid off. The Ox and a repair truck constantly moved up and down the convoy's line, fixing broken Humvees if possible and hooking them up via tow straps to other Humvees if not. At the front of the convoy, I tried desperately to keep track of all the goings-on miles behind me in spite of the patchy radio so that I could slow us down when work was being done and speed us up when it wasn't. I started swallowing my coffee grounds about an hour after our entrance into Iraq.

I also drank water furiously. It was ninety degrees outside in the Iraqi desert and I was wearing sixty pounds of gear on a Kevlar vest that didn't breathe. Soon, the high caffeine/high water combination proved more than my renal system could handle, and I found myself performing in real time the one thing that I had forgotten to practice earlier: urinating into an empty water bottle while moving at forty-two miles per hour and checking our direction with my wrist compass. Thankfully, these unpleasant exercises were the most eventful things to happen to me during the entire convoy. At 4 P.M. on the same day, the Jokers pulled into the city that would be our home for the next seven months.

amadi. The capital city of the Sunni-dominated Anbar province, it contained roughly 350,000 people, a sweltering mass of humanity packed into less than nine square miles—one of the highest population densities on earth. As we pulled into the city from the north, its alien nature struck me almost like a physical blow. No amount of training at abandoned U.S. bases could have prepared us for the rows and rows of close-packed, high-walled compounds that made up the city blocks, or the mounds of trash that lined every street, or the throngs of people who stared at us as our convoy crawled through their midst on the way to our first stop.

We pulled into Ramadi from the city's west side and made our way into a base located at the tip of a peninsula formed by the Y intersection of the Euphrates River and one of its tributaries. Called Hurricane Point, the place was one of three main U.S. bases located on the western border of the city. We were relatively pleased with what we saw. The main base head-quarters was inside an elaborately constructed former palace of Saddam Hussein's. Air-conditioning units protruded from nearly all the boarded-up windows, and the outside walls were covered in sandbags stacked five feet high. Palm trees lined a nicely paved road that ran throughout the base. Hurricane Point also featured running water in its shower areas, nearly twenty-four-hour electricity, multiple phone banks, an Internet café, and a mess hall. Though we knew we wouldn't be staying here—we had simply pulled in to drop off a few vehicles and personnel who belonged to another of 2/4's companies—we hoped it would be representative of what we'd find at our own, as yet unnamed base.

We drove on toward the far eastern side of Ramadi, an area isolated from Hurricane Point and the two other large U.S. bases next to it. As we drove from west to east down the city's main highway, Route Michigan, I realized that between our base and the closest reinforcements would be nearly the entire population of Ramadi. We hit the very eastern edge of the city, and the buildings began to taper off. I had started wondering where our base was when a gigantic wall of concrete barriers appeared to my left, on the north side of the highway. I guided the convoy into the base's entrance, denoted as such by a giant red-and-white-striped pole that blocked the opening be-tween barriers. Slowly, we approached, and slowly the Army guards next to the pole raised it vertically. Looking around there was little evidence of the relative luxury of Hurricane Point. There were no trees, no paved roads, and no contract mess halls. In fact the giant square building that would become our mess hall had only three walls and half of a roof. Most of the open areas of the base were covered in the same desert sand that surrounded it. There were no shower facilities, or Internet cafés, or phone banks. Indeed, there wasn't any running water or electricity. And we weren't housed in one of

Saddam's expansive former palace complexes. Instead, we occupied a former chemical manufacturing facility, about three hundred meters wide and five hundred long.

The compound itself was shaped vaguely like a rectangle that had had its top left corner violently removed at a forty-five-degree angle, leaving a square base at the bottom and a rough triangle at the top. Near the tip of that triangle the compound wall had crumbled, so the base's Army occupants had strung rolls and rolls of concertina wire across the gap. Inside the compound sat eleven main buildings of varying sizes and varying degrees of repair. One building had a crumbling wall and yellow-and-black warning tape wrapped all the way around it. When we later asked the Army why the tape, we were told simply that we probably shouldn't go in there—the unit we were replacing wasn't sure what the building had previously been used for, but they did know that their hazardous-chemical detection equipment went off wildly every time someone went inside. We took them at their word. For all the disrepair, it could have been far worse, I thought as the trucks ground to a halt. After all, during my previous deployment I had lived in a tent. Once the convoy was safely inside the base, vehicles lined up on a stretch of gravel that pretended to be a road, I hopped out of the cab and unloaded my weapon. Behind me, Joker One began slowly climbing out of the truck beds, and the squad leaders started assembling their men for inspection. Behind us, the other platoons were doing the same thing. As the squad leaders took charge, I joined the CO, Hes, and Quist, and we made our way into a gigantic hangar bay at the very center of the compound, where the Army captain commanding the base waved to us.

As we met up with the captain and his officers, the Gunny took charge of Golf Company. Shouting and storming about, he herded the slightly bewildered platoons into the open area inside the hangar bay. As soon as they were all assembled, the Gunny set the Marines to work building bunk beds, and the concrete walls of the bay echoed with the relentless clanking of metal on metal. Meanwhile, the Joker officers met with our counterparts in the company command room in an effort to understand better the task assigned us.

We soon discovered that our area of operations (AO), the part of the city for which we would be responsible, comprised almost the entirety of Ramadi. Looking at the photographic map beforehand, this had seemed reasonable enough, but after the drive across the city to our base, we weren't so sure. We had known before arriving that Ramadi was, to say the least, densely populated, and that we, at 150 men, were not. The Army company currently occupying the base would leave for the States in a mere two weeks, at which point in time Golf Company would be the only ones operating throughout the heart of Ramadi. Having now seen the dense blocks filled with massive crowds, we began understanding what it would really mean to try to control a city of 350,000 with only 150 Marines. We had earlier calculated ratios of one of us for every two thousand of them. Those numbers had now taken on a whole new meaning.

My eyes had certainly been opened enough to make me want to pay close attention to the Army company that we were relieving. However, after about an hour of conversation, the captain hosting us at our new base revealed that the soldiers we were supposed to be relieving had actually already left. Those remaining were just caretakers of the base, and they rarely left the gates and so didn't know much about the world we'd be entering. Over the past two weeks, an interim Army force, the 1st of the 506th, had patrolled the city; they would arrive the next day to pick us up and begin driving us around Ramadi, showing us their missions and introducing us to the key leaders with whom they had developed relationships. Our hosts did give us one bit of good news: In the six months that they had been in Ramadi, their unit had not suffered a single fatality.

Happy to hear this statistic, the three other platoon commanders and I left the command room and stepped back into the hangar bay to check on our men. The bunk beds had all been set up, and the Marines were in various stages of undress, preparing to sleep after three days' hard journey. Seeing that they were set, we tromped up to the second floor of the hangar bay and set up cots along it. I took off my boots, sat on my bunk, and stared at the cityscape silhouetted to our west. The distinctive slim minarets spiked upward at strange intervals. The city was mostly dark, but the stars in the desert sky were brighter than I'd ever seen them in America.

TEN

slept for five hours and awoke to find that our Army counterparts had shown up bright and early. They lived in a different base, about fifteen minutes away, and they had driven over to pick us up. Noriel, Bowen, Leza, Captain Bronzi, and I made our way over to the six Army Humvees (all of which were heavily armored) and readied ourselves for the pre-mission briefing. The platoon may have been fairly new to the city, but as they talked with us that morning, they seemed to know it well enough. The platoon commander, Lieutenant Mitchell, spoke with confidence, and he covered all the standard bases—medevac plans, reaction to enemy attacks, communication failure plans, and so on—just as (if not better than) I would have. His NCOs, in turn, briefed my squad leaders. The Army enlisted seemed as competent and experienced as their officer.

Unfortunately, the platoon from the 506th had room in their Humvees for only five or six of us on each of their rides. As Golf Company's first mission after turnover with the Army would fall to Joker One, my three squad leaders and I had priority on the first several trips. Zipping around the city in the thick, squat vehicles with the Army was exhilarating, even if it wasn't entirely representative of the way in which we planned to fulfill our mission. The 506th confined itself mainly to the city's major highway and a few other significant roads, and they only rarely left their vehicles to move on foot. Unlike the Marine Corps, the Army had money for massively armored Humvees, and it provided plenty of these monsters to its troops in harm's way. We, by contrast, still didn't have enough unarmored Humvees to carry an entire forty-man platoon. So we planned to walk the city on foot, exploring Ramadi in a way that no unit before us had, but on some level we envied the equipment and mobility of our sister service.

The details of how we would ultimately achieve our "security and stability" mission were still a bit hazy, but we wanted to try to get a sense of all of Ramadi's neighborhoods. We wanted to interact face-to-face with its people; to get to know its politicians, policemen, and sheiks; to demonstrate that the entire city was ours and that we cared about all of it, that no place would be a no-go area for the Marines. After all, Ramadi was the capital city of Anbar province. Over the last several months, the vast majority of Iraq's hostile incidents had happened in Anbar, which was why the Marines had been sent to the restive area. Like the rest of Anbar, Ramadi was populated almost exclusively by Sunni Arabs. While Saddam Hussein had ruled, the city's most prominent export had been officers for his army, and it had been well treated as a result. The city still retained some vestiges of his largesse — beautiful mosques, functioning traffic circles, road signs, and so on.

However, the Ramadi we saw on the Army's early tours had suffered as a result of the war's aftermath. When the Coalition Provisional Authority (CPA) disbanded the Iraqi army, quite a few of Ramadi's residents had lost their jobs. Though the city's downtown still teemed with commerce, male unemployment was high, well above 50 percent. Furthermore, in the aftermath of Baghdad's downfall, most of Saddam's civil servants had found themselves out of jobs, and most of the violent criminals had found themselves out of jail. Thus ten months after President Bush made his "Mission Accomplished" aircraft carrier landing, Ramadi's basic services were nonexistent and crime was rampant. Trash and human waste littered every street. Massive open-air garbage dumps were scattered across the city, and no one tended to them. A few of the buildings had the distinctive bullet-hole pockmarks scattered across them, and a few of the roads had the scorched and blackened potholes that indicated an IED had gone off there. Still, those things aside, most of the city had been spared war's rampant physical destruction.

Ramadi proper could be roughly divided into four quadrants. In the northwest was the souk: a vibrant, bustling marketplace with streets so narrow that it was impossible to fit a Humvee down most of them. Here a clever shopper could buy everything from the latest consumer electronics to European house music to hard-core pornography and anti-American videos. From about 10 AM onward, with the exception of some downtime in the early afternoon, the souk was jammed solid with pedestrians. Most buildings in this quadrant's southern portion were three- to four-story commercial structures; these gradually gave way to two-story residential properties as one moved farther north. Everything, it seemed, was connected by dense networks of wire that stretched crazily in all directions in rat's nests of tangled connections some ten to fifteen feet off the ground. Some of these wires tapped into the city's power supply, probably illegally; some served to hang laundry; and some did double duty. Across from the souk, in the southwest quadrant of Ramadi, the past and present were skirmishing. Multistory, relatively modern government buildings dominated the top half of the area, but butchers ruled the bottom. Here, individual two-story residences mingled with *halal* shopkeepers who slaughtered animals in the same manner as their Bedouin forefathers. Skinless, glistening pink-and-red corpses hung in front of small, dirty storefronts, and unpaved streets ran dark with blood. The air was thickly heavy with a sharp metallic tang. Packs of wild dogs—animals considered unclean by the Iraqis—roamed these streets, looking for food.

The southeastern quadrant of the city was a similarly solid urban area that we called the Farouq district, named after the volubly anti-American Farouq mosque located at the quadrant's southwestern tip. Aside from a gigantic, professional-quality soccer stadium directly across the street from this mosque, the Farouq district had little else to distinguish it; just row after row of the two-story walled compounds that serve as the standard residential structure in Ramadi. In this city, every house was surrounded on all four sides by an eight-foot-high concrete fence, with some sort of steel gate serving as the only entrance into or out of the compound. Inside the walls, an open courtyard of varying sizes surrounded each house, which usually sat at least five or so meters back from the gate. Each exterior wall was joined to that of its neighbor's, and each city block was some seven to ten houses long and two houses wide.

We realized on that first tour that this section of the city would present us with a serious challenge in the form of thirty-meter-wide, hundred-meter-long solid lines of wall. Crossing between houses was a near impossibility, for it usually meant climbing three eight-foot-high walls in rapid succession—the one in front of the nearest house, that house's rear wall, and the street-facing wall of the new compound you had just dropped into—or breaching three separate sturdy metal doors. The easiest and most practical way to transition from one block to another was simply to walk to a block's end and then use the streets that ran around each block to cut over. We would find out the hard way that this typically Middle Eastern housing array meant that if any squad was more than two blocks away from its counterparts, the squad was, for all intents and purposes, completely on its own.

Finally, Ramadi's northeastern quadrant was its industrial zone. Though the area had some residential buildings concentrated in its northern and western areas, the vast majority of the quadrant was taken up by fifteen warehouses, one gigantic parking lot, and scores of small mechanic shops. Each of these automobile repair places usually had an actual automobile on top of its flat roof, transforming what would normally have been one-story buildings into one-and-a-half-story buildings. At the zone's easternmost point, another smaller soccer stadium provided a playing field for many of the area's children, and those who couldn't get a spot inside the stadium itself could always use the dusty plain just to the north. Both stadium and plain were bounded on the east by what had previously been a gigantic trash dump, and the eight-foot-high, rolling mounds of garbage still reeked fetidly in the heat of the day.

Neatly through all of this ran Route Michigan. The city's most vital transportation artery bisected Ramadi in a perfectly straight west-east line from one end of the town to the other. On that first tour, our Army guides pointed out several important sites situated along the highway. The al-Haq mosque, located directly across Michigan from the northern stadium, broadcast anti-American rhetoric from its loudspeakers every Friday, the standard Muslim day of worship, equivalent to Western Sundays. The al-Haq had, our guides told us, distinguished itself from other mosques by the intensity of its diatribes and its propensity to advocate immediate military action against U.S. forces. Smack dab in the center of the city, perched inside a gigantic traffic circle in the middle of Michigan, stood the massive Saddam mosque, commissioned by the former dictator himself in the mid-1990s, sometime after he decided that his Baath Party would no longer be a secular, communist organization. On some Fridays that mosque also broadcast hatred of the infidel foreigners, but on most it simply exhorted devout Muslims to live their lives in a manner hewing more closely to the dictates of the Koran.

Just one hundred meters west was the city's cemetery, a gigantic triangle that extended its tip nearly ten blocks south of Michigan, deep into the butchers' area. A flat plain dotted with small aboveground mausoleums and headstones, the cemetery was considered the most sacred area in the city (outside of the mosques), according to our Army guides. Six blocks west of this cemetery, near the western edge of the city, lay the provincial Government Center, a four-block-long, five-block-wide walled compound that contained all the infrastructure necessary to support the oversight of Anbar province. Leaning over as we passed it, Lieutenant Mitchell yelled to me that it was here that the governor, the mayor, and their respective councils met every day, and here that the province's police chief held court.

After we passed the Government Center, our six-vehicle convoy ran into the western boundary of Ramadi, a wide tributary of the mighty Euphrates River. We drove south along it until we ran into the city's southern boundary, a set of railroad tracks running west to east. Turning east again, we paralleled the tracks. For nearly the entire length of the city, an open-air trash dump bordered the railroad. The stench was incredible, even inside the Humvees. After some twenty minutes of driving down a potholed, intermittently paved road, we ran into the city's eastern boundary, a wide irrigation canal. We headed north, and five minutes later we were back on Michigan, a mere two hundred meters west of our base. The rural areas outside the city were dotted with occasional housing compounds, well-tended fields, and lush greenery—as long as they were close to the Euphrates. Get more than three kilometers from the river, though, and the fields, the houses, and the trees disappeared. In their place was the vast desert.

As we drove around the city on that first day, I was struck by the living conditions endured by its citizens—they had little power, no sewers, no garbage disposal, broken-down roads, and the occasional IED that blew up on their main highway. Their country was in shambles, and I felt saddened that our country was largely responsible for it. I knew that my squad leaders and I shared the same sense of wanting to help them, and to show them that Americans were decent people who truly did desire the best for others, even if we didn't always know how to go about providing it. So I enjoyed the stops we made along the way. First off, we met with a female Christian bank manager who worried about road security. Through the Army translator, a large, fit Iraqi known only as "Monster," she told us that she needed to transfer some reserves from one branch to another and that she feared them being stolen without adequate protection. Through Monster, Lieutenant Mitchell reassured her. Later that evening, after dark, we stopped by the Government Center to meet with Anbar province's police chief. Just inside the building's entryway was a small foyer, into which were crammed about ten Iraqi policemen, all huddled around a TV set. Curious, I glanced over to see what had them so intrigued. It was hard-core porn. Noticing us, the policemen smiled and gave us the thumbs-up sign. We grinned back. Some things, it seemed, were common to fighting men of all cultures.

Continuing on, we made our way into the police chief's office. As soon as he laid eyes on the Army lieutenant, the chief—a giant, bald, mustachioed man who reminded me a little bit of a walrus—broke into a huge smile, stood up, and embraced the lieutenant in a bear hug. After exchanging pleasantries, sweet, hot chai was served in small shot glasses as Mitchell and the police chief talked about security in Ramadi and elsewhere. Four rounds of tea later, we made our way out of the building. That man, Mitchell told us, was a terrific ally.

The next day, Mitchell, Bronzi, and I visited another police chief, this one suspected of being on the take. It was our mission to warn him to change his ways or risk joining the inmates he currently oversaw. While at the station house, deep in the Farouq area, Mitchell pointed out the spot where an enemy had fired an RPG at his patrol two weeks previously. Since then, he told us, nothing major had happened in Ramadi. The story confirmed what we all suspected and hoped: Combat in the city probably wouldn't be very fierce, and the action that did occur would likely confine itself to occasional IED blasts and mortar attacks. From that day forward, all of the officers from the CO on down regularly debated whether we would ever be authorized to wear the coveted Combat Action Ribbon, since the criteria for this award demanded that fire be both taken and returned.

Another measure of our naïveté came a few days later, when, during a brief foot patrol with the Army through the packed souk, the CO and I heard automatic weapons fire from what sounded like a block or two away. Even though we hadn't heard the distinctive cracking that indicated the fire was actually close enough to do damage, for the rest of the day we twittered to each other about the incident like excited schoolboys. What we didn't realize then was that the default way to express nearly any emotion in Ramadi was to walk outside and peel off a few rounds from the family AK-47. Wedding parties wildly fired their weapons into the air to celebrate the joy of marriage; funeral parties wildly fired their weapons into the air to mourn the sadness of passing; families at circumcisions wildly fired their weapons into the air to commemorate the separation of a boy from a part of his penis.

ELEVEN

While Noriel, Leza, Bowen, and I were busy taking in the sights and sounds of the city, the Gunny was busy housing the Joker platoons. I hadn't involved myself in the process, which was fortunate because at the time I had no idea of how important geography was to unit cohesion. Fortunately, the Gunny understood this concept all too well, and he gave my platoon its own building. The "house," as we called it, was shaped like an *L*, with all of the new Marines billeted in the long arm and all of my NCOs housed in the short one. Docs Smith and Camacho got their own bunks in the NCO rooms—unlike the other platoons' corpsmen, most of whom opted to live in the main hangar bay building with the Navy doctors and their fellow corpsmen, ours docs chose to live with us. Unsurprisingly, Doc Smith fit right in with second squad. Very surprisingly, Doc Camacho fit right in with first. Maybe the hot climate agreed with him, or maybe there was more to the young man than simply the neonatal ward tender. Time would certainly tell.

Two eight-foot-high walls connected the arms of the L, forming a small courtyard where my Marines relaxed when they weren't running missions. I can't say for certain, but I believe that the combination of our own living space with our own relaxing space contributed as much as anything else to the tight cohesion that developed among the Marines of Joker One. Most other platoons had to share houses with one another, and none had their own courtyard in which to hang out. We were the only ones with this amenity. Once again, the Gunny was taking care of me in spite of myself.

While the Gunny was helping sort out the Marines, the Ox was busy screwing up the base improvement project. Shortly after arrival, the CO had placed his right-hand man in charge of all of the company's contracting, both within our walls and without. With little knowledge of the process and few other readily available options, the Ox had chosen to stick with a contractor whom he had inherited from the Army. This man—whom we'll call Achmed since it eventually became apparent that he had never given anyone his real name—told the Ox that because the Ox was such a clever, strong officer, he, Achmed, would perform a whole host of free work for us. Delighted with his shrewd negotiating prowess, the Ox immediately told all the lieutenants to ensure that neither we nor our Marines hassled Achmed, since he, the Ox, had cleverly convinced the Iraqi to "hook us up with a ton of free shit." Alarm bells immediately went off in Flowers's engineer head after hearing of this "clever deal," but his offer to help the Ox with the contracting process was rebuffed in short order.

The "ton of free shit" that Achmed had so graciously "hooked us up with" turned out to be, among other things, a faulty electrical wiring system installed by drunken vagrants and a shower complex that drained itself into the middle of our base, eventually creating a disgusting malarial swamp that sometimes prevented showering even when we had water, which was rare. Worse, the creative wiring schematic caused our breaker box, located in the medical room, to catch on fire about two months after its completion. Wounded Marines had to be quickly transported out of the burning room while doctors and corpsmen battled the fire with whatever they could find. Eventually all the wiring had to be redone by a former electrician who spent days on the task. During these failures, "Achmed" was nowhere to be found. Sources later hinted that he had taken our money and simply relocated his operation to Baghdad after finishing his work on our base.

Fortunately, not all the responsibility for internal improvements had been assigned to the Ox. The CO had put Flowers and the Gunny in charge of shoring up the base's defenses, and they got to work with a vengeance.

While Hes, Quist, and I rode around the city with the Army, the Gunny and Flowers remained largely inside our complex, trying to harden its outer walls and interior buildings against mortars, rockets, and suicide VBIEDs (vehicle-borne improvised explosive devices, otherwise known as car bombs). They created two new machine-gun positions along our perimeter to cover the crumbled portion of our north wall. Once that was done, the Gunny set the Marines to work putting sandbags over everything that mattered, from the electrical transmission lines that ran out of our generator to the portable chemical toilets that the Army had left us. Flowers, meanwhile, got division engineers to bring in tons and tons of dirt with which to fill huge ten-foot-tall canvas boxes that were placed around each platoon's living areas. Called HESCO barriers, these massive mounds of dirt would do for large objects what the sandbags did for small ones—prevent mortars and rockets from shredding them.

There was no time to waste. From our first day in our new home, the Army had told us about the local mortar happy hour, which apparently lasted from 6 PM to about 9 PM every day. During this time, the chances of the enemy firing mortars at our base were significantly elevated, and just a few days after our arrival, a couple of medium-sized 82mm mortar rounds landed outside the base walls with huge ground-and-wall-shaking thuds. Everyone walking outside the base's buildings fell flat on their faces while everyone inside instinctively flinched and looked for something to throw themselves behind. From then on, the CO mandated that all Marines wear flak jackets and helmets during those hours. In practice, this order meant wearing Kevlar vests and helmets when heading over to the bathroom area to shave or take bottled-water showers.

The sight of young, skinny infantrymen tromping around awkwardly in short shorts, flip-flops, towels, and body armor was a source of never-ending laughter for us in those early days. No mortars had landed inside our walls, no rockets had struck the base, no one had fired at us on patrols, and none of our Marines had been killed or wounded. It was still a merry adventure for the Jokers, and we were all just happy to finally be doing our jobs in real life.

By the way, our army predecessors had named our little base "Combat Outpost," and we stuck with it. It proved to be a prescient decision.

TWELVE

The Lord is my shepherd.
I shall not want.
He makes me to lie down in green pastures.
He leads me beside still waters.
He restores my soul . . .
Yea, though I walk through the valley of the shadow of death,
I will fear no evil,
For thou art with me.
Thy rod and thy staff, they comfort me.
Thou hast prepared a table before me in the presence of my enemies.
Thou anointest my head with oil, my cup runneth over.
Surely goodness and mercy will follow me all the days of my life,
And I will dwell in the house of the Lord forever . . .

Blessed be the Lord my Rock
Who trains my hands for battle
And my fingers for war.

My strong tower, and my deliverer.
My shield, and the one in whom I trust,
Who subdues my people under me.
Amen.

The prayer echoed softly through the front of the hangar bay as thirty or so kneeling Marines murmured it in unison while the rest of our platoon stood silently behind them with their heads bowed. The platoon formed a rough semicircle, and at its front I knelt, praying quietly and fervently. The sun had just winked out, the swift desert night had fallen, and all around us the city wailed as the muezzins' calls to prayer rang out in jarring ululation. The microphone-amplified chants formed a weird background to our own quiet prayers, and for a brief second the strange juxtaposition of faiths struck me with sudden clarity.

The moment passed as quickly as it had come—I was far too nervous for reflection. Three days earlier, Golf had suffered its first casualty when, on one of our last turnover rides with the Army, one of Flowers's men, Corporal McPherson, had had his face blown off from the upper lip down by an IED. Mac had lived, but our merry foreign adventure had ended in flame and smoke and a young man's jaw scattered across a city block. Now we had some sense of what it meant to "take casualties," and for the first time I wondered what I'd do if any of my men were wounded. I couldn't rely on the Army's help for a medevac; Golf Company had finally assumed full control of the Ramadi AO just one day earlier.

With these and other concerns weighing heavily on me, I'd given my gear an unusually thorough pre-mission inspection half an hour before the prayer started. All of us had plenty of equipment—the average Marine carried between fifty and sixty pounds on every mission—and if time allowed we inspected it before every single mission. That night, I'd started with the Interceptor flak jacket, the basic unit from which everything else hung. Each of these Kevlar vests covered us from the throats down to our waists, with a small add-on flap hanging over our groins. This triangular piece of Kevlar certainly wouldn't stop AK bullets and probably wouldn't stop any serious shrapnel, but just having it hanging there made me feel a bit better. Inside each Interceptor were our SAPI (small-arms protective insert) plates, rectangles made of sandwiched ceramic layers that could stop 7.62mm

AK-47 rounds. Each plate added roughly four pounds to the vest itself, and the total combination came out to about seventeen pounds.

Next, I had checked the magazines strapped to the lower left side of the Interceptor to make certain that 1) all six were filled with twenty-eight rounds apiece, and 2) the springs inside were in good working order. Often, when an M-16 jams it's due to a worn-out spring in the magazine, not a malfunction with the weapon itself. Next to the magazine pouches I had laced a grenade pouch, but in those first few weeks it was usually filled with something else, something random. We still didn't have enough grenades to give one to each man in the mission platoons, so we carefully rationed the little we did have, with twenty or so going to select Marines in the ops platoon and the other ten or so going to the QRF (quick reaction force) platoon.

A brand-new bayonet hanging handle down and a first aid kit rounded out the gear on the bottom left half of the vest. On the bottom right half, I had stuck my map/binocular pouch containing those items plus my night vision goggles (NVGs) and many, many spare AA batteries. My canteen also hung there as a complement to my CamelBak hydration pack. To the right side of my chest, I fastened my Garmin GPS and its backup, my military-issue magnetic compass, and around my waist I'd strapped my butt pack, which carried assorted survival equipment and two sets of field rations. In the desert, electrolytes are nearly as precious as water, and copious drinking without eating is a good way to wash them all out of your body and suffer a serious case of hyponatremia, which can kill just as surely as dehydration. On my back hung the CamelBak, one that I had purchased myself because it carried 50 percent more water than the standard-issue gear. Of course, this extra water came with extra weight, and, including my M-16A4 rifle and the M-9 pistol strapped to my right leg, all of my gear added up to a little bit more than fifty pounds. I couldn't complain, though. My SAW gunners carried close to thirty pounds of weapons and ammo alone, as did Yebra and Mahardy with the radio and its spare batteries.

Now, as I knelt in the hangar bay on that early March evening, praying quietly with all of that gear tugging heavily on my shoulders and back, I was glad that the platoon had spent countless hours adjusting to the load back in Camp Pendleton. Joker One was about to execute its first live mission in Ramadi, a night ambush, and the last thing we needed was fatigue from carrying unfamiliar equipment. That night would be my first time leading the entire platoon on a true infantry mission, and it was the first time we had prayed together as a unit. These simultaneous firsts were no coincidence. Over the past few weeks, I had thought long and hard over the decision to institute a platoon prayer before each live mission, and thirty minutes before our first time out of the Outpost's gates, I had decided in favor of prayer for a few reasons.

First off, I believed that if we had a pre-battle ritual, something unique to first platoon that only we performed every time we left the base's confines, then we would more quickly gain a sense of corporate over individual identity. Ideally, I wanted each of my Marines to think of himself first as a member of Joker One and only thereafter as an individual with needs and desires different from that of the team as a whole, for I believed that selfishness was the best way to destroy a unit and to get Marines killed in combat. In my mind, the best way to purge this destructive quality from my men was to replace a focus on the self—and its concomitant concern with individual happiness—with a focus on the group and an overriding concern with the service and welfare of others. A pre-battle ritual may seem a strange way to try to effect such a profound transformation, but I had already learned the hard way that sometimes the smallest things have an unexpectedly large impact. Those who felt uncomfortable praying weren't required to say the words, but they were required to stand or kneel shoulder to shoulder with those who did. Thus, Joker One stood together before the mission, and together we steeled ourselves to walk outside the wire for the first time and do our jobs come what may.

I had a responsibility to my men to provide for all their needs, and those included their spiritual as well as their material ones. Some may say that the spiritual is the province of the chaplain or the priest and that the lieutenant should stick to tactics, to fire and maneuver. My only reply is that the chaplain doesn't throw grenades alongside his men. It's not the priest who holds the hand of the Marine who's just been shot and swears to him that no matter what happens, he will make it back alive somehow, someway. Marines will only really listen to those who have suffered alongside them, and if you want any credibility as a leader, you not only have to bear the same burdens as they, but you also have to try, to your utmost ability and every single day, to transfer those burdens from their shoulders onto yours.

After Corporal Mac's face had been blown off by the IED, many of my men had serious questions. "Why did this have to happen to Mac?" and "What if it happens to me?" I didn't have a good answer for the first, and I didn't want to confront the reality of the second just yet, so I prayed and asked the Marines to pray with me for a third, more selfish reason: Deep in my heart, I believed that prayer would work without fail, that if together Joker One prayed long and hard enough, God would spare all of us from Mac's fate. What I know now, and which didn't occur to me then, was that by praying as I prayed, and hoping what I hoped, and believing what I believed, I was effectively reducing God to a result-dispensing genie who, if just fed the proper incantations, would give the sincere petitioner (me) the exact outcome desired.

As the platoon murmured the Twenty-third Psalm before our first mission on that mid-March evening, I believed that those prayers would be enough to keep us safe, to keep Henderson's heart beating on the patrol, Guzon from shooting Staff Sergeant in the back, and Feldmeir from falling asleep during the middle of our walk. I hoped the prayers would keep me from getting my men lost on our first mission, from forgetting everything I knew about ambushes at night, from losing communication with one of my squads and abandoning my men to the mercies of Ramadi. In short, I hoped that prayer would allay my fears and cover for my shortcomings.

The soft prayer ended, and together Joker One rose and walked from the hangar bay to the broad sandy area just inside the base's main entrance. We assumed our patrol formation, with Noriel's squad leading, Leza's in the middle, and Bowen's bringing up the rear. I stood just behind the base's entry barrier as Yebra checked the radio one last time and the Marines behind me strung themselves out into two long, snaking lines. Suddenly the kneeling Yebra straightened, slung the radio across his back, and turned to me. Quietly he whispered, "Sir, COC [combat operations center] says we're good to go."

I nodded, paused for a second, then looked up at Teague, the platoon's point man. He stood a few meters away, looking back at me. In the dim wash of the streetlights lining Michigan, our eyes met. He didn't look nervous—just hard, with narrowed eyes in an emotionless face. I nodded to Teague, lifted my arm above my head, and dropped it in front of my face. Move out. Teague nodded back, turned about, and calmly walked around the red-and-white-striped barrier and into the city. I crossed over five meters behind

Teague, and behind me I heard Yebra mutter softly into the radio: "COC, be advised, Joker One is departing friendly lines." Our first combat mission officially began.

As soon as Teague took those first steps into Ramadi, my general fear and anxiety vanished. I was too concerned with minute-by-minute execution of the plan to worry about much more than the next half hour or so. In the scheme I had drawn up we would conduct an ambush at a cemetery at the south end of the city, a cemetery that had an excellent view of a train station where insurgents were rumored to be meeting at night. To catch them in the act, we planned to patrol down to the cemetery on foot, heading directly south from the Combat Outpost, across Michigan, and through a thick cluster of buildings lining the highway's southern edge. Then we would cross a large open plain just to the east of the irrigation canal to keep ourselves away from the populated areas until the very last minute. With little electric light thrown off by the southern portion of Ramadi and low predicted natural ambient light, the darkness should cover our movement nicely. Bowen's squad would peel off at the extreme southern end of the canal to keep watch over a major bridge while Noriel, Leza, and I would continue on, crossing under the bridge itself at the canal's end and coming back into the city from the south.

First and second squads would then occupy the little cemetery about five hundred meters due south of our target train station, the one demarcating Ramadi's extreme southern end. We had heard reports that the insurgents used graves to hide their weapons, banking on the reluctance of Americans to search sites of such great sensitivity to the locals, so once we had observed the train station for long enough, we could give the cemetery a good once-over while the rest of the city slept.

I had conceived this plan based on a prior train station visit with the Army and a detailed study of the photographic map I had managed to scrounge from one of the departing soldiers. Golf Company had obtained just a few maps of Ramadi prior to our arrival. Even with the Army supplying us their leftovers, there weren't enough maps for each platoon commander, let alone each squad leader. As we walked out of the base's gate, I held the worn photographic map in my left hand, and Leza, Bowen, and Noriel consulted crude hand-drawn graphics they had earlier created based on my lone map.

My carefully thought-through plan held good for all of fifteen minutes. After moving quickly through the few buildings just south of Route Michigan, Joker One hit the open plain and our first set of complications. The aerial photos had shown this area as a smooth dirt field dotted with palm trees, but to our dismay we quickly discovered that the plain was scored with lines and lines of secondary irrigation ditches—most at least ten feet deep. The loose dirt sides of each of these furrows sloped down at about forty-five degrees, making it difficult for our heavily laden SAW gunners to struggle back up the slopes once they had climbed down. After twenty minutes of patrolling, first squad had managed to cross only three of these ditches, and third and second hadn't even hit the plain yet.

We pressed on for a little longer, but we were making horrible time. The Marines were starting to wear out climbing one crumbling ten-foot slope after another. Finally, after clambering on all fours out of our fourth or fifth irrigation ditch, I motioned Teague to move the head of the squad about two hundred meters west, right up against the main irrigation canal. It was a calculated risk—by moving so close to the canal and the lighted Farouq area just across the water, Joker One had a much greater chance of being spotted by locals sleeping on their rooftops. However, a nice, firm road ran alongside the canal, and the platoon could move much more quickly on it than in the open plain. If we crossed the area fast enough, perhaps no one would spot us.

Once on the dirt road, our pace picked up considerably, and I called Leza and Bowen over our intersquad radios, the PRRs, to let them know about the changed scheme of maneuver. I reached Leza, second in the patrol's column, but not Bowen; the PRRs, which had reached for close to a mile in training areas of Pendleton, apparently carried for only a few blocks in the urban canyons of Ramadi. Leza relayed the message, though, and the transition to the new route went smoothly. The platoon swiftly moved south until we hit the end of the canal. There, third squad and Staff Sergeant peeled off on their mission while first and second bumped over a set of railroad tracks, followed them underneath the bridge, and looped west, homing in on the cemetery.

A few hundred meters from the bridge, we hit an open field with waist-high grass. With no other cover in sight save a few family compounds butting right up against the cemetery, I halted the patrol and had the men lie down in a rough circle. The bulk of the Marines would remain there, hidden by the grass, while Leza, Noriel, Teague, Yebra, and I headed to the ambush site for a quick look-over. The last thing that I wanted was the whole of Joker One to crowd into the cemetery and stumble noisily around trying to get into position all at once. Loading people into a night ambush is a tricky business. After about ten minutes of positioning themselves, first and second squads had assembled a rough defensive perimeter in the field. The small recce party and I headed out.

After a hundred meters of moving, I glanced back at where the two squads lay. Even using my NVGs, the Marines were completely hidden in the tall grass, and I snapped a quick mental picture of their location so that our small reconnaissance patrol could find them on our way back. Then I turned my attention to the business of locating the little cemetery in the dark. I had driven there once before with the Army, but that had been during the daytime. Everything looks different at night and on foot. Despite the cool evening air, I started sweating. I thought that I knew where we were, but things were looking a little strange. As this was our first live mission, I was extremely worried about getting lost and inclined to second-guess myself. I briefly considered pulling out my GPS, but scrapped it as a last-resort idea. To get a reading, I would have had to illuminate the instrument. A random light in the middle of a grassy field on a clear night can be seen for miles. Nervously, I led us forward in what I hoped was the right direction.

Five minutes later, Noriel and I hit the large dirt road that signaled the approach to the cemetery. But no sooner had I breathed a sigh of relief than headlights appeared around a road bend some one hundred meters away, moving rapidly toward us. With no time to spare, we flung ourselves face-down into a small depression on the side of the road. I held my breath as the vehicles rumbled by. They turned out to be Army Humvees, but the soldiers either didn't see us or didn't deign to acknowledge us. When the coast was clear, we hopped back onto the dirt road and moved rapidly down it.

After fifty more meters, Teague and I boosted Leza to the top of a high wall bordering the road to see if the cemetery was behind it. It wasn't, and I cursed myself. Sweat was pouring off me in rivulets. We moved another fifty meters down the road and the entrance to the cemetery appeared: a dark break in the wall between compounds. I cursed my lack of patience. We darted inside and took cover in a small crypt. I settled down with Noriel and

Leza, and together we planned out exactly how we would load the ambush, identifying squad positions, fields of fire and observation, and the various egress routes we would take if compromised. With everything sorted out, I left Yebra and Teague to watch over the cemetery while the two squad leaders and I headed back to get the squads. Teague had a PRR and could easily communicate with me over the short distance I needed to travel.

As I had no desire to risk compromise again by heading down the dirt road, our reduced patrol climbed a broken wall at the rear of the cemetery and dropped into the compound abutting it to the south. Now that we had a good idea of the lay of the land, Noriel, Leza, and I would simply skirt the walls of these compounds, hiding in the shadows and avoiding use of the dirt road altogether. It was a solid plan, and it worked for about twenty meters. Then the feral dogs that slink around all the populated areas of Ramadi caught wind of us as we crept through someone's backyard. What sounded like fifty hounds started howling loud enough to wake the nearby dead. At the time, though, Leza, Noriel, and I weren't all that concerned about possible compromise. Instead, we were preoccupied trying to outrun the pack of snapping dogs that had suddenly materialized ten meters behind us. Abandoning all pretense at tactical movement, we ran full bore through people's backyards. As we ran, we tore our way bodily through the things that people in Ramadi normally left in their backyards—laundry hanging up to dry, piles of crunchy trash, small clutches of sleeping chickens, and so on. After all of our efficient, professional, and silent patrolling in, I now felt like an amateur circus clown piling clumsily out of his clown car.

With all our gear weighing us down, it didn't take long for the dogs to close the distance, and I seriously considered shooting them. Just before I pivoted around to start killing dogs, though, Sergeant Leza performed a pivot of his own. Catching his movement out of the corner of my eye, I whipped around in time to see my blocky sergeant scoop up a rock, brandish it behind his head as if to throw it, and then charge full tilt at the baying dogs. The pack broke immediately under this feigned assault and peeled off into the darkness. I congratulated myself for having a quick-thinking, surprisingly nimble sergeant who had clearly been chased by dogs before.

The rest of the mission proceeded without incident. Noriel, Leza, and I linked up with the two squads and led them back to the ambush site, where Teague and Yebra waited to guide them into position. With the cemetery

loaded full of Marines, my reduced platoon waited, watching the train station to our north for several hours. After neither our NVGs nor our thermal
scopes revealed any movement at our objective, we searched the cemetery
for signs of recent activity. Finding none, we moved out to hit the train station itself. That, too, quickly proved a dry hole, and at 1 AM the platoon patrolled back to the Combat Outpost through the quiet Farouq area. By 2:30,
Joker One was safely inside the Combat Outpost, a lot dirtier but a little
more experienced, a little more confident that we could handle ourselves in
the real world. Moreover, a number of my worries had proved unfounded.
Guzon had done well—Staff Sergeant was still alive and kicking—and
Henderson had exceeded my expectations. In fact, Henderson had proved
himself so reliable and so tough in Kuwait that we had given him one of our
precious SAWs. That whole evening, he had humped the light machine
gun uncomplainingly up and down drainage ditches, even stopping to help
out other Marines who had trouble struggling up the steep slopes. Even
Feldmeir did okay—he fell asleep a few times in the cemetery, and Teague
had to smack him on the back of his helmet to keep him awake, but he
stayed alert and ready through both the patrol in and the egress out. My
men were everything that I had hoped for.

As I headed back to my room, helmet swinging in my left hand and
weapon still slung across my gear-laden chest, I smiled a bit to myself. The
first mission hadn't exactly been a textbook ambush, but it hadn't been a
failure. The newly formed Joker One had performed well in its first time out
of the gates. I had even managed to get us where we needed to go with only
a few minor setbacks, so now both I and the rest of platoon knew that the
lieutenant, whatever his other failings, could at least steer himself in the
dark of the city. This most basic of accomplishments gave me some badly
needed confidence.

Most important, though, everyone returned from this mission. At the
time, that accomplishment was the ultimate definition of success in my
mind.

THIRTEEN

Over the course of the next week, Golf Company settled into a loose routine that would form the basis for our combat rhythms and that would give some vague shape to our new life in Ramadi. The CO created a rotation schedule guaranteeing that at least one out of every eight days was spent guarding the Outpost, which meant that, except for periodic squad-sized local security patrols, the majority of the day was spent either on or behind the compound walls. Another of the eight days was scheduled to be "off." In theory, this meant a day free of all mission responsibilities for the Marines. (The platoon commanders and platoon sergeants stood duty as watch officers—even in theory, we never had a dedicated day off.) The other six days were spent running missions, either as the platoon tasked to take the twelve to fourteen hours during sunup, the platoon tasked to take the remainder during sundown, or the platoon tasked to stand ready for twenty-four straight hours as the backup for both (the QRF platoon). Golf Company's final eight-day schedule, then, went as follows:

DAY ONE: Day Ops
DAY TWO: Night Ops/Tertiary QRF

DAY THREE: QRF
DAY FOUR: Security
DAY FIVE: Day Ops
DAY SIX: Night Ops/Tertiary QRF
DAY SEVEN: QRF
DAY EIGHT: "Off"/Secondary QRF/Gunny Duty

A few days after our first mission, on our first "off" day, I walked into the platoon's courtyard to check on the men and found eight gray Marines shuffling confusedly around. I almost fell over. In the dim light of the early evening, the strange figures looked like statues come to life, but on closer inspection these animated wonders turned out to be merely Mahardy, Yebra, Henderson, Guzon, Bolding, and three others. Shirtless, they ground to a halt when I walked into the courtyard. From stony faces eight eyeballs rolled whitely in my direction, the only proof that these now-still creatures actually lived. Even Bolding's dark black skin had succumbed to a fine gray powder that covered every square inch of him, but his hundred-megawatt-smile still shone through the dust and obvious exhaustion. As he was the first Marine I recognized, I made a beeline for Bolding to ask what had happened to turn my platoon into living statues. Before I got there, though, I was intercepted by an agitated Noriel.

"Sir, sir, sir! I finally found you. I've been looking all over for you, sir. The XO made the Marines move concrete powder bags for the past three hours. Each of the bags, he weights about fifty pounds, sir. We had to put them in one building, and we did it, sir, but as soon as we finished, the XO decided that we had to move them to another one. So we had to redo it, sir! Now the Marines is filthy, but Gunny's told the companies we can't use bottled waters to take showers. I asked Staff Sergeant if we could use him just this once, but he said no. Sir, how can the Marines sleep like this?" Noriel waved his arms at the statues.

How indeed? We had no running water, and all of the baby wipes we had brought with us from the States wouldn't even clean one of my men. At the courtyard's entrance, I peered around the corner. None of the company staff were in view. I ducked back to Noriel and told him to sneak into the mess hall and take whatever water he needed. If anyone asked my sergeant what he was doing, he was to tell them I had ordered him to retrieve some water. If they had a problem with it, they could deal with me directly.

Hearing this, Noriel grinned and was off like a shot to the mess hell. Five minutes later he returned, arms and cargo pockets full of bottles of water.

Establishing any sort of routine in Ramadi was nearly impossible. We soon learned that our missions were completely unpredictable and would arise, or change themselves, at any time, day or night. Being technically "off" was no guarantee of rest.

There was one notable exception to this patternless pattern: the morning route sweep. Because Michigan was such an important transportation artery for all coalition forces in the area, keeping it free and clear of IEDs became a high priority for our company, so almost every morning started off with a platoon patrol straight down the highway from the Outpost on the eastern edge of Ramadi to the Government Center on the city's western boundary. The mission seems sound and practicable in theory; even the term, "route sweep," sounds professional, efficient, antiseptic. The reality is anything but—a route sweep is a nasty mission that can only be accomplished by ugly, primitive, and fairly risky methods.

The Army had performed its sweeps by driving down the highway in fully armored Humvees at forty miles per hour, minimum, looking for whatever suspicious objects they could spot at such high speeds while holding their breaths, just waiting to get exploded. By contrast, we performed our route sweeps by walking down Michigan wearing body armor. Like the Army, we also held our breaths, waiting to get exploded. Walking at five miles an hour rather than driving at forty, we stood a much better chance of spotting unusual objects among the trash and other clutter littering the road. Wearing only body armor, though, we also stood a much worse chance of surviving a blast. Even at the slow speed, Marines still rarely spotted well-camouflaged IEDs until we were about thirty to fifty feet away, well within the kill zone. Each morning route sweep was an extremely nerve-racking forty minutes, to say the least. I envied the Army and their armored vehicles.

Every platoon commander had his own preferred time of morning to do the sweep, giving the recurring mission some inherent unpredictability. Exhibiting regular mission patterns is a great way to get your men killed. Quist liked to wait until midmorning, when he could be sure that the streets would be crowded with people. If they weren't, or if certain spots seemed to be widely avoided, then he could be relatively certain that an IED was in place. By understanding the ebb and flow of daily life, he used the city's inhabitants as early warning devices.

As compelling as it was, I had heard of too many times when tens or hundreds of unsuspecting civilians were blown up to trust too fully to this logic. Instead, I preferred doing my sweeps early in the morning, just after first light. The terrorists are *Homo sapiens,* and, like the rest of the species, they are subject to the very human desire not to wake up at 4 AM. Furthermore, without crowds, the insurgents were deprived of their most valuable asset: normal civilians to provide cover and concealment for their operations. Since we couldn't use civilians in the same callous manner—as mere pieces of terrain at best and as human shields at worst—I liked to level the playing field whenever I could by depriving the enemy of their inherent advantage. They could still detonate us, of course, but now they would have to do so from a nearby building instead of a nearby crowd, and a distant triggerman would be deprived of a hidden, anonymous observer. The downside to such early morning operations, though, was that the light wasn't as good as it was later, so it was a bit easier to miss well-hidden IEDs.

At 5 AM on March 14, Joker One set out on its maiden route sweep. An engineer squad had been attached to our company, and I had earlier grabbed two of these explosives experts and asked them to walk point during the mission. They moved on the sidewalks on the north and south sides of Michigan, and Teague's team followed closely behind. Walking on the median, straight down the center of the road, were Noriel, Mahardy, and I. Someone had to investigate the area, but walking in the middle of a four-lane highway with no cover for thirty meters on any side was a dicey business. I wanted the smallest number of Marines possible exposed like that, so on that day the leaders walked the medians while everyone else stayed on the sidewalks, closer to the buildings and cover. Later, Noriel and I traded off center responsibilities to give the enemy a less concentrated target, but on this first unpleasant mission we wanted to send a signal to the Marines about what they could expect from their leadership going forward.

By the time we made it to the road's center, Bowen and Leza had already peeled off to our south and north, respectively—in addition to being a juicy bomb magnet, first squad also presented a tempting target to potential ambushers holed up in the multistory buildings bordering the highway. By patrolling one to two blocks off Michigan, second and third squads protected our flanks and provided some early warning in the event of an enemy staging to attack. For forty-five minutes, Joker One walked the city this way. I alternated between using the PRR to monitor all of our squads' positions, scanning the median for bombs, and trying not to hyperventilate.

Finally we hit the Government Center, and I relaxed a bit. The sweep part of the mission was over, and I leaned my head back to tell Mahardy to call in the checkpoint. He was already on it. He was more than on it: Not only was Mahardy telling the COC our current location, but he was telling them where we were headed next and that he would let them know when we hit our follow-on checkpoint. This kid was a keeper, I thought. The more I could rely on my RO to communicate with the COC in my stead, the more I could focus on controlling my platoon.

At the Government Center, Joker One wheeled south, deep into the butchers' area. Incredulous Iraqis stopped everything to stare. In the past, U.S. forces had rarely, if ever, ventured down here, and they certainly had not done so on foot. We walked past butchers who halted in mid-chop, schoolchildren who stopped walking to school, shopkeepers who completely ignored their customers, customers who completely ignored their shopping. Smiling and waving when we could, we pressed on, moving quickly through the area. I wanted to say something, to talk to the locals, to reach out to them, but without any translators in our platoon it was impossible. Bowen tried his rudimentary Arabic a few times, but the Iraqis couldn't understand him. He had apparently learned a different dialect.

When we hit the Farouq district, the stares intensified, and some took a harder edge. We still smiled and waved, and after about ten minutes a crowd of children formed around us, all shouting at once in broken English: *Mister mister, give me, give me. Give me Pepsi. Give me soccer ball. Give me Frisbee, pencil.* We handed out all the candy and writing utensils we had on us. I started thinking that no matter where you went, little kids still acted like little kids. It was reassuring that in this crazy city, at least something translated across cultural lines. I broke out in a wide smile. Then Carson called me over the PRR:

"Sir, they're starting to throw rocks at us back here." He was at the tail end of second squad.

"Who, the men?"

"No, sir, the kids."

The smile vanished. "What? The kids are throwing rocks at you?"

"Yes, sir."

"Okay, well, let them throw rocks for now." Five more minutes passed, then:

"Sir, they're pretty good at throwing rocks. These rocks, they really hurt, sir. Some of them are big, too, sir."

I was at a complete loss as to how to respond. We had come here to win hearts and minds, and I had never envisioned a scenario where I would have to choose between roughing up ten-year-old kids or forcing my Marines to endure some serious punishment at their hands. If anyone could take it for a little while, though, Carson could. Walking, I pondered our response, but after about two minutes of enduring a vicious pelting, Carson solved the problem for me.

"Hey, sir," he radioed, "we fixed it."

"What?"

"Yeah, I grabbed some old man standing by, pointed to the little kids throwing rocks, and he chased them away. We're good to go, sir."

"Oh. Good work. Thanks, Carson. Keep it up."

"Roger that, sir."

When we made it back to the base about half an hour later, I was still unnerved. What kind of child tries repeatedly to stone someone who has just given them a present?

Maybe children all over the world weren't the same after all, and maybe we needed a more nuanced understanding of the various neighborhoods and of the attitudes of the Iraqis who inhabited them. For the first time, I wondered whether our smile-and-wave tactics would be sufficient to win the hearts and minds of the adults (and keep them from attacking us with rockets) if they couldn't even prevent the children from stoning us.

FOURTEEN

Three days later, intelligence came down that an internationally wanted Sudanese terror cell was operating in our AO, far on the western edge of Ramadi proper. Three platoons were to snatch these terrorists in the dead of night, and those of us participating were excited. During our first week in the city, a corporal had been badly wounded and all we had done since then was wander around, smiling, waving, and handing out candy and soccer balls, waiting to get shot at or exploded. We didn't want revenge per se, but we did want to take the initiative away from the enemy, to go on the offensive, to be proactive rather than reactive. Now we would be moving on our own terms.

The CO mapped out our mission. Joker One would head out first, early in the afternoon, patrolling through the city on foot until we got to the target location. Our main purpose was to get human eyes, and human judgment, on the actual buildings that the company would be hitting that evening, hopefully limiting the number of surprises in store for us later. I was given verbal descriptions of the known terrorists—middle-aged, middle-height, and, most tellingly, black-skinned—and their names on the off chance that I recognized an opportunity to take down the Sudanese while we were patrolling. We would disguise this reconnaissance mission by conducting Information Operations (IO) in the vicinity, a task that sounded sophisticated at headquarters but that on the street simply meant handing out flyers explaining in Arabic that we were the good guys and the terrorists were the bad guys. In case the text wasn't engaging enough, the missives also had a few pictures of Marines building schools, surrounded by smiling children. We had about seventy flyers in all, enough for one per every 4,300 people in our AO.

Once my platoon returned from the patrol, we would share whatever we had found out with Joker Two, the raid force itself. Joker Three would be the cordon force, and they would set out an hour earlier than everyone else. Remaining concealed in the darkness, their mission was to surround the target site before the mission kicked off so that no one could flee the raid force. Once they had set in, Joker Three would call back, and Jokers Two and One would launch out in Humvees and seven-tons to hit the target houses. Two would be the door kickers while my platoon set up machine gun positions in case things went really wrong. Leza and Raymond, the human cannonball, were also on standby to lend Joker Two a hand if necessary. Joker Four had security; so they would remain at the Outpost.

With the company plan set, I issued the necessary orders to the squad leaders. Three people per squad would get about five flyers apiece. They had strict instructions not to hand them out until I gave the order. I didn't want us running out of Information Operations material before we got near the target site. The rest of us stuffed our pockets full of candy to hand out in lieu of the flyers. A few hours later, after rehearsals and final inspections were completed, Joker One stepped off on our target reconnaissance mission.

The patrol initially went smoothly. We moved quickly through the warehouses and automobile repair shops of the industrial area to the north of Michigan, avoiding the hostile Farouq district to our south altogether, and we crossed over the highway near the Saddam mosque in the center of the city. From there, the platoon pushed to the edge of the butchers' district, to the major street demarcating its western boundary. That road would take us right by the target compound, and second squad and I hopped on it while first and third moved along our flanks. With another five minutes of walking to go, I called Noriel, Bowen, and Leza and instructed them to slowly start handing out the flyers.

As we passed the compound, I glanced around second squad to make certain that my men were still handing out flyers and candy and waving. They were. I slowed my pace to get a better look at the target complex. One thing became apparent: There were more buildings inside the compound than were shown on the company's photographic map. Without being too obvious, I pulled out my own map and consulted it to make certain that I was remembering correctly. I was. Sure enough, where the photographic map showed two large open patches, my eyes showed two new buildings. Whatever imagery we had been provided was dated, probably by a few years.

I made a mental note of the buildings, then quickly moved over one block, from second to third squad, to get a look at the compound from another angle. Aside from the unexpected buildings, everything else seemed pretty straightforward—the walls were the normal height, the gates were located in the usual locations, and there was no evidence of heightened security. The patrol moved through the area, and I rejoined second squad. When we got two hundred meters away, I started to relax a bit. I could detect no evidence that the patrol had spooked our quarry. Then Teague called me:

"Sir, you said that our targets were three black people?"

"Yeah, Teague. What've you got?"

"Well, sir, I've got three black people walking down the street right here. Sir, I ain't seen no black people in this city yet."

Leza chimed in. "Yeah, sir. I see 'em too. They're about to pass me. Sir, I think they look like North Africans. Want me to have Raymond's team grab them?"

Briefly, I was stymied. On the one hand, Teague was absolutely right. In our nine days in Ramadi, we had yet to see a single black Iraqi. Every Ramadian, it seemed, was an ethnic Arab. And Teague's black-skinned, North African–looking males were well within walking distance of where our targets supposedly lived, so we could grab the three men now and perhaps complete the entire mission in one fell swoop. However, if these men were not the ones we wanted, then my platoon would just have snatched three black guys off the street in broad daylight within two hundred meters of a suspected terrorist residence. If the Sudanese truly were internationally wanted terrorists, it would take them less than an hour to put two and two together and move to a different safe house or a different city. It would take us more than an hour to figure out if we had the right guys, and the whole raid would be blown in the meantime. Or we could grab the streetwalkers and hit the houses ourselves, but there was no guarantee that 1) with just one platoon we could prevent fleeing terrorists from escaping or 2) our targets would even be home in the late afternoon.

With real-time dilemmas like this one, you generally have about five seconds, maximum, to make a crucial decision if you want to have any impact on the outcome of events. After that, a changing situation or your enemies usually make the decisions for you. I didn't have time to radio the CO for his input, and I wasn't sure that I wanted to. I was the only one on the scene, and no one was better positioned than me to make the call. I wasn't going to offload my decision-making responsibility to a distant headquarters. Still, I was painfully conscious that if I screwed this one up, a trio of international terrorists was going to continue killing innocents.

About five seconds after Leza called me, I radioed him back and told him to stand down. We'd wait until we had the entire company.

As the patrol continued uneventfully, I knew that I had just rolled the dice. When I got back to the Outpost, I explained to the CO what we had seen and the rationale behind my decision. He looked extremely dubious, and he asked me, rather pointedly, whether I had ever seen any black Iraqis in the city before. When I admitted that I hadn't, he then asked me why on earth I had hesitated to snatch the only three men in Ramadi who fit the description we had been given of the Sudanese terrorists.

This less-than-subtle Socratic questioning made quite clear the intended point: The CO thought that I hadn't been aggressive or decisive enough.

However, what we didn't know then was that the western edge of Ramadi had a large North African population. Hundreds, maybe thousands, of black-skinned residents answering to our targets' descriptions lived in the area, which was why, of course, the terrorists had located their safe house there. I never found out if the three men I saw on the street that day were our targets or not, but the odds were in my favor.

Fortunately for me, events soon caused the CO to forget all about my decision. When Golf Company hit the buildings early the next morning, all our targets were inside. Joker Two raided the complex hard and fast, and pretty soon they called us for some extra manpower. The additional buildings meant that the men they had planned to use for prisoner security were instead tied up kicking down doors. Leza, Raymond, and the rest of second squad took off at a dead run from where I had positioned our vehicles. Soon they radioed back. They'd collected a whole clutch of terrorists, and they'd be bringing them back presently. Along with their targets, Joker Two had also found loads of IED-making material, tens of thousands of dollars shrink-wrapped in compact bundles, and a large cache of anti-American hate videos commingled with hard-core pornography.

I could tell by Leza's tone that he was enjoying himself, and I was happy for him. After all, how many twenty-four-year-old, high-school-educated, Mexican American immigrants could say that they had played a crucial role in capturing internationally wanted terrorists? While I was monitoring the goings-on over the radio, the Gunny sidled up to me.

"Hey, sir, looks like you might have made a decent call back there, earlier today."

"The CO didn't seem too pleased," I replied.

The Gunny's creased face broke out in his big, heavy-lidded smile, and he pantomimed a shrug, hands held straight out from his sides. "All I know, sir, is that those terrorists are there now, sir." He nodded at me and walked off.

FIFTEEN

We had indeed gotten all of the terrorists, and we later learned that word of our success aired on every major news network. At the time, though, we were virtually sealed off from the world outside Ramadi. We had no telephones save the one satellite cellphone, no e-mail, no computers, no network television, and only sporadic electricity. For us, communicating with home meant writing or receiving a good old-fashioned letter. At nearly any time of day or night, then, anywhere between three and ten of my men sat shirtless and tattooed on their stools in the courtyard, smoking and writing back home to wives, girlfriends, mothers, and so on. I did the same in my free time, only I did it in my room, and usually by myself—the relentless pace of the missions meant that at least one of us was always out on patrol.

The Ox, redeeming himself at least to some degree for the contractor fiasco, managed to procure two TV/DVD combinations for each platoon. Even without live television, they were among our most highly valued possessions, and a recently installed generator provided sporadic electricity to power them. Soon after that first raid, Golf Company received a towering, six-foot, six-inch, 250-pound Iraqi translator named George. During my first conversation with him, George wrapped up our meet-and-greet by blandly informing me that he hated all of the Iraqi people, apparently seeing no contradiction between his hatred for Iraqis and the fact that he himself was one of them. He then began a fairly sizable side business selling pirated DVDs to all the company's Marines. As valuable as his translation service was, his movie business had at least as much worth in our eyes. No matter that the movies had been shot by someone holding a video recorder in a movie theater, and you could occasionally see people arriving or getting up to leave.

It's amazing what a lack of choice and access can do to your taste in movies. Most of the Marines were so eager for something from home that they'd watch anything at all so long as it was made in the United States. Toward the middle of our second week in-country, Noriel walked into his squad's room to find the long, skinny Mahardy and the short, fireplug-like Guzon lying together on a lower bunk bed, both wearing nothing but their short green nylon shorts and watching *The Notebook*, a romantic tear-jerker starring an exceptionally beautiful actress. It's hard to picture a more unlikely couple than the skinny, pale, blond Irish kid and the squat, dark-skinned, dark-haired Hispanic. About the only thing they had in common was the fact that both sported tattoos on their backs and shoulders— Mahardy a Celtic cross and Guzon the USMC logo. Noriel, of course, immediately ridiculed the odd couple for their supremely unmanly choice of movie. Cuddled next to Guzon, or so Noriel described it to me later, Mahardy defended his masculinity fiercely: "It's a fucking good movie, Sergeant. Watch it."

My feisty squad leader swore he'd never do such a thing, but four days later, having exhausted his own entertainment supply, he surreptitiously made his way into an unoccupied squad room, snagged *The Notebook*, and brought it back to a packed NCO room. Half an hour later, I found him, along with Leza and Bowen, watching the movie with tears running down their faces, engrossed in the story of star-crossed love. Some things, it seemed, cut across all ranks.

The downtime after our first major success was short-lived. On March 18, one week after our triumphant capture of the terrorists, Captain Bronzi let us know that he needed to revisit the corrupt Farouq police chief because intelligence reports suggested that, surprisingly enough, the man hadn't changed his ways at all since the previous Army visit. Joker One was slated for the next day's patrols, so we would take the CO down to the station. As far as missions go, it wasn't all that complex—just a quick platoon walk down through the Farouq district and back. Nothing seemed amiss or unusual about the operation, and I woke up on March 19 feeling fine about the day and what it held.

We left the base at 10 AM. Even in March, it was already getting hot— the temperature hovered around ninety degrees that morning. Using a technique borrowed from the British, the "bomb blast," Raymond's four-man team sprinted out of the base as fast as they could, dodging cars as they bounced south across Michigan. Moving out of a base is a particularly vulnerable time for any patrol, and the bomb-blast technique minimized that time. I followed Raymond's team with the next team, and, bomb blast by bomb blast, Joker One crossed the highway and settled into a quick, smooth rhythm. The CO and I walked with second squad while first and third shadowed us, a block or two off to our right and left. We needed to keep them tight—we still didn't have enough high-powered radios to equip each squad, and my communication with Bowen and Noriel was limited to the four-block range of our PRRs. For the most part Captain Bronzi stayed silent, which relieved me. I didn't enjoy having senior officers out with Joker One, for they often forgot their proper place and usurped the role of the platoon commander by making decisions better left to their better-prepared subordinates.

As the platoon moved off Michigan toward the police station to our south, we passed into the thick maze of high-walled compounds of the Farouq district. I constantly scanned the areas all around us, trying to pick out any potential threats. All that I could see were two-story, flat-roofed buildings hiding behind compound walls that ran in smooth, unbroken lines down to the end of each block. Once we entered this part of the city, we were hemmed in for the hundred meters it took to get from intersection to intersection. Moving down different streets, each squad was cut off from the others, and as I entered the first walled block with second squad, first and third had already disappeared into their separate corridors. Losing sight of them made me slightly uneasy, but I quickly turned my attention back to my own surroundings. To my front, I saw Leza's solid bulk moving just behind his point fire team, watching the roofs, expertly keeping second squad on line and moving. Just behind me walked the CO, still silent, and behind him trailed the rest of Leza's men.

The first few blocks we crossed were deserted, but after five minutes Iraqis began to emerge from their houses, apparently to get a better look at us. At first I noticed them only peripherally—I was far too preoccupied with navigating the patrol, maintaining communication with first and third squads, and scanning the rooftops around us to pay much attention to the slowly crowding streets. Indeed, I was so busy that I didn't feel anything other than hyperfocus. After all, it was the first time that Captain Bronzi had come out with Joker One, and I wanted everything to run as smoothly as possible. After another five minutes, though, I began paying more attention. The residents lined the sidewalks, gawking at the fourteen Marines walking through their neighborhood. One man waited until I was even with him then asked, "Army?"

"No," I replied with a smile, "Marines."

He pondered this answer for a few seconds, then pointed at Yebra, walking, as usual, just ten feet away from me. "Little Army," he said.

I moved on. I was too busy trying to get all of my men to the police station to spend too much time winning hearts and minds, something I didn't really know how to do without a translator present. And I didn't like being referred to as a diminutive sister service.

A quarter of a mile before we reached the police station, Noriel radioed me. He had found a suspected IED and was going to cordon it off and investigate it. I acknowledged and continued onward toward the police station. A few blocks later we reached our destination, and the CO went inside to try and sort out the crooked chief. The rest of us took cover where we could find it—in doorways, behind small concrete blocks, next to parked cars—and waited outside for Captain Bronzi. On general principle, I didn't like having to stand still in the middle of a foreign city in a war zone, but I wasn't too worried. The last attack in the area had been well over two months ago.

After about ten minutes, Noriel called me on the PRR. The signal was weak and the transmission garbled, but I got the gist of his message. On closer inspection, the suspected IED had turned out to be trash. He was coming to link up with us at the police station. Roger that, I told him. No reply.

Five minutes later, the CO emerged and announced that it was time to return to the base. I explained that we were awaiting first squad's imminent arrival. Ten minutes later, however, they hadn't returned, and unable to raise Noriel on the PRR, Joker One got ready to head back to the base. I was beginning to feel uneasy that one-third of my platoon was missing, but I wasn't terribly worried for their safety. We hadn't heard any gunfire or explosions, so first squad wasn't in any immediate danger. The idea that an isolated squad might be attacked flitted briefly through my mind, but, again, nothing had happened recently in the area, so I doubted that anything would happen to Noriel and his men.

We had a plan for this type of situation, and it dictated that any separated unit head straight back to our last checkpoint, in this case the major traffic circle five hundred meters away from the base. If the squad wasn't picked up there within fifteen minutes, it was to head straight back to the Outpost. I was betting that without a map (we still didn't have enough of them to give ones to the squad leaders), Noriel had simply gotten turned around in the narrow city streets, missed the police station, and was now on his way back to the base. I gave the order to move out and the reduced platoon set off, this time with second squad leading and third squad following directly behind, on the same street. It gave us no depth to our flanks, but I was willing to take the risk—the last thing I wanted at this point was yet another lost squad with no communication. The return patrol went smoothly enough, and as second squad started entering the base, I had Yebra call headquarters just to make certain that Noriel and his men had made it back. The report came back negative. No signs of first squad anywhere.

When I heard the news, I was standing just inside the Outpost's gates, watching the tail end of second squad enter the compound while third patrolled along the south side of Route Michigan, just across the street from where I was standing. My heart sank and my mind began racing, trying to sort through what could have happened to my lost squad. Noriel should have had more than enough time to make it back. If he hadn't yet, he was far more lost than I thought and probably wandering aimlessly in the unfriendly Farouq area. Grabbing Yebra, I ordered Leza to finish getting his squad back into the Outpost and Bowen to halt in place. Third squad was still about one hundred meters away from entering the base, and they were going to turn around and start looking for the lost first squad. Yebra and I were going with them.

The CO wished me luck and told me that he'd monitor our progress closely on the radio back in the COC. Yebra and I nodded to him and then re-exited the base at a dead sprint. Despite his extra thirty pounds, the little radio operator had no trouble keeping up with me. Linking up with Bowen, we turned third squad around and headed back into the Farouq area, looking for any signs that first squad had passed through. Every forty seconds or so, I would call out over my PRR: "One-One, this is One-Actual. Come in, One-One." If first squad was truly in serious trouble, we would probably have heard gunfire and explosions by now. The fact that we hadn't yet was somewhat comforting, but we needed to find them quickly.

Third squad and I wandered the Farouq area for nearly an hour, moving quickly from block to block and occasionally breaking into a flat-out run whenever I pumped my fist twice, which I did every four blocks to give our movements more randomness. We kept heading south, toward the Farouq police station. After about ten minutes moving along one street, we moved either east or west to the one paralleling it, again to give our movements more randomness. This was the third time we had passed through the area, and I was worried that anyone with hostile intentions was by now fully alerted to our presence. With each passing minute, my nervousness ratcheted up slightly.

As we zigzagged through the dense housing compounds, I noticed that the streets were nearly empty. The few people who remained didn't seem friendly. Some stared and then turned away. One man even spat on the ground after we passed.

We had almost reached the police station when I heard the Ox's voice on the radio: "Uh, One-Actual, be advised we have your first squad back here at the base. We, uhhh, must have missed them when they got back. Over."

The Ox signed off. I swore to myself. We had been wandering the Farouq area for close to two hours now, confined to a small, fifteen-block box, giving any potential attacker ample time to take note and track us. I pumped my fist twice at Bowen, and we began running again, north this time. I wanted us to move very quickly for a few blocks until we popped out of the dense housing compounds and hit Michigan.

Third squad ran for about a minute, then stopped as our point man hit Canal Street, the main north-south road running just west of the al-Haq mosque, a giant structure located at a traffic circle a mere five hundred meters away from our base. We almost could see the Outpost from our position, and some of the tension that everyone was feeling fell away. I made a brief joke to Bowen over the PRR, and he joked back. His rear fire team leader, Corporal Brooks, chimed in, and immediately banter was flying back and forth between all three team leaders. "Hey, Carson, this is Brooks. Did you see what that old guy looked like when we passed him? I thought he was gonna have a heart attack or something."

"Yeah, I don't think I've ever seen anyone so wrinkled. What do you think he was, like, forty-five years old . . ."

I was horrified at what I had started.

"Break, break, break. All Jokers, this is One-Actual. This is the fourth damn time that we've crossed this area. Stop talking, damn it, and pay attention. If anyone is going to hit us, it'll be now."

Everyone shut up. Our point fire team, the one leading the squad, bumped quickly across the street, Yebra and I covering their movement, rifles held up to our shoulders, squinting eyes tracing the pavement back into the Farouq area. Bowen moved up behind me and tapped me on the shoulder. It was the signal to get going; he and the second team would cover our movement across the wide-open pavement, a fairly dangerous area as there was nothing nearby to give us cover in the event of an attack. Yebra and I jogged across the road, rifles still held high. Two by two, the squad repeated this process until Corporal Brooks and his trailing fire team started moving across the street.

I was up near the head of the patrol when I heard two booms, in quick succession. I whipped around. Where Brooks's team should have been was a large cloud of grayish smoke, about ten feet high and ten feet wide. Its center was nearly black. Outside the cloud, just fifty meters away, chunks of concrete began raining down. I had just lost three of my Marines.

had imagined how I would react in this situation. First I would be over-come by emotions, which I would have to tamp down quickly. Once I'd done that, I hoped that I'd then make cool, dispassionate decisions about how to maneuver the rest of my Marines against our enemies. But looking at the smoke where Brooks's team used to be, I felt nothing at all. In fact I wasn't even aware of making any sort of conscious decision to react. I found myself running, as fast as I could, back toward the scene of the explosion, with Yebra trailing a few feet behind me, shouting into the radio as he re-ported the situation to the COC. I remember thinking that I'd never heard my RO speak so loudly before. Looking over to my left, I could see Bowen and his Marines crouched down in a long line near the wall in front of the al-Haq mosque. As I sprinted past them, part of me noticed the distinct bull-whip-like sounds of bullets cracking their way along as they passed close by. For the first time, I understood on a gut level what it meant to "take fire." I sped up the run—despite the shooting, I couldn't be bothered with taking cover. I needed to get my missing fire team; it was possible that if they weren't dead, then they were badly wounded and unable to take cover. I also needed to sort out who was attacking us, and from where, so that I could make decisions on how to maneuver third squad. About three seconds into the run, in which time I had covered about twenty meters, I called Bowen on the PRR, panting from the exertion.

"One-Three . . . Flip the squad around . . . Patrol column . . . We're going to see what's happened to Brooks . . . and then push back into Farouq to pursue. Over."

"Roger that, sir," Bowen replied crisply, without any hesitation at all.

Still running, I looked over, saw him rise, grab his point man, and shove the Marine toward the smoke. Shouting at the rest of the squad to get up, damn it, Bowen started running backward as well, getting everyone else fol-lowing him toward the explosion. About two seconds later I heard a voice talking through the PRR. It was Brooks.

"Sir. I'm good. My team is good. No injuries. We've spotted two guys fir-ing an RPG about two hundred meters south, down the street into the Farouq area. They're gone now, sir, but someone's shooting at us from the west."

I was so sure that Brooks was dead or seriously wounded that at first I didn't believe my ears. Then he appeared out of the smoke, a magician's apparition, running toward me, his team emerging one by one behind him. Their eyes were as big and white as dinner plates. Approaching them, I slowed down. The front of third squad caught up with me, and Brooks and his team fell back to their usual place at the rear of the column. Together now, we all pushed right back the way we had come, running through the now-settling dust of the RPG explosion. We were still taking fire but I couldn't hear the rounds cracking nearby anymore. Our enemies had either stopped aiming at us or had stopped getting lucky—probably the latter, given what I now know about the typical insurgent's spray-and-pray marksmanship. What they lacked in accuracy they made up for in volume.

With most of third squad across the road, I paused my advance briefly and grabbed Yebra. It was the first time anyone in the company had come under fire, and I wanted to report what happened to the COC myself. Everyone there was likely on high alert, having no doubt heard the explosion and the rifle fire and Yebra's shouted reports, and I didn't want them to launch the QRF because I had failed to communicate. Every time someone left the base they put themselves at risk, and I didn't want to put Quist and his guys in danger unless I absolutely couldn't manage the situation myself.

It had been at least a minute since the first explosion, and Yebra was already getting hounded over the radio. "Joker One, this is Joker Six. What the hell is happening out there? I say again, what is happening out there? Give me a SITREP [situation report] now! Over."

I stopped moving and tried to slow my breathing. It was my first firefight; I didn't want to sound frantic or panicked on the radio, since how you sound when you call in during your first enemy contact can come to define how you're viewed by those above and below you for the rest of your tour. Frantic-sounding lieutenants lose everyone's confidence immediately; they end up getting second-guessed a lot. Calm-sounding lieutenants make everyone believe that the situation is well under control, and people listen to their recommendations and take them seriously. The underlying reality in each case may be the same, and the lieutenant's state of mind in each case may be the same, but on the radio, appearances are everything.

I quickly composed a contact report in my head, then grabbed the handset from Yebra. I took a deep breath and began talking. I thought my voice sounded steady and calm, but it was hard for me to tell. I hoped that I was coming across the way I needed to.

"Joker COC, this is One-Actual. Be advised we have just taken one RPG and some small-arms fire from an estimated three to five enemy about two hundred meters south of the mosque, in the Farouq area. Break. Still under some light fire from the west, estimate no weapons heavier than AKs. Break. I have no casualties at this time. Break. We are going to pursue west and search for the enemy. Break. Recommend QRF be mounted, ready to go. No need for them yet. Over."

"One-Actual, this is Six. I copy all. QRF is mounting as we speak. If you need us, give me a call."

"Roger that, Six. I am pursuing at this time. Over."

"Roger, One. Six standing by."

"Roger. Out."

By now, third squad had nearly passed me up, and I motored my way back up to the front, about thirty meters to the west in a narrow alleyway. The two men at the very front of the squad, Dotson and Cabrera, had taken cover behind a large mound of dirt, and they pointed out the location where they thought the AK-47 fire had been coming from. The shooting had just stopped; it looked like the enemy had broken contact. Bowen, meanwhile, maneuvered the rest of the squad deeper into the Farouq area, trying to cut off our attackers' escape route. Third squad was now strung out in a narrow column along an entire north-south city block. Along with Dotson and Cabrera, I now stood at the very rear of the squad.

I picked up again and moved south, resuming a position near third squad's front. We moved again, farther south, gliding along through the late afternoon sun in the bent-kneed combat crouch, weapons held up against our shoulders, heads pressed to our buttstocks, looking over the sights, daring someone to take a shot at us. Unlike earlier when we had been smiling and waving, we now looked ready and eager to shoot, and everything that moved had a muzzle immediately swiveled toward it. The streets were mostly deserted, but the few Iraqis who did see us took off running.

We managed to open a few compound gates near where the fire had come from, and we gave their inner courtyards a quick search to see whether the gunmen had holed up inside. We found nothing. We patrolled for a few more blocks, but by now our chances of catching our attackers were close to zero. There were literally hundreds of houses in which the gunmen could have hidden, and Brooks had told me that the RPG team had taken off west on a motorcycle immediately after firing their weapon. We were learning the hard way that in this city, all that an enemy had to do to escape was simply drop his weapon and step around the nearest corner. After about half an hour of searching, we turned around and headed back to the Outpost.

"Joker Six, this is One-Actual. Be advised, we have found nothing here. The attackers escaped. Over."

"Roger, One-Actual. I'm going to take the QRF out and look around the area. Over."

I was so surprised that I forgot all tactical dialogue. "Why? You're not going to find anything."

Captain Bronzi's voice came back, tight with anger. "One-Actual, we're going out because I fucking think it's necessary. Last time I checked, I was still CO. Over."

I shook my head. I thought he was putting people at risk unnecessarily, but it was his call.

"Roger that, Six. Anything else? Over."

"Negative, One. Come back to the Outpost. Six out."

"One out."

We patrolled the half mile back to the Outpost as quickly as our heavy gear loads would let us. Once inside its gates, we pulled off our helmets, unloaded our weapons, and started the quick inspections to make certain that we had all of our sensitive items—spare barrels for the SAWs, for example. Everyone was drenched with sweat and still breathing hard. Brooks's team was covered in the dirt and dust from the explosion that had stuck to the exposed, sweat-laden skin of their necks and faces.

Inspections completed, we headed back to the platoon's house for a debrief session. When we got to the platoon's courtyard, we found first and second squads already assembled, silently waiting as we trooped in. Their men had already stripped out of their gear, so as the sun set behind us, a mixed crowed of hard-looking, armored warriors and pale, skinny high school kids gathered in a tight half circle around me for the after-action question-and-answer session.

Strangely, I still didn't feel anything—no relief at our lack of casualties, no anger at first squad and the mix-up with the COC, nothing. I was still in that strange emotionless combat mode, totally focused on the event and on understanding fully what had happened so that we could better forestall being ambushed again. I didn't know why COC hadn't registered first squad's arrival or why first squad hadn't been able to find us at the police station. I didn't know how our enemies had hit us from two directions at once or exactly how far away from Brooks that RPG had exploded. My sole concern was answering as many of these outstanding questions as I could, and that concern took all of my attention.

So, M-16 and gear still slung across my sweat-soaked chest, I began the debrief with my assembled platoon. First I summarized the events as best I understood them—after all, as the commander I had the best overall picture of the fight because my primary job was to build that picture. Next I asked what the rest of third squad had seen that I hadn't. I was amazed at how many of the young Marines spoke up, and as the entire picture of the day's short firefight emerged, we learned a couple of things. First, RPGs travel slowly enough that you can see them in flight, and they'll skip off the pavement like Frisbees if they don't hit it at a steep enough angle. We learned this fact because Brooks had seen the RPG warhead zipping at him as he crossed the road, and he had somehow managed to jump as the rocket passed beneath him, skipping off the pavement just a few feet in front of him and continuing on to impact the traffic circle just five meters away.

This is how we learned the second thing, which is that the rocket warhead can tear concrete to pieces. An RPG warhead looks much like an American football with a finned cylinder about eighteen inches long sticking out of one end. That football can carry a lot of explosive, all of which detonates as soon as it hits something. The RPG that Brooks had hopped had dug a huge divot out of the foot-wide concrete traffic circle, much as a golfer does to the fairway on a bad drive.

Third, any proper RPG makes two explosions—one when it fires, and one when it detonates. If you hear only one boom, then no need to worry. The warhead hasn't been armed, or it's a dud. Though we had already learned a decent amount about RPGs in training, such as how many millimeters of rolled homogenous armor they can penetrate and how their shaped charge mechanism spews molten copper in a thin stream upon detonation, these smaller, equally relevant details were news to us.

We also learned something else, something far more important and far more disturbing. During the fighting, I had thought that no one had gotten more than a quick glimpse of our attackers, but I was wrong. Bowen informed me that he thought Dotson and Cabrera—the point men—had both had a chance to observe the gunmen for at least twenty seconds. Puzzled, I asked them about it, and they told me that yes, they had indeed seen two of our attackers. I immediately asked them if they had fired. Nervously, Dotson and Cabrera looked at each other; then Cabrera replied simply, "Uh, no, sir. We didn't fire our weapons, sir."

I was furious. "What the hell is wrong with you? We're Marines—we kill people who attack us. Why on earth would you not shoot?"

Dotson and Cabrera glanced at each other again, then Dotson replied, quietly. "Uh, sir, we didn't fire back because the guys were surrounded by a crowd of little kids, sir. Maybe twenty, they were all around. The guys, they were just holding up their AKs in the middle of the kids and firing them wildly our way. Without a scope, sir, I was worried that if I fired, I would hit the little kids." He looked down at his feet, shuffled them, and then looked back up at me and said softly, "I thought that was what you wanted, sir."

My heart swelled with pride in my Marines at exactly the same time that I kicked myself for yelling at them before I had all the facts. Dotson and Cabrera had done exactly what we had trained them to do—stop, think, and put themselves at greater risk if they believed that there was any danger to innocent civilians from their reactions. Immediately, I publicly backpedaled.

"Guys, I didn't know that. You did exactly the right thing. I'm proud of you. Everyone else, if you find yourself in that situation, do exactly what Cabrera and Dotson did."

Hearing this, all of the Marines nodded, and I ended the debrief and let them disperse. We had learned something more valuable and disturbing than the flight characteristics of an RPG. The insurgents would use kids for cover. We knew that the militias in Somalia had used this tactic to great effect during their street battles with Rangers in Mogadishu, but we hadn't heard many reports of it happening in Iraq. The idea that someone would use small children—both girls and boys—as nothing more than disposable body armor is so foreign, so beyond the pale of basic morality and decency, that you have trouble believing it until it happens to you. It's kind of like a car crash: Until you're in one, you can know that they happen and perhaps even sympathize with the victims, but you can't fully internalize it, or accept it as entirely real with painful, ongoing consequences, until you're sitting in a wrecked vehicle and staring at your broken leg.

As the Marines walked away, I did something that I now regret. I pulled Bowen aside and asked him how I had done during the fighting. How had I seemed under fire? Did I not do something that he had needed me to? Could he help me be a better lieutenant, please?

What was Bowen supposed to say? I had put him on the spot, but, professional that he was, Bowen managed to smoothly answer at least some of these questions. Halfway through our conversation, the Gunny suddenly appeared off to my right, about ten feet way, smoking a cigarette and leaning against the hangar bay wall. When Bowen and I finished up, the Gunny stubbed out the smoke and walked over. He stood silently next to me for a while, watching my third-squad leader walk away. Then he spoke up.

"Your first firefights, right, sir?"

I nodded.

"You brought all the Marines back this times, though, right, sir?"

I nodded again. "But I think mostly it was because the enemy sucks at shooting. Plus, we didn't even shoot back. I don't think that's a really good performance, Gunny. I probably should have done something differently." Again, I was seeking validation.

"Hey, sir, you kept your heads, you brought the Marines back, no civilians was killed. Hard to argue with that, sir." He clapped me on the back. "Hard to argue with that. They'll be time enough to shoot back, sir. Don't worry." The Gunny gave me a little crooked, squint-eyed smile, then wandered off on another of his never-ending projects.

As I reflected on his words, the implications of the day's events began to sink in. No longer did I wonder whether we'd ever earn the coveted Combat Action Ribbon. I suspected that we might be in for more fighting than originally anticipated. Exactly how much fighting I didn't know, but I still hoped that it would be the exception rather than the rule. My men had performed well, but, going forward, I didn't know how we could fight an enemy that clothed itself with children, particularly while trying to win the favor of the local residents. I took some solace in the fact that the other side couldn't shoot straight, but even incompetent enemies sometimes get lucky. At some point, we'd be forced to use our weapons. Until then, though, we'd have to muster some of the most difficult strength of all—the strength not to fight back.

SIXTEEN

The second time we came under attack, a mere two days later, we took several RPGs all at once. We were walking along Michigan to the Government Center when the engineers at the head of our patrol located an IED in the middle of the road. It was a dull olive artillery shell, and it looked much like a gigantic, two-foot-long bullet. As we moved quickly to cordon it off, I heard several explosions in rapid succession—several RPGs, all launched at us. One of them drilled a neat hole through the thin armor of the passenger door on our lead Humvee and continued onward to drill another neat hole through the two off-white blocks of C-4 that our engineers had placed on the vehicle's center console. Fortunately, neither block exploded. Two of our engineers took shrapnel from the blast: One had minor cuts on his hands while the other, a six-foot, three-inch giant named Canouck had a sizable chunk embedded in his right leg. When I arrived at our damaged Humvee, Docs Smith and Camacho had cut off Canouck's pant leg, bandaged his wound, and tried, unsuccessfully, to prevent him from standing and shouting obscenities at our vanished attackers. Shortly thereafter, a medevac vehicle from the Outpost and an Explosive Ordnance Disposal (EOD) team from Hurricane Point arrived. We sent Canouck back, blew up the IED, and continued on to Ramadi's Government Center. An inauspicious way to start the day, but we had handled it with no serious casualties or loss of life.

If the point of our mission was to bring stability to Ramadi, the city's Government Center was often the focal point of that mission. Inside a double layer of ten-foot-tall concrete barriers, roughly eight buildings housed all the administrative and logistical machinery necessary for the governance of the entire Anbar province. We were primarily concerned with one building, a large, four-story, L-shaped monstrosity where the governor, the mayor, and various other high officials met daily, but we couldn't completely ignore the rest of the compound. With its front butting up against the teeming souk and its rear extending halfway to the butchers' district in the southwest quadrant of the city, the entire complex was, to say the least, a security nightmare.

We had left the Outpost early, at 7 AM, and after the RPG attack we made our way on foot to the Center, walking straight down Route Michigan until we reached its huge concrete barriers, nestled securely in the heart of Ramadi's downtown market area. The crowds were fairly light as we passed through, but by 10 AM they had become so thick that the one-squad security patrols we ran out of the Government Center every two hours could barely thread their way through the clogged sidewalks. Snarling traffic jams replete with the ubiquitous orange-and-white taxis packed the previously empty Route Michigan—the highway ran directly in front of the Center's double concrete walls.

As the day wound on, hundreds of people necessary to keep Anbar province functioning would pass into and out of the front of the building we were protecting, and searching every one of them was clearly unworkable and likely counterproductive. We decided to concentrate our efforts on repelling any direct attacks on the building, positioning ourselves at stationary posts around the L of the building's roof, watching the crowds of people and cars just dozens of meters away, wondering whether one of them might explode, marveling at how everyone went about their mundane daily business in such an uncertain environment. These crowds, and our anxiety level, remained high until well after sundown.

The private security contractors operating in Iraq have occasionally come under criticism for their excesses, but on that day—and most others following—we felt incredibly fortunate to have help from the men of Triple

Canopy, the company that had received the contract from the U.S. government to protect key American personnel and infrastructure facilities in Ramadi. For the Center, this mandate meant setting up a series of guarded checkpoints (using Iraqi forces) along the two approaches to the building's entrances and periodically sweeping its halls with bomb-sniffing dogs. It also meant occasionally training and equipping the fledgling Iraqi police and national guardsmen who operated out of the provincial police headquarters just west of our L-shaped government building.

Mostly ex–special forces types, the Triple Canopy guys probably had regular names like Joe or Frank, but we knew them simply by their colorful call signs, among them Highway, Pigpen, and Pipebomb. The Triple Canopy guys seemed equally happy to have our help, and they had quickly equipped us with their own long-range Motorola radios so that we could communicate with them at all times. The first time I used them, I was ecstatic — the Motorolas beat our U.S.-issued PRRs hands down, and there were enough of them to equip each squad leader with one. We were finally able to send our squads more than two blocks away and still keep in contact with them (we still didn't have enough long-range radios to give any more than one to each platoon).

So, shortly after arriving at the Center on that early March morning, I rendezvoused with Highway, collected the radios, and trudged tiredly up to the roof with Noriel and third squad to man our fighting positions in the hundred-degree heat. It had already been a long day. As Noriel and I popped out into the blazing sun and clomped across the sticky tar slathered around on the building's roof, I was less than enthusiastic about what lay ahead. Security duty on the Government Center roof involved cramming yourself and another man into a four-foot-by-three-foot sandbagged plywood box and then sweating for two hours underneath the 120-degree desert sun while having to maintain constant vigilance. But I soon found that being up there meant I could sweat side by side with my Marines, mostly free of the pressures of navigation and constant communication that defined our patrols. Sometimes we talked about Ramadi, sometimes about life in general, and sometimes we just sat there, watching the streets together in companionable silence.

During those early days I learned a great deal about my men on that roof. Feldmeir told me of his troubled past, of the series of foster homes he'd grown up in, of his constant fear each time he was moved. Mahardy told me about growing up in upstate New York with a tight-knit Irish family of seven and how he and his siblings were still best friends.

It was on the roof that I learned that Noriel had enlisted in the Marines at age twenty because he saw no future in busing tables as a green-card immigrant in Lake Tahoe. Shortly after his enlistment, my fiery squad leader had been charged with assault with a deadly weapon. Sometime during his infantry finishing school, Noriel had been pulling guard duty, carrying an M-16 and a full magazine of ammunition (as all guards do) when one of his fellow privates began "screwing" with him. Noriel being Noriel, he had immediately pulled back the bolt on his weapon, locked and loaded a round, and proceeded to threaten the offender with grievous bodily harm if he continued. The next day, Noriel found himself arraigned on some very serious charges and assigned to a disciplinary platoon whose sole purpose was to beat down its members by making them perform such Sisyphean tasks as carrying a boulder on a five-mile round trip, painting and unpainting rocks, and, the all-time classic, digging a trench only to immediately fill it in again. For a year, my future first-squad leader endured the treatment, refusing to quit because he knew he had nothing to go home to. Then one day all charges were inexplicably dropped, and Noriel was sent right back to the school to finish his infantry training.

Less remarkable but slightly more amusing were PFCs Niles and Ott, the two team members led by the giant Carson. In their shared bunker up on the roof, they interacted in the unique way that only the pressure and close confines of extended combat can produce. The two Marines were as opposite as the day was long, and stuffed together into the little pillboxes up on the Government Center roof, they played off each other like a two-man comedy act. Nineteen-year-old Niles was one of the smartest, quickest, and lankiest Marines in the platoon, and he probably had the most expansive vocabulary of any of its members. He was also possessed of endless reserves of twitchy, nervous energy. By contrast, the short, solid Ott was one of our slowest, most laid-back men—by his own admission, he had smoked a lot of weed before joining the Corps, and I suspect that the drug combined with his own God-given personality to make him Niles's polar opposite. Typically, Niles would take Ott around and around, tying him in verbal and intellectual conundrums until Ott finally broke out with "Ah, shit, you're making fun of me again, aren't you, Niles?" It was their own game, and they played it endlessly to help ease the strangely tense monotony of watching a particular patch of city for hours on end.

Whenever I made my rounds on the roof, walking from sandbagged bunker to sandbagged bunker as I checked on each team, the two often as not broke off their practiced dialogue, and I found myself fielding Niles's incisive questions, questions that ranged from the feasibility of representative democracy in Iraq to why the blatant disconnect between the CPA in Baghdad and those of us on the ground tasked with executing its apparently half-baked policies. My answer to the latter question, by the way, was that if Joker One also lived in a mini-America (Baghdad's Green Zone) with discos featuring half-naked women, bars, movie rental parlors, swimming pools, and the like, and that if we only rarely ventured outside its four walls, then maybe we, too, would lose all contact with reality and concoct fantasyland plans of stock market exchanges before bothering to turn on the water. Maybe we, too, would prefer the comfort and the safety of something that mimicked America, and maybe we, too, would prefer to leave the dangerous, dirty work of policy implementation to nineteen-year-old lance corporals.

Niles, however, wasn't the only one with incisive questions. Most of my Marines were pretty savvy, and it didn't take them long to figure out that we rarely, if ever, saw any Americans other than Marines and Triple Canopy contractors at the nerve center of Iraq's most volatile province. Up on the roof with them, I learned that to a surprisingly deep degree, my men understood the greater purpose of our mission in Ramadi, and they wondered why, if stability in Anbar augured well for stability in Iraq, we never saw any of the country's civilian U.S. overlords. Being normal nineteen-year-olds (and me being a mostly normal twenty-four-year old), though, we usually didn't dwell on these strategic questions for very long, and the conversations generally wandered to topics closer to our hearts. Ott, for example, was very curious about what types of music I listened to and who my favorite bands were. Henderson wondered if he had a future in NASCAR or as a professional stuntman, and Guzon usually wanted someone to listen to his relationship issues with his now-distant fiancée.

On that late March day, I spent about an hour up on the Government Center roof, checking on the Marines, fortifying myself with their boundless energy, and amusing myself with their absolutely absurd banter. As Noriel and I were walking back to our makeshift command post inside the Government Center after a few hours of observation, we came upon a tall, red-haired, red-faced, red-mustached Marine major whom we hadn't met before. Immediately, he pulled us both aside and began to lecture us about safety. The nameless major was from one of the Marine Civil Affairs Groups (CAGs), the military units tasked to respond to local concerns and to slowly rebuild the infrastructure and institutions necessary for some semblance of normal life to resume.

As he held forth, the major moved around nervously, his head swiveling back and forth the entire time. He began his impromptu instructional by telling us how we had to keep our guard up at all times, how every patrol was a combat patrol and how we had to be constantly ready to engage. After a few minutes, I realized that our new major friend wasn't so much lecturing us as he was reassuring himself, so I let him ramble on and then thanked him politely for his advice. As he walked off, Noriel turned to me and grinned, and I grinned back. All of the major's bravado had revealed only one thing—that he hadn't really seen any combat yet; indeed, judging from his nervous lecture, this might well have been his very first mission. Four weeks into our tour and we were already beginning to feel like combat veterans. For the first time, I began to understand why in the Marines there's the infantry, and then there's everybody else.

An hour later, just after noon, first squad and I completed a local security patrol and headed back to the roof. Walking through the gates of the compound, I saw our helpful Civil Affairs major nervously preparing to mount his Humvee and head out of the Government Center, back to whatever base he had recently come from. Noriel saw him, too.

"Sir, he looks kind of scared. Maybe I should go over and asks him to give us some useful combat tips? You know, take his minds off the fears . . ." He was grinning widely at me again.

"Behave, killer, behave. He's got enough to worry about without you screwing with him. Let's just get out of this damn heat."

"Roger that, sir . . . Maybe just one little questions?"

Noriel was irrepressible. I couldn't help smiling back. "No, not even one little questions, you Filipino nut. You've got work to do. Get your squad back inside and let me know when they've got all their sensitive gear."

Noriel trotted off, smiling. As he went, he glanced over at the major, then back at me. I shook my head and pointed to our building.

Ten minutes later, the Civil Affairs convoy roared out of the gates, and a few seconds thereafter, a massive explosion shattered the calm afternoon air. I had just taken off my vest and helmet inside our Government Center headquarters, and I immediately threw them back on. As I adjusted the helmet and the PRR headpiece, Bowen called down from the roof.

"Sir, it looks like that Civil Affairs convoy just got hit pretty bad by an IED. They might need some help, sir."

"Roger that, One-Three. On it."

I dashed out of the room. Leza and Noriel already had their guys suited up and heading for the compound's side gates. I joined them, found Teague, and assumed my normal position just behind his point fire team. Then I gave the order to head out, and first squad, followed by second, blasted out of the Government Center and set off at a run, heading south into the butchers' area. It had been less than a minute since the explosion.

We traveled two blocks and came upon a scene straight out of Dante's *Inferno.* In the middle of a deserted four-way intersection, four groaning, screaming, badly wounded Marines lay on the concrete, rolling around in swiftly congealing pools of their own blood. Some already had various parts of their uniforms cut off to better expose their injuries, but others were bleeding right through the cloth. A Humvee was burning brightly, and several of the Civil Affairs officers were frantically running around like chickens with their heads cut off. The streets around were nearly deserted.

Immediately, Docs Smith and Camacho jumped on the wounded, and I ordered Leza and Noriel to position their men to secure the intersection. The IED attack had not, as yet, been followed up by small arms and RPGs, but we needed to be prepared, and the Civil Affairs convoy did not have enough people to defend the intersection properly. When I was satisfied with our positions, I went to find the major to see what else he and his men needed from us.

What I found was the embodiment of all I had hoped to avoid becoming, a frantic and nonsensical officer, clearly in shock though not wounded, repeating over and over that he had taken wounded as he dashed randomly about to check on the various reports coming in over his PRR. After trying unsuccessfully to penetrate his shell shock, I walked off and immediately ran into the Marine artillery lieutenant who was the convoy's security commander. He, too, was agitated, but he was in much better shape than the major, and he told me that though the casualties were stable for now, we needed to get them out soon. They were urgent medevacs, bleeding badly from severed arteries.

Five minutes later, we had helped load the wounded, and a subsection of the CAG convoy roared off to Junction City, the massive U.S. base just west of Ramadi, right on the other side of the Euphrates. The remaining Civil Affairs folks were preparing to load up, and I radioed Noriel and Leza, instructing them to head back to the Government Center as soon as all the vehicles had left. By this time, the stricken Humvee had burned so fiercely that very little remained—just a five-foot-by-five-foot black, smoldering cube. There was nothing our enemies could do with it, so we decided to leave it in place for the time being. However, just as the CAG convoy was mounting its men to leave, I heard the now-distinctive double boom of an armed RPG ring out, very close to our positions.

I whipped my head left. A fully armored Civil Affairs Humvee guarding an intersection two blocks to our east had just been struck by an attack from its south, and Marines were piling out of it, taking cover behind its heavy doors. Small-arms fire erupted from their assailants, and the Marines started firing back. Unaffected just yet, I yelled over the PRR for Noriel and Leza to collect their squads and meet me in our intersection. Then I ran over to the frantic major to see if I could get a better idea of where the attack was coming from. If the attackers were close enough, we stood a good chance of flanking the insurgents with our two squads if we could move quickly.

Pulling up at the major, I asked him for any information he could give us, but he just stared back, wide-eyed and stunned; then he turned away and began shouting into his PRR headset. I glanced back at my squads. Teague was ready and waiting, and he motioned furiously at me to get on with it and move out south. I held up my hand. Wait. I turned back to the major and tried again to elicit information, but his response hadn't changed. Blank stare. More yelling into the PRR. Getting information from the man was a lost cause, so I turned around and furiously motioned for Teague to go.

It was like watching a greyhound released from the racing gate—Teague streaked smoothly south, vaulted a wall into a small cemetery, and continued running without any hesitation at all. The rest of first squad, me included, trailed him by about fifteen meters, with Leza and his men running behind us. Up ahead, Teague leaped onto a four-foot-high crypt, and, without breaking stride, used the grave's height to launch himself over yet another wall. I thought for a second that I was watching an action movie, but it was just twenty-one-year-old Corporal Brian Teague from Tennessee doing what he did best while wearing fifty pounds of gear.

Ten seconds later, the rest of us caught up with him, but I had been too slow giving the order to pursue. Teague had seen only one of the attackers—the rest had escaped by car—and he had raised his weapon to fire, but the man had dropped his AK and merged into the surrounding crowd before Teague could take a clean shot. He took off after the insurgent, but trying to find a particular Iraqi dressed in everyday civilian clothes among several thousand Iraqis also dressed in everyday civilian clothes was like trying to find a needle in a stack of needles. We searched a few houses in the vicinity, but the opportunity to cut off our attackers was long gone. Dejectedly, I ordered us back to the Government Center. We patrolled north, the carbon-black cube that used to be an American Humvee smoking bleakly as we passed.

I cursed my slow decision making.

SEVENTEEN

he next morning found me back at the Outpost, disappointed and frustrated with myself. Thrice now we had been attacked, and thrice now we had failed to shoot back. For several hours, I intermittently second-guessed my decisions of the previous day, wondering what would have happened if I had just listened to Teague and set off south across the cemetery immediately instead of waiting for nonforthcoming information from a nonsensical major. Instead of four badly wounded Marines and an enemy who escaped scot-free, we might have had four badly wounded Marines and a dozen dead insurgent attackers. I spent the early part of that morning moping, until it was time to saddle up and relieve the evening guardians at the Government Center. As usual, we had begun squad-sized security patrols immediately upon arrival, and when noon rolled around I had just returned from a walk through the teeming marketplace with Bowen and his men. As we stood inside the QRF room at the Government Center, on the roof above us stood Noriel and first squad, and second squad and Leza were strapping on their gear in preparation for the next patrol. As I watched the men ready themselves, I unstrapped my gear, dropped the body armor and helmet to the floor, and rubbed my hands up and down my thoroughly sweat-soaked blouse (the official Marine Corps term for our camouflage shirt) and trousers. I glanced around at third squad; everyone else looked as if they had just taken a shower with their clothes on. It was definitely starting to heat up. That's when I heard the two explosions, in rapid succession.

Today the enemy had chosen to attack us directly at the Center. An RPG slammed into the wall next to the gates leading into our building, gouging a dinner-plate-sized chunk out of it. Another rocket immediately followed. As the warheads detonated, I was standing in the large, open Quick Reaction Force room on the first floor of the Government Center. Outside the compound, I could hear AKs chattering on full automatic and the rapid pop-pop-pop of my Marines on the roof returning fire in three-shot bursts. A tense Noriel called me over the PRR as I struggled hastily back into my armor:

"Sir, we've been hit from the east. I think there's at least five or ten of them on two different roofs. Tig's got eyes-on and he and Feldmeir is returning fire. No further info, sir."

"Roger that," I shouted into the PRR as I ran out of the building toward the compound gates. "Let the COC know." Then I pushed headquarters out of my mind entirely and focused on the situation at hand. Ahead of me, Staff Sergeant was already at the compound entrance, leaning on the sheet steel gates as he braced his rifle up against one of the doors and fired at a building just across the little alleyway to our east. As I ran up to him, Staff Sergeant stopped shooting and turned to me.

"Sir, there are at least three of them on that roof right there, sir," he said, pointing out of the slit in the gates. "I've returned fire, but I'm not sure whether I got any of them." He leaned back in over his weapon.

Irritated, I briefly wondered what good all of that Rifle Team shooting had been if Staff Sergeant couldn't even hit a man-sized target less than one hundred meters away, but I pushed it aside, edged my way around him, and stuck my head out of the gates. Immediately, something heavier than an AK opened up to our north. It had been set up so that it fired perfectly down the length of the street that we now had to cross, and the rounds were cracking nearby again. Damn it.

I recoiled back through the gates and glanced behind me. Leza had second squad stacked up against the compound wall, ready to go. I met his eyes. He nodded coolly back—he and his men were ready. Bowen's squad was behind them, waiting for the order to proceed. I hesitated. I knew we had to attack, but we had to get across a fire-swept, two-lane street first. I radioed up to Noriel to see if he had any idea where the suspected machine gun position was so that he could lay down suppressing fire while we dashed across. "Negative" came the reply.

As Leza's squad stacked up behind me, I froze at the metal compound gates for a few seconds. Then, somehow, I found myself outside the open doors, running for my life across the street while waving frantically at second squad to follow. The machine gun kicked up again, and the rounds started snapping by.

My clever plan had been to dash across the street and then leap over the double-stranded concertina wire that lined its eastern sidewalk, but I clearly wasn't thinking straight—my vertical leap is in the single digits on a good day, and weighed down by my gear and tired out from the patrols, what little athletic ability remained wasn't nearly enough to get me over the obstacle. Running up to the barbs, I jumped anyway. Predictably, both legs landed squarely in the middle of the tangled coils of wire. Flailing frantically, I managed to free my left one immediately, but my right was caught firmly by the little razors. The machine gunner had aimed in on me now, and a detached part of my mind noticed that the concrete sidewalk in front of me was erupting in little puffs of dirt. That same part of my mind absently recorded Sergeant Leza screaming behind me, "Someone get in front of the lieutenant, goddamn it. Someone get up there."

I have no idea how long I was trapped in the wire. It was probably only a few seconds, but that was one of those moments when the flow of time froze solid and the whole world was reduced to a single moment, to a life-and-death struggle between me and the inanimate razors. Intently, I focused in on my own private battle until a sudden movement to my left caught my eye. It was Raymond. I turned my head, and it seemed like I watched in slow motion as somehow he catapulted himself over both strands of concertina wire, putting his body between me and the machine gun. Then the world opened up, and I watched as the rest of his team followed his lead, vaulting the solid concertina wire one after the other. A solid wall of four of my

Marines interposed themselves between their lieutenant and his attackers, and my Marines stared firing back.

All of a sudden, time started up again and I ripped my leg out of the razors, shredding both my trouser legs and my lower right thigh in the process. Raymond and his men had silenced the gun, and Teague's insistent voice in my right ear finally registered through the confusion around me. Hearing it, I responded.

"Send it, Teague," I yelled over the PRR as I hustled to the cover of a building's entrance.

"Sir, I missed a guy on a roof as he ran away, but I know what building they're attacking from. Can you see the building with the orange soap sign on it?"

I looked at all the buildings within my line of sight. "No, Teague, I can't."

"Well, just keep moving east and I'll guide you on."

"Roger that. Moving."

I motioned to Raymond to move his team off the sidewalk and into the cluster of buildings next to us, and I glanced back at Leza to see if he had followed the conversation. He had, and he gave me another silent thumbs-up. Second and third squads moved deeper into the buildings, hunting for the one with the orange soap sign.

Within about five minutes, we found it, and I ordered Bowen to cordon off the building's rear while Leza and I hit it with his squad. Swiftly, second squad ran to the building's entrance as third snaked around its rear, and, arriving at the building's sheet steel door, Raymond battered it with his body until the locking mechanism broke. We poured inside, only to discover that the orange soap sign building was a student dormitory. After a thorough search, we had found nothing other than frightened male college students hiding behind locked doors. Frustrated, I made my way out to the building's balcony to call across the city to the Golf Company COC. That morning, I had been given a smaller version of our long-range radios, a version that we had never seen before, and I just happened to be carrying it on my vest as we hit the building. Time to test it out, I thought.

"Joker COC, this is Joker One-Actual. Be advised, we have the situation at the center well in hand. Break . . ."

"One-Actual, this is Six-Actual," came Captain Bronzi's near-shouted reply. "If you ever put that moron on the radio again, I will fucking kill you. I repeat, I will fucking kill you. I have no idea what's going on over there. I've had to listen to a driveling idiot for the past ten minutes. I have no idea how many enemy you are facing, how many casualties you have, or what the hell is going on in general. You had better start talking right fucking now and fucking fast, Joker One!"

"That moron" referred to Feldmeir. Unbeknownst to me, during our entire brief firefight he had been manning the radio, for in an earlier moment of lunacy I had agreed to Noriel's request to let our narcoleptic take the platoon's sole 119. It was a last-ditch effort to find some continuous activity that would keep our somnolent Marine awake, but I clearly hadn't thought through the implications of making Private First Class Feldmeir the critical lifeline to our higher headquarters. Nearly the entire time we had been under fire, the PFC had been screaming frantically into the radio: "They're attacking us, they're attacking us! The fire's all around! Everywhere!! Aaaah-hhhh!!" The CO had been frustrated, and rightfully so. He hadn't hesitated to let me know.

Once the tirade ended, I responded with a detailed situation report. It calmed the CO down a bit to hear that no one had been hurt and that the enemy had been chased off, but he was understandably less than pleased with my choice of radio operators. He reiterated his threat to physically kill me if I ever let Feldmeir on the radio again. After the day's performance, I couldn't dispute the judgment, and I signed off, somewhat chastened.

Heading back down from the balcony, I rejoined my platoon. Somewhat pleased with ourselves for finally firing back, we returned to the Government Center, and second and third squads settled back into their rooms while I trudged up to the roof to try to sort out what had actually happened during the fighting. On the way up, I ran into Highway, the leader of the Triple Canopy group. It was the second time in as many days that Joker One had responded to an attack on the compound, and the former Force Recon Marine pulled me aside.

"Hey, lieutenant, your guys are really solid. You move quick and you're not afraid to attack, which is more than I can say for some of the other folks who have been here. You fight well. I'm glad the Corps is here."

I took Highway's kind words as high praise, and was again proud of my men. Then I moved up to the roof, hunted down Noriel, and, sighing, told him that never again was Feldmeir to touch the radio. If he did, I might die.

My first squad leader agreed readily, and together with Teague we began to reconstruct the afternoon's attack. After comparing notes, we determined that the insurgents had struck from the roofs of three different buildings just across the street, and that they had covered this head-on assault with supporting fire from a machine gun position somewhere to our north. Before the main force fled, Teague had gotten four shots off at one of the rooftop attackers, but his bullets had gone wild. We had just learned the hard way that our three newly issued short-range scopes (called "ACOGs") did not retain their accuracy when we took them off our weapons, even though we had been told that they were supposed to. Never mind that, Teague told me. He now knew the adjustment he had to make—he'd be good shooting from here on out.

After spending some more time on the roof with each Marine, I tromped back down to our makeshift headquarters rooms. We were scheduled to spend the night at the Government Center, pulling security and posting a squad-sized observation position to our east to prevent IEDs from being planted along the highway. I drew up the specific rotations for the evening's mission and then spent the rest of the afternoon shuttling between the roof and the squad rooms. Near 5 PM, the CO and fourth platoon dropped off George the translator on their way over to a meeting at Hurricane Point. After that, though, the early evening passed uneventfully. George smoked and talked with the Iraqi police.

When twilight finally came around, I moved myself to the roof for the rest of the mission. It was the best place for me to command and control my various forces, and, now that the sun had gone down, I could endure the heat for more than two straight hours. The temperatures hovered just above one hundred degrees Fahrenheit, and after the day's events, our cammies were soaked, our boots squelched with sweat, and our heads ached from dehydration and exposure.

Once the darkness had enveloped the city completely, Noriel and first squad left the Government Center and headed to their Route Michigan observation site: an abandoned multistory parking garage four blocks to our east. There the squad planned to remain until we picked them up on the next morning's route sweep home. For an hour after their departure, the night proceeded uneventfully. The streets cleared of the evening shopping rush, the tea tables across from us slowly emptied, and, one by one, the lights in the storefronts to our north winked off. With the cessation of civilian activity in front of us, I had just relaxed a bit when I heard one AK shot followed immediately by three quick shots from an M-16. I braced for more fire, but none came. A few seconds later, Noriel called me on his Motorola. Teague had shot an Iraqi, he said, but other than that the situation report was somewhat cryptic and guarded. He requested my presence on the scene immediately, so I ran down from the roof as quickly as my tired legs and the unevenly spaced steps would allow.

Five minutes later, second squad, George, and I met a subdued Noriel on the street with his men in tow. I walked over, and my first-squad leader silently handed me a black plastic grocery bag. I took it. It was heavy.

"Noriel, what is this?" I asked.

"Look inside him, sir. Just look inside."

I opened up the bag, and found, winking back at me, four sticks of PE-4 (a powerful military-grade explosive), two blocks of dynamite, and at least fifteen different blasting caps. Everything needed to make several IEDs, or to level a small house.

I looked back up, stunned. "Where did you find this, Noriel?"

"Sir, he was in the car of the guy Tig killed."

"How did you know what car was his?"

"The locals pointed it out, sir."

"Okay, where is the dead guy?"

"Don't know, sir. Before we could get to him, some peoples loaded him into a taxi, and he took off. But we need to search that house across the street, sir—the guy Tig killed was running out of it when Tig shot him. Maybe more bombs in there, sir."

Puzzled, I turned to look at the building directly across the street from us, and, after a moment's consideration, I ordered second squad to enter and search it. The structure in question turned out to be a gym, and it was filled with nothing more menacing than pictures of Saddam on the walls and used hypodermic needles on the floors. When we finally finished turning the place upside down, I rejoined Noriel's squad and demanded a full explanation of what had just happened. They quickly explained in hushed tones.

en minutes earlier, shortly before the shooting, Corporal Brown, Noriel's second-team leader, had noticed a soft scuffling sound at the stairwell leading up to the squad's position on the garage's third floor. As he leaned in for a closer look, the scuffling picked up, and Brown began to suspect that someone was trying to creep up the stairs to fling a grenade or a homemade bomb into the scattered squad. Using his PRR, the team leader softly called Noriel over to the gaping stairwell entrance. Quietly, the first-squad leader picked up his gear and crept across the floor.

As soon as he had made his way to Brown's position, Noriel, who was carrying the heavy long-range radio as he crawled, located the nearest Marine to hand it off to. Unfortunately, that nearest Marine happened to be Feldmeir, and even in the dark Noriel noticed his head bobbing. As quietly as he could, the sergeant smacked Feldmeir on the back of the helmet to wake him up.

"Feldmeir," he hissed. "Take this radio. I have to check on something. No matter what happens, Feldmeir, don't fucking say anything on the radio. I will fucking kill you if you do." Wide-eyed, Feldmeir nodded his mute agreement.

Not fully satisfied but with time for a decision ticking away, Noriel reluctantly handed off the radio and crept the few feet over to where Brown knelt. On arrival, the squad leader heard the same scuffling sounds, and he quickly pulled out his single grenade, removed the thumb clip, and pulled the pin. Now the only thing keeping the device from detonating was Noriel's thumb pressed firmly up against the grenade's spoon, the long rectangular flange that extends downward off the top of a grenade, curving over the device's circular body. Holding the grenade away from his body, Noriel leaned out over the gaping hole and peered into the darkness with his NVGs. He didn't see anything, but the scuffling only continued, and at the first sign of an attacker Noriel determined that he'd simply drop the grenade down the stairs and then take cover.

As Noriel and Brown knelt tensely over the entrance to their floor, waiting for the split second in which an attack would materialize, Teague noticed a commotion in the building immediately opposite him. Perking up, he focused his attention on the building's entrance just in time to see an Iraqi run out of the building followed by a giant wielding an AK-47. The huge Arab seemed irate, and without warning he suddenly raised his rifle and fired a shot into the back of the fleeing man. The Iraqi fell and began twitching spasmodically on the ground. His assailant strode over and raised the rifle to his shoulder, clearly intending to apply a brutal coup de grâce and finish what he had started.

Teague was shocked, and he called Noriel over the PRR. "Ser'ent. Ser'ent! A hajji just shot another hajji in the back. He's gonna shoot him again, Ser'ent."

("Hajji," by the way, was our generic term for the Iraqis. Its formal use is as an honorific bestowed on someone who has completed the hajj, the pilgrimage to Mecca. I'm afraid our use was more in the grand tradition of soldiers faced with a populace with whom we couldn't communicate and who often seemed difficult to understand, to say the least. In most instances the term wasn't meant to denigrate the Iraqis—we simply used the two-syllable "hajji" because it was easier than the three-syllable "Iraqi.")

His concentration broken, Noriel was briefly nonplussed by the sudden commotion. The live grenade still hung out over the stairwell entrance. After about a second's consideration, Joker One's first-squad leader radioed Teague back.

"Well! Fuck! What are you waiting for? Shoot back, Tig!"

Teague took action. Correcting for his errant ACOG sights, he aimed at a point three feet above and to the right of the Iraqi's head and loosed a three-round burst. All three caught the man in the throat, and he fell to the ground like a marionette whose strings had been severed. There he lay, boneless and unmoving.

Through it all, Noriel knelt by the stairs, still waiting with his grenade at the ready. As the gunfire faded, he realized that the scuffling had ceased, and, as Noriel's attention diffused, he noticed something horrifying: Feldmeir was talking on the radio, again babbling uncontrollably to the COC a vague account of Iraqis shooting Iraqis and us shooting Iraqis and something about a grenade. Furious, Noriel rose and whirled to confront Feldmeir, the live grenade in his right hand completely forgotten. Brown, however, hadn't taken his eyes off the explosive, and his face went white as his squad leader stormed over to Feldmeir with his arms swinging furiously. Before Noriel could snatch the radio away from the self-appointed radio operator, though, he was intercepted by a slightly wide-eyed, slightly agitated Teague.

"Ser'ent, Ser'ent. I shot that guy, Ser'ent. I think I killed him. He was laying on the ground, Ser'ent, just laying there, dead I think. He's dead. What should we do, Ser'ent?"

At that exact instant, Noriel had Golf Company's first dead Iraqi lying in the middle of Ramadi's main thoroughfare, a young man who had just killed his first human being asking for advice and guidance, a live grenade clutched tightly in his own right hand, and Corporal Brown tugging at his cammies, holding the grenade's pin and trying urgently to get the squad leader's attention so that they could reinsert the pin and defuse the bomb.

"But, sir," Noriel later told me, "you know what the only thing I could think about at the time was? How much trouble I was going to get into cuz Feldmeir was talking on that damn radio again."

A few minutes later, the grenade's pin reinserted, first squad had collected themselves and their gear and moved out of the observation position and down to the street to get some more information and collect the body. It was gone — a few passersby had loaded both Iraqis into a taxi just minutes after the shootings — but others had approached the squad and told them that the man they had just killed was very, very bad. "Saddam, Saddam," they repeated, shaking their heads and pointing at the man's car.

As I sat outside the gym and listened to the story, it seemed fitting to me, somehow, that our first kill had come not in our own defense but in defense of a citizen of Ramadi. It was too bad we hadn't been able to recover the body, but at first glance, it looked like we had not only saved an innocent life but also killed an actual insurgent in the process: after speaking more extensively with the locals, George confirmed that the car's owner was indeed the now-dead giant. He then nonchalantly informed me that my platoon's first kill had been Iraq's champion bodybuilder, aka "Mr. Iraq," which left me with one dead celebrity insurgent and a plastic grocery bag filled with explosives. Maybe the situation wasn't quite as black-and-white as I had initially assumed, but I was still happy.

Finding nothing else, I ordered first squad to hunt down another building and continue the observation mission. I returned with second squad back to the Government Center, where I called the CO and explained everything to him. He was as puzzled as I was, but very pleased that Golf Company had killed its first apparent terrorist. When I finished the transmission, I took my little special grocery bag down to the Triple Canopy guys. They were all ex–special forces, so they should know a bit more than I about what we were dealing with. I found Pigpen and proudly showed him our catch. His eyes widened.

"Nice work, lieutenant. Those are some nasty explosives. Let's see here, yep, PE-4, some TNT, oh, what are these? Blasting caps, I see." He paused, then swallowed hard. "Well, lieutenant, I only have one recommendation. You might want to put the detonators and the explosives in two different bags. The explosives are stable, but those blasting caps are not, and they'll probably go off if you drop or shake them. If that happens next to one of those blocks of explosive, well, it would probably be bad."

Oh. Important safety tip. I should have known about the caps—we'd all had a decent amount of explosives training—but the night's events had moved the little detonators down to a much lower priority in my mind.

"Yeah, right. Thanks, Pigpen. You got another bag?"

"Sure, I'll get it for you. By the way, some of those blasting caps are electronic squibs, which means you can set them off remotely. These are some nasty things with some nasty uses. I'm glad they're not floating around anymore."

"Yeah, and I'm glad I haven't exploded yet." Pigpen handed me a bag. "I'll see you later."

"Yeah, good night."

We made it back to the Outpost early the next morning after the usual harrowing route sweep. However, what I didn't know at the time—but found out a few days later from our Information Operations officer—was that Mr. Iraq had been considered a hugely pro-American personage by U.S. forces, and he had played some role in their current public relations efforts. In their eyes, my men had just killed an important Iraqi spokesperson. Even the CO started doubting despite the fact that, when we killed him, Mr. Iraq had been about to pump several rounds into the head of an unarmed man, and his car had contained a few kilos of military-grade explosive and detonators. The CO repeatedly pointed out to me that since the Iraqis were known to use explosives for fishing, maybe all of the so-called "IED material" that we had found was simply fishing gear. My response was simple: It was highly unlikely that an urban gym owner played at rural fisherman in his spare time, and if Mr. Iraq was such a pro-coalition figure, then why was he transporting enough explosives and remote detonators to destroy several of our partially armored Humvees?

Questions surrounding the IED material aside, the laws of war and general morality compelled us to intervene to prevent atrocities, atrocities like an armed man shooting a wounded, unarmed man in the head. All of this and more I explained to Teague when a few days later he asked me whether I thought that he had done the right thing by killing Mr. Iraq. He had, I told him, and I was very proud of his quick thinking, his straight shooting, and the life he had saved. I should have told Teague all of this sooner, though, because watching a man fall to the ground as he spurts blood out of his carotid arteries because you just put three pieces of metal through them is no small thing for a twenty-one-year-old to handle. Though the killing is easy and emotionless in the moment, it can sometimes comes back, especially if the man you killed wasn't shooting at you when you shot him.

And, though I kept it solely between Teague and myself, my final response to all of our doubters, from the CO to the Army, was simple: Welcome to the world of deception and shifting allegiances that is Iraq, Golf Company. Only a fool would take a person at his word and at face value in this place.

Aside from the mystery terrorist's celebrity status, there was one more relevant fact that I didn't know on March 30, and it was that our platoon's aggressive actions on that day were too little, too late. To date, nearly every unit in the battalion had been involved in at least one, if not several, enemy attacks, and 2/4 had responded with our own fire on fewer than five occasions. Our hesitance to engage our enemies spoke volumes about both their willingness to sacrifice civilians in pursuit of their aims and our willingness to sacrifice ourselves in pursuit of ours, but this powerful message had somehow been lost in translation. At the company and platoon level—the units actually on the street day in and day out—we had done almost no work with our Iraqi counterparts, the police and the national guard. Aside from

George, there was no one to help us explain our seeming passivity in the face of repeated attacks to a population largely on the fence. Therefore, our kindness quickly became perceived as weakness by the insurgents and by most of Ramadi's citizens, and by late March, 2/4 had earned itself the nickname *awat*, an Iraqi Arabic term for a soft, sugary cake that crumbles easily to the touch.

We didn't know it then, but the insurgents had decided to touch us, to crumble us just like the soft cake that had become our namesake. The battalion had extended the velvet glove, and it was about to get its hands severely bitten.

Part 3

FIERCE

EIGHTEEN

By early April, Golf Company had developed a solid feel for Ramadi's daily pattern of activities, an understanding that allowed us to gauge the city's normalcy. In the early morning, just after sunrise, men gathered at the local tea shops to drink shot glasses full of steaming chai; women began walking their children to school; and storefronts all across the city raised their locked steel doors and opened for business. The hustle and bustle of daily life reached its peak shortly before noon, with thousands of people thronging the souk and the industrial area, shopping, working, or, more probably, looking for work. At noon, the streets and marketplaces emptied as most people retired to their houses to try to sleep during the scorching afternoon heat. A few hours later, around 3 or 4 PM, commerce resumed until nightfall. Then the streets became largely empty again, and strict Islam, it seemed, took a backseat to practicality. During our early curfew enforcement patrols, the vast majority of erratic Iraqi drivers whom we pulled over at our checkpoints were inebriated.

Governing these rhythms of life were the muezzins' chants. Five times a day they rang out across the city, in a ritual unchanged since the ninth century, save that in the twenty-first, electronic speakers magnified their sound.

Before people arose, while the city was still dark, the muezzins invited them to wake and pray. After everyone retired, just after darkness returned to Ramadi, the muezzins closed out the day with their chants. And three times in between, as life ebbed and flowed according to the heat and commerce, the muezzins reminded everyone to pause, just for a bit, and to pray.

Normally, we had no idea what different sentiments these chanted prayers contained as they competed with one another for the attention of the faithful in a furious cacophony of noise. We simply walked on through the babel and perhaps gave our own quick thanks that the streets were clear. At 10 AM on April 6, though, Golf Company knew that something was wrong, because for the first time since our arrival, we knew exactly what each mosque was saying during its call to prayer. From every minaret in the city, the same word rang out, over and over, in short, chanted blocks:

"JIHAD, JIHAD, JIHAD."
  Pause.
"JIHAD, JIHAD, JIHAD."
  Pause.
"JIHAD, JIHAD, JIHAD."
  Pause.

Every single muezzin in Ramadi was calling for a holy war against the Marines.

Unbeknownst to us, during the previous week several hundred hard-core insurgents had infiltrated the city with the intent of attacking head-on, and ultimately crumbling, the weak American Marines. Implementing a tactic that was currently working for them in Fallujah, the terrorists went from one house to another, staging weapons at each and telling the head of the family that if the caches were not there when the fighters returned, they would simply behead the family in front of the father before torturing the man to death. This prestaging of fighting positions eliminated the need to carry weapons openly in the streets. Knowing that we would not shoot unarmed individuals, the insurgents could thus use our rules of engagement against us by fighting from one house until they were overwhelmed, then leaving their weapons and retreating—unarmed and thus relatively safely mixed with the civilian populace at large—to the next house and the next fighting position. There they would take up arms again and repeat the process.

Making matters worse, the ranks of these "professional" insurgents were swelled by thousands of part-time volunteers, local Ramadi residents who grabbed the family AK-47 and ventured outside their compounds to take potshots at nearby Americans before returning and continuing with tea or television. Of course, not all Ramadians took part in the fighting, and estimates of the size of the force that we faced on April 6 vary widely, but consider the following: In the city of 350,000, it would have taken only 1 percent of the total residents to field some 3,000 volunteer fighters, a number easily four times that of our battalion's roughly 800 able-bodied infantrymen. And one thing is certain—far more than 1 percent of Ramadi resented the American crusaders enough to take a relatively risk-free shot at them.

Thus, on the morning of April 6, Lieutenant Hesener and his platoon, Joker Three, were patrolling a wide swath of the city on foot, en route to the Government Center as the jihad prayers drew to a close. Suddenly they started taking sporadic fire. Within half an hour, the sporadic had turned intense, and Joker Three soon found itself separated into three isolated squads, each pinned down in a different house in the middle of Ramadi, taking fire from and returning it at an enemy that seemed to be everywhere. As we were on QRF that day, Joker One was sent in first to relieve them and to extract the dead and wounded, but it soon became apparent that every man who could be spared from the Outpost was needed, so the CO called in Joker Four and the battalion's Weapons Company to reinforce us. To our east, Porcupine, the sister company sharing the Outpost with us, was also hit by numerous well-coordinated, well-planned ambushes. Eventually every available man in the battalion would be deployed into the fight, and by the time the sun set on April 6, twelve Marines had lost their lives. At least twenty-five others were wounded in the bloodiest day of the Iraq War since the fall of Baghdad.

For Joker One, though, the events of April 6 began well before we launched into the city to relieve third platoon. In fact, for us April 6 began precisely at 12 AM, as we were once again wide awake on the roof of the Government Center when midnight rolled around. We had arrived there seven hours earlier, in the late afternoon of April 5. I had taken first and third squads out on foot to guard the complex while my second squad rested back at the Outpost. While at the Center, I planned for us to run a few squad-sized security patrols during the early evening; then, after nightfall, I wanted to alternate first and third squads between resting and standing security up on the roof. On our return to the firmbase, early on the morning of April 6, we would sweep Michigan for IEDs so that Joker Three, the day's operation platoon, didn't have to. When the sweep passed the northern soccer stadium, my plan called for second squad to meet us there and beef up our security as we patrolled through them during the last stage of the sweep.

Like most of my plans, this one didn't survive very long. First off, while on patrol with Noriel during the late afternoon of April 5, I received radio reports that a substantial crowd was gathering south of the Government Center and that a violent protest would likely soon be headed our way. I was pleased—a mass of people willing to stay in one place and assault us meant that we finally stood some decent chance of fighting back. We hustled back to the Center, and I put both second and third squads on security, splitting them between the roof and the two entrances to the compound. For several hours we waited on 100 percent alert, but the predicted protest never materialized. When the streets finally cleared, well after sundown, I stood third squad down so that they could get some rest. However, no sooner had I done this than another "intelligence" report came down from battalion: Insurgents had packed a vehicle full of explosives, and the suicide bomber driving it was definitely headed our way with the intent to trade his life for several of ours. Third squad stood right back up again, and Bowen and I frantically positioned commandeered vehicles in front of the two gates to the Government Center to prevent a high-speed car impact from penetrating our quarters.

We waited for another two or three hours, nervously scanning every vehicle that passed for signs of erratic driving, but, once again, nothing happened. Disgusted with our intel, I finally sent third squad inside to rest and then bedded myself down on the Government Center roof. Not more than an hour later, battalion called again with yet another report, one that claimed an IED had been placed in a local middle school five blocks to our south. We were the nearest forces; go check it out, came the order. I felt like a jack-in-the-box—up, down, up, down, up, down. Wearily, I sent first squad with Noriel down to the school while third took over security duties. Soon enough, first reported back that, finally, battalion had gotten it right. There was indeed an IED at the school, and the squad cordoned it off and waited for EOD, the explosive disposal experts, to clear it.

Three hours later, they were still waiting, and I was getting very nervous. Finally, at 2 AM, first squad returned, and Corporal Teague gave me some bad news. EOD's little robot was dead—that was why the bomb disposal had taken so long—and the explosives experts had no idea when the robot would be fixed again. Hearing that, I hoped desperately that we wouldn't find any IEDs during the morning's route sweep, because I had no desire to sit in a cordon in downtown Ramadi for an untold number of hours, waiting for a robot that might or might not be fixed sometime in our near future.

So, of course, we found an IED almost immediately. The reduced Joker One had assembled blearily at about 4:15 AM—no one had really slept—and headed down Michigan ten minutes later. First was on the northern side, third was to our south, and the engineer, Corporal Aiken, and I were walking squarely down the middle of the highway. After about five minutes of patrolling, Aiken turned to me.

"Sir, I just kicked a really heavy piece of trash. Trash isn't normally this heavy, sir. I think it might be an IED. What do you want to do, sir?"

I looked around rapidly. The streets were completely deserted.

"Well, Aiken, if they wanted us dead, we'd be dead by now. No sense in cordoning off something that we don't know is an IED, especially if the stupid robot is down. Let's cut open this trash bag. If you've got a knife handy, I'll hold a flashlight up so that you can see." It was still fairly dark out.

"Roger that, sir."

So, somehow I found myself bending over a suspected IED, a red-lens LED flashlight in my mouth, holding steady what appeared to be a full black plastic trash bag so that the engineer could cut it open with his bayonet (if we moved it too much, an antihandling device might set the bomb off). Aiken proceeded slowly and cautiously and he unveiled a huge block of explosive with wires, circuitry, and other nasty bits wrapped all around it. As soon as we grasped what we were looking at, Aiken and I bolted away in an absolutely reflexive, completely thought-free reaction. Once we were a moderately safe distance out, I radioed Bowen and Noriel, told them about the IED, and instructed them to hold in place for a bit.

Two quick assents came back, and staring at the little bomb in the median, I briefly had no idea how to proceed. Standard doctrine called for us to cordon off the bomb and wait for EOD, but standard doctrine didn't take into account the fact that EOD wasn't working that day. We could be in a cordon for hours, perfect static targets, and if the enemy didn't get us, the heat very well might. However, I couldn't just leave the bomb where it lay and hope that some other unit would cover for my lack of responsibility and my fear, and after my earlier nervous experience carrying around a much smaller quantity of explosives, I had no desire to pick up this IED, put it in my butt pack, and take it home with us like some twisted version of an adopted pet.

I hesitated to call the COC for guidance, though, because the Ox was on watch. I knew that in lieu of a careful evaluation of the various available courses of action, he would simply instruct me to do what he perceived as the toughest thing possible: Cordon off the IED and wait. As I pondered the situation, Corporal Aiken, a little shaken but still thinking, sidled up to me and suggested that we blow the bomb in place with the sticks of C-4 he was carrying.

Problem solved. If anyone was watching that bomb, it would have gone off by now, so there wasn't a lot more risk to be had by sending someone out to it again (or so I judged at the time). I radioed the squad leaders with our plan, and, once they had gotten everyone behind some solid cover, I gave Aiken the go-ahead to move out with the mission. Immediately he trotted out, disappearing into the blackness between two nearby buildings. Meanwhile, I watched the IED site intently, and, about a minute later, Aiken suddenly darted out of the shadows to my front. He ran up to the IED, put something onto it, fiddled for about ten seconds, and then took off again in one of the fastest runs I have ever seen. Maybe a minute later, a huge explosion rocked the street, and great gouts of concrete flew up into the air. The patrol picked up again, and I got on the radio to let a no-doubt nervous COC know what we had just done. "Joker COC, this is Joker One-Actual. Be advised, that explosion you just heard was us blowing an IED in place about three hundred meters east of the Government Center. Break. We are continuing the route sweep mission now. Over."

Better to ask for forgiveness than permission.

Immediately a furious Ox started shouting at me out of the handset. "Joker One, be advised, what the fuck did you just do?"

"Five, I say again, we blew an IED in place. Break. The engineers detonated it with some C-4, and we are now continuing the route sweep mission. Over."

"One, did you not listen to the fucking presentation that we were given by that fucking guy back in the States? A lot of fucking engineers have been killed doing that. You should've waited for EOD. Over."

"Five, I will repeat what I told you earlier today. EOD's robot is down indefinitely. Over."

"Whatever. You could've cordoned off the area like you were fucking supposed to. Over."

I pulled the radio handset back from my head and glared at it for a second. Then, in my most detached, professional voice: "Five, be advised we are proceeding with the route sweep mission at this time. Out."

"Yeah, well, we can talk about this when you get back. Over."

Fortunately, first and third squads made it to the northern soccer stadium without any further incidents. There we linked up with Leza and second squad at 6 AM, passed them as they provided overwatch for us, and continued into the Outpost. Fifteen minutes later, I was waiting for second squad to report back into the base when Leza called me over the PRR. He sounded uncharacteristically nervous, and after a brief bit of fumbling with his words, he spit it out: Raymond's team was nowhere to be found—not in the base, not in the soccer stadium. They couldn't be raised on the PRRs, and they had no other radios with them. For all intents and purposes, they were lost and completely cut off from friendly forces.

My heart fell through my chest. Terrified, I ran back to the platoon's house and reassembled all the men on the slim chance that somehow the team had simply been missed by everyone, but it didn't pan out—our lost Marines were still nowhere to be found. Next, Leza and I climbed the walls of the Outpost, calling over our PRRs time and time again for Raymond and his team to report, but all we got in return was dead silence over our earpieces. Fearing the worst, I ran to the COC to report that I was missing four of my men and to check and see whether any other friendly units out in the city might have found them.

They hadn't, and I was getting more anxious by the minute. In the COC, the Ox was incredulous, and he peppered me with question after inane question about how a group of Marines could possibly have been so dumb as to have gotten lost well within sight of our base. Eventually I snapped and told him to shut the hell up. I had the same questions, the same disappointment in my men, but the Ox's rambling, cursing commentary wasn't doing anything other than distracting everyone around from the useful pursuit of my lost team. After I determined that there was nothing left to learn from our battalion, I left the Ox and his useless ranting and ran back to the platoon's house to get my men ready for a sweep through the northern part of Ramadi. We were halfway through assembling to leave again when a headquarters Marine came running into the house with the news that Raymond's team had been found: They were at Hurricane Point, the Marine base all the way on the other side of the city. A weight fell off me, and suddenly I felt very, very tired—it had been over twenty-four hours now since any of us had slept. The platoon stood down, and slowly and wearily the Marines started peeling off their heavy gear load. Meanwhile, I trudged back to the COC to get the full story.

Half an hour later I learned that Raymond's four-man team had simply gotten themselves turned around in the predawn darkness and walked in the exact opposite direction from the Combat Outpost, somehow traversing the entire length of Ramadi unscathed. When they finally caught sight of the base at Hurricane Point, they realized their mistake and continued onward inside friendly walls, even if those walls weren't exactly where they were supposed to be. I was too relieved and exhausted even to begin feeling angry, so I arranged for the team's return on the morning's logistics convoy and then headed off to the platoon commander room to try to rest.

An hour and a half later, someone shook me awake, shouting breathlessly that third platoon was pinned down and taking casualties and that I had to go and rescue them quick, quick, quick, sir. As I stumbled groggily downstairs, tripping on damn uneven steps again, it slowly dawned on me that I could hear sporadic fire well out in the distance. My body started up the familiar adrenaline drip, quickly eating away the sleep. By the time I had strapped on my gear and headed out to the vehicles, I was more or less fully awake, and most of my Marines were mounted in two Humvees and two seven-ton trucks (we still didn't have enough Humvees in the company to mount a single platoon). The CO was near the front vehicle, and, catching sight of me, he immediately ran over.

"One, you know what's happening?"

"Yeah, I was told briefly that third's pinned down and taking casualties. We've got to go relieve them and get the wounded out of there, right, sir?"

"Right. Now, get in the lead vehicle. We need to leave immediately."

"Sir, I can't lead us out. I have no idea where third is right now. I can't take us where we need to go because I don't know where we're going."

The CO stared at me for a second, then said, a bit sharply, "Fine then. I'll take us there. Just get in the second vehicle. We're getting out of here to go get third."

Five minutes later, the convoy roared out of the gates en route to the southern part of the Farouq district. The CO, Teague, Doc Camacho, and Mahardy, who was carrying the only long-range radio in the platoon, were in the first vehicle, and everyone else followed behind them. As fast as we could, we drove straight toward the sound of the guns.

NINETEEN

wish that I could tell the story of the battle as it happened—give some sort of traditional, blow-by-blow account of the different troop movements within the city, where the various units were engaged, how the enemy forces arrayed themselves—but I can't. In fact, I can't even give a reasonable account of my own platoon's fighting, because most of the time my squads were separated from one another, without communication, in the middle of an urban jungle that had suddenly sprouted fire from all directions. I can't begin to describe the chaos, let alone try to make sense of it. My Marines and I fought house by house and block by block in a series of small, intense, mostly separate battles, and we experienced that day not as a linear, understandable progression of events but as a jumbled array of brief, intense snapshots. All that I can do is share some of these snapshots and hope that they at least convey faithfully our experience of the all-out fighting of April 6.

We piled out of the vehicles at the very bottom of the Farouq area, along Baseline Road just north of where the train tracks ran along the very bottom of the city. Baseline was entirely deserted, and where its northern sidewalk ended, the dense housing compounds sprang up, forbidding and seemingly impenetrable. The fight had gotten more intense, judging by the brief pauses between bursts of gunfire. Based on how distant that firing sounded, I guessed that the fighting was still several hundred meters away, to our north. As I was about to hop out of the Humvee, it suddenly struck me that we couldn't take the seven-tons off the wide Baseline Road and into the narrow streets of Farouq. They'd assuredly get stuck somewhere, and then we'd be tied down defending hunks of metal instead of rescuing our trapped comrades.

Still, I couldn't just leave the vehicles and their four drivers all alone in the most hostile part of town. I used the PRR to radio Bowen, who was standing one hundred meters behind me on Baseline. If anyone could handle being isolated in this dangerous area, protecting a stationary target without any communication with other friendly units, it was he.

"One-Three, this is One-Actual. I need you to provide vehicle security here. One-One and One-Two will move with me farther north."

"Roger, sir. You need me to stay with the vehicles. Uh, sir, do you have a 119 [long range radio] I could have?"

"No. Mahardy's got the only one for the entire platoon, and the CO needs it. There's no fighting here, so you might be safe. And if you take any casualties, at least you can perform your own medevac with the vehicles. That's the best I can do, One-Three. We don't have any time to wait. I've gotta leave you—somewhere in this city Joker Three's got a couple of Marines bleeding out, and we've got to get 'em. If anyone can handle this shitty mission, it's you."

"Roger that, sir. I'll make it happen. Don't worry about us. Get Joker Three. I'll see you in the fight."

During our conversation, the rest of the platoon had finished dismounting. I jumped out of the Humvee and looked up ahead. The CO was sprinting west down the road with Mahardy in tow, so I took off after them. Once again I heard someone screaming for Marines to get in front of the lieutenant, and suddenly Teague passed me and positioned himself directly in front of me.

The CO called me over the PRR: "Hey, One. Third platoon isn't where we thought they were, and we don't know exactly where they are now. I bet we're too far south. We've gotta move north, and quickly."

"Roger that, sir. Moving."

Neither of us had any idea where, exactly, to go, so first squad, second squad, the CO, and I did the only thing we could. We ran straight toward the sound of the guns as rapidly as our feet would carry us.

Ten minutes later, we had made our way into Farouq, and we found ourselves running toward a major north-south road called Easy Street. The sounds of fighting were much closer now. I was functioning mainly on autopilot and adrenaline—there were no decisions to be made until we either found third platoon or got attacked. The CO was leading the way, and he and Mahardy suddenly popped around the corner of a house, jumping out onto the sidewalk lining Easy Street. I was about thirty feet behind, and the two disappeared from my view. Suddenly firing erupted, very close now, and Mahardy and the CO immediately reappeared, backpedaling as fast as possible. Teague ran up to join them; arriving there, he, too, dived for cover.

My PRR erupted with the CO's voice: "One . . . they've got us pinned down with some heavy fire . . . Probably at least one machine gun position . . . Get off this street . . . Move south, try and flank."

The last bit was redundant—I had already backtracked to the closest north-south street, and now I was running south as fast as I could with the back half of first squad following. The front half was still pinned down, and second squad had somehow gotten separated from the rest of us. We moved down one block, then I stuck my head around the corner of a compound wall to get a visual on the houses across Easy.

Less than a foot to my left, the wall suddenly exploded in a solid line tracing up from the sidewalk to well above my head. The left side of my face was peppered with shards of concrete that pinged off my sunglasses and scraped the skin where they hit. Reflexively, I jumped backward around the corner so quickly that I almost fell over. There was at least one machine gun position directly across the road—I had seen the flashes out of the corner of my eye—and we needed to somehow get rid of it. I glanced back and spotted Corporal Walter, one of Noriel's team leaders.

"Walter," I yelled. He couldn't hear me above the din, so I caught his eye and motioned frantically for him to come alongside me. "We've got a machine gun right across the street; first house you see, second story. We need to get some fire on it so we can cross the street and hit it hard. Grab one of your Marines and get him ready to go. You and I are gonna suppress and cover him."

"Roger, sir," Walter screamed back, then turned around and grabbed Lance Corporal Boelhower, a Marine who had joined us only one month before deploying, from where he was kneeling behind a parked car. Ten seconds later, Boelhower and Walter were both standing behind me.

I put my mouth right next to Walter's left ear and yelled, "Okay, on the count of three, we're going to pop out and fire. Watch my tracers—they'll tell you where that gun is . . . Got it?"

"Got it, sir," he screamed back.

"Okay, one, two, *three.*"

We lunged around the corner, out into the open again, and I started pouring fire at the window where I had seen the enemy. Corporal Walter followed suit. Immediately the gunner opened up again, then went silent; our combined fire had eliminated him. I felt nothing at the possibility of having shot my first human, just the need to continue pouring fire on the other houses across the street and a distant irritation that I could no longer hear anything out of my right ear since Walter had placed his muzzle right next to it before opening up with his weapon.

I kept pulling the trigger as fast as good shooting allowed, and Walter turned around and waved Boelhower forward, screaming, "*Go, go, go.*" Without any hesitation, the Marine set off across the street at a dead run, and Walter and I started opening up again on more enemies who had suddenly appeared on a nearby rooftop and begun shooting at our runner. Tracers were streaming back and forth across the road, but somehow Boelhower made it safely across. More of the squad moved up alongside me and added their fire to Walter's and mine. I briefly stopped shooting and looked to my south, trying to figure out where on earth my second squad had gone. I spotted them about fifty meters away, crouched down behind a gigantic mound of dirt right in front of the southern soccer stadium. Tracers from more enemies across the street were pouring into the mound, and it looked strangely as if a laser light show had suddenly started, with all lasers converging to a single point two-thirds of the way up the large mound. Carson later told me that while he was crouching behind that mound, he suddenly became certain that he wouldn't live through the next five minutes.

I tried calling Leza and Staff Sergeant over the PRR, but got nothing in response. I wondered if they had been killed, then I started shooting again.

Somehow, I had made it across Easy with the back half of first squad, and I paused to shift the receiver of the PRR to my left ear after realizing that the hearing in my right one still hadn't returned. The radio squawked to life with Noriel's voice, and it distantly occurred to me that it could very well have been squawking at me this entire time without my knowing. He and the front half of first were still pinned down on the opposite side of Easy Street. I could hear his shouted instructions.

"Tig, above you, Tig, above you!"

Corporal Teague's voice came back. "Ser'ent, I can't see him. I can't see him!"

"He's on the balcony, Tig, one house down, on the balcony! Throw the damn grenade there. Throw him!"

I looked back across Easy Street, one block north of the way I had just come, and I spotted Sergeant Noriel standing on the roof of a house, completely exposed and totally heedless of the bullets that were clearly zipping all around him. One hand was on his weapon, and the other was on his PRR. I glanced farther up Easy on my side of the street just in time to see Teague heave a grenade up in the air. A balcony above him exploded, and I saw a flash, smoke, and dark redness suddenly splashed all over the balcony's railing.

Boelhower was trying to get into a house, the one from which most of the enemy's fire had come, but first he had to kick in the metal gate that opened up into the house's courtyard, and several kicks failed to produce the desired effect. The rest of the Marines were stacked up behind him, along the compound wall, waiting for the gate to break so that they could pour into the breach. I was still on the sidewalk, trying to raise Leza on the PRR but having no success. I had no idea whether any of his second-squad Marines had made it across the street, or whether any of them had been killed or wounded in the fighting. After ten or so attempts failed, I gave up, and I ran down the street to rejoin the fragment of my first squad as it finally entered the house.

No sooner had we gotten inside the wall than the CO called me. "One, this is Six. I'm across Easy with part of your first squad. Where are you?"

"Six, I'm also across Easy. I'm about to go into a little housing compound that we're breaching."

"Negative, One. We need to keep moving. Third platoon isn't at the south water tower like we thought. It's at the north one [a distance differential of roughly half the city]. We've got at least ten more blocks to go. I'm moving north on the sidewalk now."

"Roger, Six, I'll pick up the rest of the squad and move to you."

I could see Walter, so I yelled at him to get his guys out of the house—whose door Boelhower had finally bashed in—and to follow me back to Easy Street. He gave me a thumbs-up, and I did an about-face and started running back the way I had come. A stream of tracers passed smoothly through the spot where I had just been standing. Corporal Brown stared at me wide-eyed as I ran past him.

When I got to Easy, a beautiful sight greeted my eyes. Weapons Company, the battalion's QRF—and its big guns—which lived at Hurricane Point, had arrived on the scene with Humvees equipped with heavy .50-caliber machine guns and Mark-19s, our automatic grenade launchers. The Marks were dusting off the rooftops of the buildings lining Easy while the .50-cals slammed through their walls in their wonderful, slowly rhythmic thumping. One block north of me, I could see the CO, Noriel, Teague, and Mahardy. Weapons Company Marines were streaming out of the Humvee to join them, and the sidewalk in front of me suddenly filled up with at least five of them. I glanced back—the rest of first squad was behind me on the street—and started moving north to rejoin the CO.

With Weapons's arrival, the fire had slackened, but it was still snapping around us from all directions, and I had taken maybe five steps along the sidewalk when the Weapons Company Marine directly in front of me suddenly doubled over, crouched down, and then fell on his side in the fetal position. He had just been shot through the stomach. Time stopped, and all sound seemed to fade away again. I looked across the street just in time to see another Weapons Marine spin around and sit down heavily. I could see tracers zigzagging crazily in front of me, creating almost a lacework pattern of light across the street directly in front of me. At that exact moment, all I remember thinking was *Wow. This is just like in the movies.*

Then time kicked in again, the gunfire and the cracking resumed, and I ran like hell to the wounded. A corpsman got there first and started work. As I passed him, I realized that my current magazine was running low on ammo, and I should probably change it. I did, and kept on moving.

We were nearing the end of Easy, about four blocks south of where it ended at Michigan. Teague's team was walking point, and I was right behind them. Two grenades came tumbling over the wall of the nearest house, neatly splitting the team in half. Without thinking, I turned around and sprinted for the nearest corner, even though it was probably futile; the grenades had landed only about ten feet away. One of Teague's team members, I don't know who, tossed his own grenade back over the wall. I heard one explosion, then nothing, so I turned back around. There, lying nicely in the middle of the sidewalk, were the two enemy grenades. For some reason, they hadn't exploded.

Everyone stopped moving. With half of Teague's team in front of the grenades and the rest of first squad behind them, I was briefly at a loss for what to do—should I risk moving past the unexploded little bombs, or try to get everyone into cover and then shoot the grenades, or wait in place for something else to happen? I stood motionless, just staring at the sidewalk for about five seconds, then Noriel solved my problem. Appearing out of nowhere, he streaked past me, spewing a mixed stream of English and Tagalog curses as he went. With no hesitation whatsoever, he ran up to the grenades, bent over, grabbed one, heaved it as far as he could into the houses to our west, then grabbed the other and did the same. Finished, he turned around and shouted at the rest of us.

"Well, what the hell are you alls waiting for! Move, move, move!"

We did, continuing north for another block until the CO reached me via PRR.

"One, we need to move west. I don't know exactly where third is, but they're somewhere in the next couple of blocks. Move west, off of Easy, and do it quick. Third's got one dead and some badly wounded. We've gotta get to them soon."

"Roger, Six."

The PRR sprang to life again, this time with a broken transmission from Staff Sergeant. "One-Actual . . . moving where you are . . . moving . . ."

"Say again, Staff Sergeant. Say again." I was desperate for news. I still had no idea where my second squad had gone or whether they had any killed or wounded.

"Moving to you. We're moving to you . . ."

"Do you have any wounded, do you have any wounded, Staff Sergeant?"

"Negative . . . Okay . . . no . . . hurt . . . see Weapons. We're coming."

"Okay, come find us. We've gotta keep moving to third. Marines are dying."

I listened, but didn't hear anything else. Teague was looking back at me, so I motioned him to head west down the nearest street. He nodded, then moved off at quick patrol pace. The rest of us followed, and when I turned around to make certain that the squad was still together—that no one had been wounded without us knowing—I saw something amazing. Citizens were standing at the entrances to their houses, watching us pass them by. The gunfire down the street had slackened, but it hadn't died away altogether, and just a few blocks away we could hear fierce, unremitting fire from wherever third platoon was pinned. None of that seemed to matter to the locals. Now that the worst of the fight had passed their street by, they wanted to see what was going on outside their front doors. Some of them even darted across Easy to get a better look, and, amid all the running, I noticed a few people calmly carrying sacks of goods across the main street.

I shook myself loose from the surprise of this outbreak of everyday life in the midst of our war. Teague and first squad were still moving, and the insurgents were still ferociously attacking third platoon somewhere nearby. I turned around and trotted off, again moving straight toward the noise of heavy firing.

The sounds of continuous fighting were very close now, perhaps only a few blocks away. As I pressed myself up against a compound wall located somewhere in the middle of the city, about four blocks due south of the Saddam mosque, I again heard the cracks of passing bullets. The fire seemed to be coming from behind us, from our east, not from our west, where third platoon was still fighting desperately. Noriel swung around and spotted a window with some flashes, and he pointed it out to Feldmeir, who aimed his grenade launcher in its general vicinity and somehow managed to put a grenade right through that window. The opening filled up with smoke and the firing ceased for a moment. Then it picked back up again. First squad stopped advancing and took cover as best it could.

I ducked around the nearest corner, intending to head toward this most recent fire to get a better picture of our attackers' positions. Suddenly, I saw two men dressed head to toe in black, from the ski masks on their heads to the black tennis shoes on their feet, standing twenty feet away and staring at me. The all-black getup was the standard battle dress of the hard-core insurgents, the uniform they favored for the all-out, stand-and-fight battles. The men and I made eye contact, and in that quick instant both they and I knew exactly what I was going to do next. Before I could lift my muzzle high enough, though, both men ducked through the open steel gates in front of which they had been standing; then they clanged the doors shut. I loosed off about fifteen shots, hoping to hit the men through the thin sheet steel, and I called for a grenade. Walter ran up and slapped one into my outstretched hand. I carefully popped the thumb clip off the spoon, pulled the pin, and then lobbed the little round, smooth object over the compound gates. We ducked up against the wall and waited for the explosion; when it went off, I screamed at Walter for another.

"We're all out, sir. No more left," he shouted back.

"Roger that. Let's hit this house."

We charged the compound, kicked down the door, and streamed through, weapons raised to fire. Nothing was inside save a large hole in the dirt, some dark streaks on the wall, and some dark dribbles on the ground. They had probably only been wounded. We cleared the courtyard and then turned around and headed back the way we had come.

We headed west again, still trying to locate the beleaguered third platoon. Coming around another corner, I saw Corporal Hayes—a third-platoon team leader—and one other Marine crouched down on our street's sidewalk, just one block to our north. Finally we had linked up with at least part of the missing unit. I ran over, and, as I got closer, I noticed that Hayes was white-faced and shaking slightly. He was bleeding from one of his hands.

"Hayes, where are the rest of your guys? Are any more wounded? Who do we need to get?"

He stared blankly at me for a bit, then, despite his pain, pointed out a spot one block to our north. "Sir, last I saw them, they were somewhere around there. We got separated early on. Now all of us're wounded." He stopped talking after that, exhausted and in pain.

The Marine to his right was also injured, and he was crying and rocking to himself. As I walked off, Noriel walked up.

"Hey. It's gonna be okay," he told them, and knelt down and put his arms around the crying Marine. "Now give me your magazines," he said, more softly. "I'm low on bullets, and you won't need them anymore."

Doc Camacho moved up and immediately got to work on the wounded Hayes, so I moved off, trying to locate the rest of Hayes's team, including the one dead Marine that I knew about. Ten feet in front of me, another wounded third-squad member suddenly staggered around a corner toward us. It was third's Lance Corporal Gentile, and he was weaponless. Both hands were pressed against his face and neck; they were covered in blood, and blood was seeping through his closed fingers. Gentile had taken a round through the back of his neck, and it had blown off part of his nose and most of his right cheek when it exited his body through his face. I motioned Gentile back toward Doc and then moved up to the street from which he had emerged. Glancing down it, I saw the dead body of Moises Langhorst sprawled out, arms akimbo, in the middle of the street, maybe thirty feet away from me. Even from that distance, I could tell that Langhorst had been stripped of his weapon and all gear, leaving a strangely naked-looking body clad only in cammies and boots.

Noriel came up alongside me and, glancing over at Langhorst, asked, "Sir, do you want to go get him?"

I pondered the question briefly, and, right at that moment, two Army ambulances appeared out of nowhere and started rolling down our street. They stopped right at Doc Camacho, and an unknown Army colonel jumped out of the vehicles, ran up to the CO, and offered to evacuate our wounded for us. Seeing this, I turned back to Noriel.

"No. My concern right now is for the living. Let's keep moving north. Let's find the rest of third."

We were still missing half of Hayes's squad and two other full squads from third, and I knew they had at least one other seriously wounded Marine in their ranks. We couldn't do anything for Langhorst now, and, even though the firing around us had ceased, our first priority was still breaking through to the besieged and helping the people we could. Noriel and I moved off north, to the end of the block, and I called the CO over the PRR to see if he knew where to go from here. He was still the only one with a long-range radio, and still the only one who had even some idea of where the rest of third was located.

When the CO didn't reply, I glanced back, only to discover that he and the Army colonel were busy conferring at the entrance to the street containing Langhorst's body. They suddenly straightened, and the CO and one other Marine, probably Mahardy, took off down the street to retrieve Langhorst. Behind them, the Army colonel started firing down the same street with a shotgun. I had no idea what he was shooting at, since the enemy guns around us had halted altogether, and I hadn't seen any worthwhile targets on that street thirty seconds ago. Maybe it was random covering fire.

No help was going to come from this quarter for the time being, so I turned my PRR to third platoon's channel and started calling out to them. After the third try, I heard Sergeant Holt, Corporal Hayes's squad leader, bark back at me.

"Goddamn, sir, it's good to hear you guys. How close are you?" he said.

"Holt, I don't know. I don't know where you are, but you've gotta be within a few blocks if I can hear you on this."

"Well, sir, can you fire something in the air? Maybe we'll see it."

"Wait one."

Sergeant Noriel had heard the whole exchange, and before I could turn to him, he slapped a red star cluster—a small aluminum canister that fires a red flare one hundred feet into the air—into my hand. "You can shoot this, sir." Then he started tugging at my cammies, but I was too engrossed with finding the rest of third platoon to pay attention to him. I fired the pyrotechnic up into the air, and Holt informed me that we were only a block and a half away, just to his south.

I set off again, Noriel following me, still tugging at my cammies—later he told me that he felt like a little kid, tagging along after a distracted parent. Finally it dawned on me that he had something to say.

"What do you want, Noriel?"

"Just wanted to say, sir, that you're a pretty tall guy. Maybe you should think about kneeling or taking cover occasionally. You keep this up, you'll get shots soon."

Shortly after we arrived on the scene, the firing at Sergeant Holt's squad slackened enough to allow them to leave the housing compound where they had taken refuge. The seven remaining able-bodied men moved just behind my first squad, and shortly after all of them had left their building, yet another third-platoon squad emerged from a nearby housing compound. They, too, inserted themselves among us, and I told Noriel to head off again, farther into the city. I started walking again before being stopped dead in my tracks by one of Sergeant Noriel's team leaders, Corporal Brown, calling over the PRR.

"Sir," he said, "I'm standing next to a dead Marine here. What do you want me to do?"

Dead bodies are classified as routine medevacs, but there's never anything routine about zippering up the lifeless husk of one of your comrades and loading him like so much cordwood into the nearest vehicle. For three minutes, that's exactly what we did. Then we headed west again to find the still-living—the priority and the urgent medevacs.

By midafternoon I had managed to hook up with my full platoon as well as most of third, and all 1,200 of 2/4's Marines had deployed in force into Ramadi to crush the fighters. We had now been fighting for almost five straight hours, and I felt tired and frantically busy. Fire would erupt fiercely and die down again just as quickly as small pockets of resistance all around us sprang into life, then disbanded. During one of those quick firefights, I was moving with Leza when the bullets started snapping all around.

"Get the guys into a house. Strong-point and return fire," I yelled, meaning they should guard the doors and windows.

"Roger, sir," came the reply. "Carson, get us inside the gate."

I looked behind me, and, sure enough, Lance Corporal Carson had just rammed his entire body against the sturdy metal gate of a compound wall. He rebounded, then shook his head just like a bull in a bullfight and charged again. This time the gate exploded inward, and second squad streamed inside to relative safety. Leza started running inside, then paused, turned around, and grinned at me despite the heavy fire.

"Hey, sir. That's Carson for you, huh?"

For the first time, I found myself grinning during a firefight. "Yeah, it sure is. Let's get the hell inside, huh?"

We poured into the building and climbed up to the roof, ignoring the people inside, if there even were any. Rows and rows of nearly identical housing compounds surrounded us, and, looking at them, I realized we were on the very western edge of the Farouq district, almost at the edge of the gigantic aboveground cemetery that marked the city center. Hes and the final squad from third platoon had taken cover among its tombstones.

Half an hour later, Hes and the rest of his men were found at the very western edge of the cemetery. It was early evening, and by now the fire inside the city had ceased altogether. The CO worked out a grid containing most of the butchers' district and all of the Farouq district, and he put fourth platoon, mine, and the remnants of third into action searching every house along the east-west streets of the grid. The streets of the city were devoid of traffic, but the occasional pedestrian walked the sidewalks, sometimes even passing us, and from every third or fourth compound we passed residents stared at us from their rooftops or their open doors. Seeing them silhouetted against the evening sun made me slightly nervous, but I was still numb to most emotions outside my extreme focus. Once citizens had been identified as nonthreats, I lost all interest and moved on to the next task and/or suspicious person.

I walked by an open compound gate and glanced briefly inside. I saw a kid, about fifteen years old, with curly black hair and the very beginnings of a mustache tracing his upper lip, dressed in a black Adidas jacket and black nylon pants. Both hands were in his pockets. If he had been standing upright, he would have been leaning almost jauntily against a wall, with one leg crooked at the knee to rest on the other. He wasn't standing, though. He was lying down, and his legs were twitching spastically. He had a neat red hole between his eyes.

I walked on.

After an hour we finished searching the grid and patrolled back into the base on foot. I was trudging back inside the base's walls, right next to Hes, carrying my helmet in my left hand with my right dangling limply at my side. My M-16 hung neatly across the front of my chest, suspended by its three-point sling, and all of my gear was still on. It had been a long day of fighting, roughly eight hours, and we were exhausted and filthy, covered with dirt, sweat, and gunpowder residue. Hes had blood all over his cammies, but he wasn't visibly wounded, so it likely wasn't his. We walked in silence for a bit, then he spoke up.

"I've got a hell of a headache, One."

"Dehydration, huh?"

"Yeah, well, that and the fact that I got knocked out by a bullet."

"What?"

"Yeah, we were fighting on a roof near the cemetery when an AK round must have caught my Kevlar at an angle. Look here, you can see the divot it made in the thing. Anyway, I fell over—must've been knocked out. I woke up and found my Marines dragging me off the roof, screaming that I had been killed. Man, were they surprised when I jumped up and told them I was okay. You should've seen the looks on their faces."

"Hell, man, you gonna see the docs?"

"Nah, they'll just treat me and put me in for a Purple Heart. I lost two guys today, One, and a bunch of others have got bullets all through 'em. Those guys rate Purple Hearts. Not me . . . Not me." Hes shook his head and put a lit cigarette up to his lips and took a deep drag. (Hes was as good as his word: He never told the docs, and he never received the Purple Heart he rated.)

I could only stare at Hes in reply. I tried to think of something witty to make light of the situation, but my mind was moving too slowly for humor.

By now, most of the adrenaline had worn off, and I hadn't slept or shaved in thirty-six hours. I felt dirty, grizzled, and exhausted, and I narrowed my burning eyes to slits after I took off my sweat-blurred sunglasses. Still, I had made it back with my entire platoon, and I felt proud. And about one hundred years older than when I had left that morning.

Each of us, I guess, had something to be thankful for. Hes, that that round hadn't hit him straight on. Me, that none of my men had been wounded. As far as I knew, Joker One was the only platoon that had fought all day long without a single casualty, major or minor. I couldn't believe it when all my squad leaders had reported none wounded upon our return to the base, so I had made them check the Marines again. Unsurprisingly, the report came back the same: None wounded, sir. Still, everyone was exhausted, so I postponed the usual debrief. Besides, I wanted to check with the CO and the other platoon commanders to straighten out the day's big-picture events before I got back to my men.

I was pretty shaken up, but I was relieved that we had made it through unscathed and happy that we had killed a substantial number of our attackers. I had no idea how the Marines felt, though, until Mahardy asked me a question sometime later that night. He was in the hangar bay, smoking, and he pulled me aside as I passed him en route to the COC.

"Sir," he said, "do you think we fought well today, sir? I mean, that was our first big fight. Would the Marines who fought at Iwo Jima and Okinawa, you know, be proud of us?"

On hearing this, I almost broke down crying. I had to turn away, choke back tears, and steady my voice before I answered.

"Yeah, Mahardy. We fought well. The Corps is proud of us. We did fine."

And we had done fine indeed. Despite being ambushed by well-prepared, highly motivated fighters all across the city, and despite being substantially outnumbered and outgunned for a good chunk of the day's fighting, Golf Company had hit back hard, ultimately recovering our own and repelling our attackers in some of the fiercest street battles since Hue City in Vietnam. And we had managed to kill, by most accounts, several hundred of our enemies. It would be nearly two months before the insurgency was again able to amass that kind of combat power in Ramadi. And the locals no longer thought of us as easily crumbled *awat.*

B ack in the States, though, our families had no idea of what we had just been through. When Christy turned on the television early on April 7 after returning home from a twelve-hour, all-night shift at the Children's Hospital of Orange County, the first thing she saw was the headlines screaming that twelve Marines had been killed and well over three times that number wounded in fierce fighting in a strange city called Ramadi. There was nothing else—no official calls or e-mails, no contact from the other company wives, nothing from me and nothing from my men. Just the news banner endlessly scrolling across the bottom of the TV screen, announcing the deaths of the nameless over and over. Christy collapsed and spent the next few hours on the floor, unmoving.

It would be two days before she knew that I was alive.

TWENTY

espite their heavy losses, the enemy fighters weren't finished; they launched another round of fierce attacks early the next day. April 7 went much the same as its predecessor, only this time it was second platoon, not third, that was pinned down inside the city, and the enemy seemed less widespread but more focused, more deliberate. There were fewer local volunteer fighters, but the professionals had worked straight through the hours of darkness to set up more fortified ambush positions. Fortunately, most of us had been able to rest during the night of April 6, so we went into the day's fighting at least somewhat refreshed, even if we were somewhat casualty-debilitated by the previous day's battles. By the time April 7 was over, Golf Company had returned back inside the gates of the Outpost sometime in the early evening, but two more Marines had lost their lives, among them one of Quist's men.

To take the initiative away from our enemies and preempt yet another round of casualties and citywide battles, 2/4's commanding officer, Lieutenant Colonel Kennedy, decided to launch a massive battalion-wide surge through the Farouq area on April 8. Titled "Operation County Fair" after a similar mission in Vietnam, the operation called for all three of the battalion's infantry companies to search house to house in predesignated sectors of Farouq while Weapons Company, along with bits and pieces of an Army brigade, provided a mobile cordon to prevent fleeing insurgents from escaping the hunt. The battalion expected the fighting to last for twenty-four to thirty-six hours, so everyone was told to take extra food and water.

Joker One and I had spent most of April 7 guarding the Combat Outpost and skirmishing in its immediate environs, so we were the best-rested and least casualty-debilitated unit in Golf Company. After all, we hadn't had any wounded, and we had slept for three or four hours on the evening of April 6. Therefore, Captain Bronzi tasked us to infiltrate the city a few hours before the rest of the company left the Outpost. Under cover of darkness, we were to move quietly through the alleyways and backstreets until we reached a series of tall houses on the western edge of Farouq. There we would set up rooftop positions, acting as a backstop for the rest of our company as it swept through the area from the east to the west. With any luck, we would be able to spot enemy ambushers as they set up their attack positions and put them between a rock and a hard place as they fled the platoons sweeping in our direction.

Thus, 4 AM on April 8, 2004, found Joker One praying, accompanied by a few attachments: a sniper team called Headhunter Two, which had been sent to us to assist in our efforts to shoot our enemies from a distance. I was happy to have them. The sniper platoon worked for 2/4, and my friend Nate Scott commanded it, so I knew all of the Marines, and I knew that they were extremely tough, competent, and professional. Additionally, Headhunter Two came complete with one long-range M-40A3 sniper rifle and, equally important, one long-range, PRC 119 radio. Once our prayer was over, I reminded my Marines and the newcomers to push water and to eat something every now and again to keep their electrolytes up for the lengthy fighting ahead of us. Final advice dispensed, the three squads dispersed and headed out of the firmbase on foot, moving as silently as possible through the sleeping city, each squad taking a different, predetermined route to its final objective. I walked with Leza and second.

The patrol into the city for once went smoothly. All squads made it to their objectives within a half hour and announced that they were proceeding to occupy their respective fighting positions. Bowen and his third squad were the farthest north, on a seven- or eight-story building just across Michigan from the cemetery that marked the center of Ramadi, the same one where Hes and part of third platoon had holed up two days earlier. The snipers moved with Bowen—since third squad would be on top of the tallest building with the best view of our zone, I wanted them to have the high-powered rifle and the high-powered optics of the Headhunters. A few blocks south of them were Leza and me with second, in the middle of the platoon sector, and two blocks south of us were Noriel and first.

We wanted to maintain the element of surprise for as long as possible, so, rather than move into a house, wake up the family, and use up a whole fire team guarding them, we had decided to try to climb the outside of the buildings. Squinting up at the second story of our tan, nondescript housing compound and its long, flat roof some twenty feet above us, Sergeant Leza sighed and turned to me.

"We gotta play Spider-Man again, huh, sir?" he whispered.

"Looks like it."

Leza nodded and spat on the ground, then ordered Raymond to scale the housing compound's outer wall while Leza, I, and another Marine braced the corporal from below. In anticipation of the all-day battle, everyone had loaded themselves up with excess ammo and water, so hoisting the muscular Raymond and his sixty extra pounds even a few feet off the ground was a task, to say the least. I have no idea how he managed to pull his way up to the top of the roof after we let go of him—all the weight lifting he did finally came in handy, I suppose—but somehow he did, and he hopped from that wall onto the flat roof of an offshoot of the house itself. The next thing I knew, Raymond was hauling me bodily up the compound's outer wall. Together we made our way across the narrow roof of the house out-cropping, scaled another small wall, clambered across the red-tiled roof of a pigeon coop, and dropped onto the roof proper.

I heaved a sigh of relief, and just as I did so, I heard a crashing sound and a loud thump. I whirled around. One of our SAW gunners had been crawl-ing across the pigeon coop when the tiles beneath him collapsed under the weight of a combat-loaded Marine and his machine gun. Pigeons flew everywhere, and an embarrassed, cursing lance corporal fought his way out of the cage's wire mesh. I flinched at the noise, but I couldn't help sup-pressing a small smile. Whoever the owner of the house was, he was certainly going to get a surprise later on that day when he came to the roof and found that his pigeons had been replaced by twelve heavily armed Marines.

After about fifteen minutes of graceless, sweaty climbing, the whole twelve-man squad finally made the building's top. I radioed Noriel. He and Bowen were both set up on the roofs of their respective buildings. Hearing that, I knelt down behind the waist-high parapet that ran along the edge of our roof and waited for the sun to rise and the day's action to begin. About an hour and a half later, the standard early morning calls to prayer rang through the city, and the Farouq search kicked off in earnest as the last chants faded away. We waited, keyed up for the first sounds of gunfire that would indicate the fight was beginning, but nothing happened. An hour later, the city was still deadly silent, and I started to wonder where the insurgents had gone and if we would see any action at all that day. Suddenly, Bowen called me over the 119.

"One-Actual, we've got a man out here with an AK. It looks like he's trying to hide it under his jacket. Over."

"Roger, One-Three. Where is he?"

"He's on Michigan, on the southern side, on the sidewalk. He's just standing there. Over."

"Is he wearing all black, or does he look like he's communicating with someone? Does it look like he's getting ready to attack? Over."

"Negative on the all black. Can't tell whether he's communicating. Other than that he's just standing there. Break. The Headhunters tell me they can take him out. What do you want us to do, One-Actual? Over."

I pondered the question for a bit. We had just come through two days of fierce fighting during which we had been attacked from all sides by enemies disguised as civilians and civilians volunteering as enemies. Nothing had happened just yet, but that didn't necessarily mean that nothing was planned or that attacks wouldn't break out soon enough. It was early, maybe the enemy was still staging; after all, the fighting of the previous two days had not begun until well after 9 AM on each, and the time was just now approaching 8. Maybe this man was a scout, or some sort of first mover. Maybe he was simply waiting, unaware of us watching him, for Marines to come around the corner so that he could unleash on them with his AK before hopping into a car and speeding away. If I hesitated to take action until the man opened fire and perhaps killed or wounded some of our comrades, then their blood would be squarely on my head.

But maybe the man was simply a local government official's bodyguard who was illegally carrying his AK-47 openly, or an off-duty police officer carrying his weapon out of uniform, something they had all been told repeatedly not to do but something that they routinely did anyway. Maybe he was just an unthinking civilian. There was some sort of punishment in place for carrying an AK-47 when one shouldn't, but, as far as I knew, that punishment wasn't death. This train of thought, or some jumbled, blurred version of it anyway, ran through my head for about thirty seconds. Then I made my decision.

"Kill him," I said into the radio handset.

No reply came, but less than a minute later I heard the long, low boom of the sniper rifle followed by three high, quick pops from an M-16. Then the report came back.

"One-Actual, this is One-Three. Be advised, Headhunters say that target is dead. I say again, target is dead. Break. He was hit low, through the liver, so we had to finish him with the 16. Break. Some civilians are loading the body into a car now. Over."

"Roger, One-Three. Tell the Headhunters good work. Out."

"Roger. Out."

Nothing else happened that day. The predicted attacks never materialized, and the battalion found a few minor weapons caches but nothing other than that—no insurgents, no terror cells, and no key civilian organizers. The only violence on April 8 was that which we had inflicted on the anonymous AK-wielding Iraqi, and I spent much of the rest of the day's downtime on the roof wondering if I had ordered the death of a potential attacker or an off-duty police officer.

A few months later, the battalion intelligence officer, Captain Towle, stopped by our base for a meeting with the CO. Afterward, he spotted me and came over to chat, and we talked for a bit, one intel officer to another, about recent events in Ramadi and elsewhere. The conversation was winding down when, out of nowhere, Towle said, "Oh, by the way, you remember that guy you had the snipers take out?"

"Yes," I replied hesitantly. It wasn't something that I thought about all that often, probably because I didn't particularly like to think about it.

"Well, we later figured out who he was. Turns out, he was the bodyguard of a notorious thug sheik with suspected ties to organized crime and terrorism. After you guys killed the bodyguard, the sheik got scared and left Ramadi. We haven't heard from him since." He nodded his approval as the words trailed off.

I nodded back but didn't bother to reply. It's one thing to shoot an insurgent who's trying to annihilate your men with a machine gun or a rocket, but it's something else altogether to order an unsuspecting man's death from two hundred yards away and then to follow the results dealt out in real time. Right then I didn't know how to tell the captain that the decision to kill that Iraqi didn't feel either right or wrong when I made it. It just felt hard either way, and the understanding now that the man was a known bad character still didn't really change my choice, its weight, or my feelings about it. It seemed a waste of time to try to explain that sometimes, on the front lines, there are no great options, just bad ones and worse ones, so you do what you can in the knowledge that you're dealing life and death no matter which way the decision swings. Then you live with the results and shut up about the whole thing.

TWENTY-ONE

"What do you think happens when I die, sir? I think now that I might."

The question came from Lance Corporal Williams, one of my youngest Marines. Joker One was now a million years away from early March of 2004, when we used to debate whether we'd ever be awarded the coveted Combat Action Ribbon. As we lived through our bloody April, Joker One and I had no idea of the larger picture in Iraq. We didn't know that a combined Marine/Army force was slugging it out with Shiite militias among the tombstones of the Imam Ali shrine in Najaf, or that our fellow Marines just down the road were bitterly disappointed after having their rolling invasion of Fallujah halted in midstride by civilian politicians. We didn't know that 134 coalition soldiers would be killed that month in Iraq. And we didn't know that many people were beginning to realize that the insurgency might be more than just a few isolated hotspots of violence. All we knew was that one morning we had woken up to find that our city had exploded around us, and that when the dust finally settled a few days later, many of our friends had simply ceased to be. Their deaths hadn't been easy; we knew because we'd recovered some of the bodies ourselves — Langhorst had been shot through the head, and Hallal, the Marine whose body had been found by Corporal Brown, had had his throat slit and his gear stripped. For the first time we understood that Golf Company wouldn't be returning home whole.

Friendly deaths weren't the only ones that affected us deeply, though. From the boy I had seen kicking in the courtyard to the woman carrying groceries that Hes had seen wither under machine gun fire, the citizens of Ramadi also paid a steep price in blood each time violence broke out. Civilians always suffer—it's an inescapable fact of war, it always has been—and you may very well have an intellectual understanding that these things happen. But until you see a boy with a red third eye, it's hard to fully understand what "collateral damage" really means. Now we knew. For us, then, April proved a turning point of a different type, a psychological one, and it profoundly changed the way we thought of ourselves, our situation, and the Iraqi citizens surrounding us.

For many members of Joker One, death took on a very real persona on April 6, and thereafter many of my Marines' questions mirrored Williams's: "Sir, what do you think happens when I die?"

There's an old saying that in war there are no atheists in the foxholes. It's not true. There are indeed atheists on the front lines—there were a few in my platoon—and even after the events of April some of them clung to their faith as steadfastly as did those of us who believed in God. A more accurate saying, then, would be something along the lines of "In war, no front-line soldier can ignore the inevitability of his own death." Most nineteen-year-olds have the luxury of avoiding such thoughts altogether, or at least of distracting themselves if the idea does arise, but, having watched some of their closest friends killed and maimed traumatically, my Marines no longer did. They couldn't reflect on tragedy for a time and then push it aside as a life of relative comfort in America slowly anesthetized them; there was no comfort, no America, no familiarity to take the edge off life. We still had six more months to go in our deployment, and now we feared that whenever we ventured outside the base, death would stalk us relentlessly.

In this psychologically wearing climate our pre-mission prayers took on an even more serious tenor, and became, I think, increasingly important to the men. I believe that, in some small way, the prayer helped my Marines focus their attention on the job at hand and on protecting one another, rather than on worries for their own death. The brief moment of togetherness gave all of us purpose in the face of chaos and random violence. To those who sought it, the prayer also provided some comfort that God was in control, that their lives had worth and meaning stemming from an absolute source.

And we needed meaning, because after April 6 we lost all faith in our tactics as emissaries of kindness and in the willingness of the people of Ramadi to help us. It would have been one thing, we thought, if, during the fighting, the citizens had simply cowered fearfully in their homes. Having been brutalized by Saddam Hussein for the past three decades, most had learned that survival meant never seeing evil, never volunteering for anything, keeping your mouth shut and your head down when neighbors mysteriously disappeared. So we would have understood if they had decided to stay at home and sit this one out, but they didn't.

Instead, despite our daily kindness, despite the relief projects, the money, the aid that we had already poured into the hospitals, despite the fact that we routinely altered our missions to make ourselves less safe in order to avoid offending them, the citizens of Ramadi had come out of their houses and actively tried to kill us. Multiple intelligence sources later told us that hundreds, if not thousands, of males ranging from teenagers to fifty-year-olds had grabbed their family's assault rifles, and, using the chaos caused by the hard-core insurgents as cover, they had taken potshots at U.S. forces as we passed by. Maybe it was one of these bullets that tumbled through Gentile's face and neck or through the back of Langhorst's head, we thought. And when these local Minutemen returned home, we were told, many of them had bragged of their exploits to their friends. For the younger ones, shooting at the Americans had apparently become a sort of coming-of-age ritual; for the older ones, it was probably a way to express anger and frustration with the misery of life in Iraq, a misery that, for better or worse, U.S. forces kicked off with the 2003 invasion. It also occurred to us that some, if not most, of them may have also felt humiliated by an occupying Western power carrying guns with impunity on their streets, or that others may have thought we were there as neoimperialists, come to steal their oil. Occasionally, I wondered what I would have done if the situation were reversed, and the Iraqi army had invaded Texas. I probably wouldn't have sat idly on the sidelines.

Making matters worse, the institutions that had formally agreed to assist us in our efforts, such as the local police or Ramadi's national guard battalion, not only abandoned their posts but also refused even to pass along the message that an attack was pending. It didn't take a trained official to figure out the signs of the assault; anyone could have done it—after all, on April 5, the insurgents had posted flyers in the marketplace and elsewhere, flyers that warned businesses not to open and residents to stay at home on the following day as attacks on U.S. forces were planned. It would have taken only two or three people out of 350,000 to warn us, but no one, to my knowledge, did. Again, there were some reasons for this—the insurgents would kill them if they found out, and we wouldn't—but we didn't know in early 2004 that for most Iraqis the decision to help coalition forces often meant death. All we knew was that no one seemed to be on our side.

So on April 6, 2004, the 2nd Battalion, 4th Marine Regiment flipped the switch of its default settings and settled firmly on kill. The insurgents, along with large swaths of the civilian population, had wanted a jihad, and a jihad we had given them. We had poured the full weight of our battalion's combat power into the city, and if the enemy decided to stand and fight again, then we would do the exact same thing, only more quickly. And if the citizens who refused to help us, or even to warn us, suffered during the fighting that ensued, then so be it. We never believed that we could win without their support, but if they wanted to help the enemy put bullets through our stomachs, then they had to be prepared to live with the consequences. Maybe they needed to fear us a little bit before they'd help us. Maybe kindness wasn't enough.

But though we stopped believing in open kindness as a sufficient condition for mission success, we never eschewed basic morality. No matter how much we despised our opponents for killing the weak and terrorizing the defenseless, and no matter how well their methods seemed to work, we could not, and would not, emulate them. We wouldn't fire artillery indiscriminately into the city (indeed, during our entire time in Ramadi, we never used this most devastating of weapons), or use our tanks and jets to level buildings hiding suspected insurgents and civilians alike. Even if it meant more risk, we'd go in and get them ourselves, using only whatever we could carry. We wouldn't beat or torture our prisoners, or routinely threaten uncooperative local families. We wouldn't descend to the level of Abu Ghraib.

There was undoubtedly quite a bit of altruism in our stance, but I believe that we were equally driven by hard practicality. From my first deployment, I knew that whatever we did during the day we had to live with at night, and whatever acts we committed in Iraq we had to carry home with us to America. I repeated this idea over and over to the men, reminding them that we had joined to protect those who couldn't protect themselves. If we interposed ourselves between an unarmed child and a thug with a machine gun and got wounded or killed in the process, so be it. That was our job, and we had all volunteered for it. If we opened fire randomly, or out of hatred and a desire to kill those who had refused to help us, then, quite frankly, we did not deserve the title of United States Marines, and we did not deserve to be able to meet our own eyes in the mirror.

We replaced open kindness, then, not with terror of our own but with fierce readiness. No longer would we smile and wave on patrol; no longer would we appear soft and weak. From that day forward, smiles vanished, wide eyes turned to slits, and both hands remained firmly on our weapons at all times—waving ceased altogether. If someone wanted to attack us, then they needed to see in our visages that we would attack right back, fiercely, unhesitatingly, and mercilessly. No more soft cake.

We also replaced our faith in the people of Ramadi with faith only in one another, with the idea that, no matter what happened and no matter what the circumstances, we would look after our comrades before looking after ourselves. Sometimes we talked about this concept, but most of the time it went unsaid; we just knew what we'd do for one another. If a man went down, another would be there to drag him away or to cover his body with his own; if someone started veering out of control, into the dangerous area of hatred and vengeance, the rest of us would come alongside to bring him back. And we replaced our belief in the idea that Ramadi would be made a stable bastion of democracy with the hope that we could somehow, someway, make life better for at least some of its residents.

Personally, I felt my own sense of mission shift, from stabilizing and transforming Ramadi to simply returning home with all of my men alive. Even though many of my Marines had grasped the possibility of their own deaths, I really hadn't at that point in time. There was no real reason underlying my avoidance of reality, no reason other than that death hadn't yet happened to me, to my platoon, to Joker One. There wasn't any particular skill or fortitude to this—we had simply been lucky. But I didn't know this at the time. Instead, I reasoned that if we had made it through the fierce fighting of April unscathed, then we could, and probably would, make it through anything and everything that the rest of the deployment would throw at us. After all, how could the fighting get worse than what we saw on April 6? After the battles of the Seventh and the Eighth, my platoon was, I believe, the only one in the battalion that had yet to suffer a single wound, and I took that respite as a clear sign that the prayers were working and that God would certainly bring all of us home safely.

I communicated these sentiments to Christy—we eventually got a satellite set up on the roof of the hangar bay and three laptop computers rigged for shaky Internet access—and she responded with cautious optimism. She was glad that no one was hurt, she said, but she reminded me that God wasn't a cosmic slot machine that came up sevens every time for the pious believer. He doesn't guarantee us health and prosperity, or even safety for your men in this life, she told me. All He guarantees you is your relationship with Him in the next. They were hard words of truth, to be sure, but ones spoken in love.

And I completely ignored them. They weren't what I wanted to hear. I didn't recognize yet that my steadfast dismissal of the idea of casualties in my platoon stemmed not so much from a belief about God's grace but from a refusal to consider the very real possibility that someday I might be responsible for the death and wounding of the men I loved so much. I still thought that I could have my cake and eat it, too, that I could accomplish the mission and bring everyone home unscathed. I thought that if I was just good enough, that if we just prayed hard enough, then my responsibility to make one of the worst choices in war—the mission or my men—just might be avoided.

However, there was something that I was right about, something that I understood well, and that something was that Christy didn't need to know about a change that took place in me after April 6. I didn't share it with her then, but ever after that day, some part of me took a grim satisfaction every time Joker One killed cleanly in the heat of battle. After a month of walking around Ramadi feeling as if we were more or less unsuspecting targets, it felt good to hit back strongly, to regain some of the initiative, to kill our enemies in large numbers. It felt good to know that someone else was doing the dying, too, and that if we were suffering, then maybe we could make our enemies suffer even more.

This realization hit me fully on April 9, when we were patrolling down Michigan during the normal morning route sweep. As I walked down the median in the middle of the road, I noticed huge pyramids of white bags stacked in front of the Saddam and al-Haq mosques. I had never seen anything like them before, so I looked closer. Each pyramid was roughly twenty bags long, five bags deep, and at least three stories high. I had no idea what they were, so I called Leza over the PRR.

"Hey, One-Two, what the hell are those stacked white things? Are they rice shipments for the mujahideen brethren in Fallujah or what?"

"No, sir, those stacks, they're body bags, sir. They're all body bags."

I pulled out my binos to check closer. Sure enough, some of the white bags were mottled with huge, rust-colored stains. There must have been hundreds of dead bodies in front of the mosques, I realized.

As the rest of the patrol wound its way past al-Haq, I found myself smiling.

espite the quiet of April 8 and 9, our enemies weren't altogether finished with large-scale operations. After the battalion's sweep through Ramadi, 2/4 received reports that although the hard-core insurgents had largely been driven out of the city proper by the fierce battles of the Sixth and the Seventh, sizable forces had re-formed in the rural areas just to its east. We would go and find them.

On April 10, then, I found myself rushing around among a long line of vehicles staged in our hangar bay. All three of my squads were staged near different trucks in preparation for an impending sweep of the area east of the city, and early in the morning, in the predawn dark, I was hurriedly giving my men one last check before we set off out of the base's gates. Halfway through the inspection, it dawned on me that words were ringing out in unison near each of the trucks. I stopped all that I was doing and stepped backward, away from the vehicles, until I could see my entire platoon. In three tight little groups, all of my Marines save one were kneeling with their heads bowed over weapons that hung down across their chests; the one standing Marine was praying the Twenty-third Psalm strongly, leading as everyone else muttered softly along with him. It was our platoon prayer, the one that

I had instituted as soon as we arrived in Iraq, the one that I had forgotten to pray with my men before they saddled up for the movement out. Now they were doing it themselves, and, at that exact moment, I knew for the first time that my individual Marines had become entirely Joker One. There are very few profoundly beautiful moments in war, and that morning was one of them.

I certainly needed it, because the rest of the day would be difficult. Like the last battalion-sized operation, we had been told to prepare for a twenty-four- to thirty-six-hour firefight, and this time we'd be starting the broad-brush sweeping mission with targeted raids on two to three houses per platoon. We had specific intelligence linking these places to insurgents, so all males inside the houses were to be detained and brought to a common company collection area, where a small guard detachment could watch over them while the rest of the platoons moved on with a general search of all compounds within our assigned sector. Every resource we had was to be expended on the operation; back at the Outpost, the cooks and mechanics would stand guard atop the walls of the base to free up more infantrymen.

Bronzi had decided to move our company to the target houses, some three miles away, on foot, so we woke early, at around 2 AM, and by 3:30 the company was preparing to set out on the patrol. For the first time, Joker One would carry a 60mm mortar, a weapon capable of leveling a small house, into combat. The battalion commander wanted each platoon to initiate its raids by firing several illumination rounds into the air from a launch site within one hundred meters of the target compounds. It was certainly an intimidating way to begin. The illum rounds would light up the predawn sky and make terrific noises, but, practically speaking, the battalion CO's wishes meant that one of my Marines had to carry a twenty-pound mortar tube (in addition to his other fifty pounds of gear) on his back for roughly two and a half miles.

Bolding had volunteered for the job. As it turned out, he was my platoon's senior mortarman, and ever since arriving in Kuwait, he had dropped all vestiges of his stateside immaturity. Now his easygoing manner, his constant self-sacrifice (he continued to help our brand-new Marines on their onerous working parties), and his trademark smile had made him one of the most well-liked Marines, if not the most, of Joker One. I still called Bolding "Lance Corporal," but, as he was the only African American in the platoon, the rest of the men, with typical affectionate irreverence, called him "Black Man." In the infantry, the measure of a man's respect among his peers is often directly proportional to the frequency with which an affectionate nickname is used ("The Ox," by the way, is an example of a nonaffectionate nickname). Using that as a rule of thumb, then, Bolding and "Gooch" Guzon were running neck-and-neck for the title of most-loved member of the platoon.

Furthermore, ever since we deployed, Bolding had proved himself so responsible that we had given him leadership over the other mortarmen— Henderson and Guzon. He was to command them when we needed mortars fired and to teach and mentor them at all times as a sort of secondary team leader. It was the sort of responsibility that we had taken away from Bolding earlier but that he now needed and deserved. Unsurprisingly, when the squad leaders had explained the mortar mission to their men, Bolding immediately asked to carry the heavy tube. He was the team leader, he said, so humping the pig was his job, plain and simple.

Shortly before the platoon stepped off on the mission, I paid him a short visit. "Hey, Bolding, how are you feeling?" I asked. Bolding was a stocky five-ten or so, solidly muscled with almost no fat on him, but carrying a mortar tube was no joke for anyone, regardless of how fit they were. When added to the rest of the gear we carried, the total load must have been roughly half of Bolding's 160 pounds.

He smiled widely back me.

"Hey, sir! I'm doin' fine. This mortar tube ain't shit, sir. Don't worry. Gooch, Henderson, and I'll get this thing taken care of. Just tell us when, sir, we'll fire those mortars."

He was still smiling, and his cheerful fortitude reminded me that whenever my men were asked to carry more, or to patrol one more time, or to fight unexpectedly yet again, they simply shrugged, complained, laughed, and then got it done come what may. A broad smile crept across my face, and I clapped Bolding on the shoulder and then walked up to the head of the patrol to wait for the order to head out. Joker One was at the head of the company patrol, and we were tasked to lead the way to the point where each platoon would peel off and hit its individual targets.

Roughly fifteen minutes later, an angry CO called me over the radio, demanding to know why we hadn't left. I was briefly nonplussed. We had been about to set off earlier, but I had been stopped by the Ox and told that the CO's radio was having trouble, that we needed to wait for him, and that the CO would call me when he was ready. I hadn't heard from either of them since.

Suddenly the radio squawked. It was Captain Bronzi, furious that we hadn't started moving yet. "What the hell is wrong with you, One? Every other company is already moving."

I bit back the urge to lash out in kind, acknowledged the command, and thirty seconds later the platoon was moving. We exited the firmbase via its little-used northwest exit and patrolled smoothly through the housing compounds that lay just to the Outpost's west. We made it all of one hundred meters before being stopped dead in our tracks by a thick, extensive barbed-wire fence that hadn't appeared on the photographic map. The entire company halted as we probed it for an opening, and, sure enough, one minute later the CO was back on the radio.

"One, Six. What the hell are you doing? Over."

I told him that we'd hit a fence, but it didn't seem to matter. He was still angry.

"Hey, One, we don't have any fucking time to waste. The rest of the companies are almost at their objectives. We're going to be the last ones to make it to ours. Hurry it up."

"Well, Six, that's because all of the other companies are driving, and we happen to be walking," I wanted to say, but once again I kept my mouth shut. Sure enough, less than a minute later, we found an opening through the wire and moved through quickly. The company stretched out from the firmbase, snaking rapidly in a twisting, half-mile-long column through the waist-high grass covering the open fields to the Outpost's north. Two-thirds of the way to our target houses, we hit another obstacle—a wide drainage ditch filled with waist-deep water. The ditch's slopes were steep and long, extending down for about ten feet before the water began. It would take forever for 140 Marines to wade the obstacle, but this time I had planned for our encounter. There were two main bridges over the water, and I had plotted Joker One's patrol route to arrive at the ditch about fifty meters south of the first bridge. Checking my GPS quickly, I knew we were somewhere very near the crossing point, so I halted the patrol, called the CO to let him know the situation, and then set out with Mahardy to find the bridge. Yet again, within thirty seconds, the CO was back on the radio.

"One, Six. Why aren't we moving yet? Over."

I was getting exasperated. "Six, One, be advised that the bridge isn't exactly where we thought it was, but we should be close. I'm looking for it now. Break. We should be moving again within five minutes. Over."

"You have one minute, One. After that, you are going fucking swimming through that ditch. We have got to move. Every other company is at its objective already. Out."

Hearing that, I had to restrain myself from losing my temper altogether and demanding that the CO come up and swim through the ditch himself to see how well that tactic would work out for us. Ultimately, though, his impatience didn't matter because shortly after his call Mahardy found the bridge, and Joker One moved out again, the rest of the company in tow.

Once everyone had made it across, the CO ordered all platoons to run the final half mile or so to our objectives, so the whole company finished the movement in a tripping, cursing half-run, half-fall over rough, broken ground in the dead of night. At least one Marine in Joker Two twisted his ankle so badly that he was rendered useless for the remainder of the operation. In fact, he had to be medevaced. However, the rest of us made it to our targets reasonably quickly, and, somehow, Bolding and his mortar tube managed to keep up with the rest of us. The illumination launches went off without a hitch and reasonably on time, and with them we began to hit our target houses.

By then, most raids had become fairly standard, fairly routine affairs, with none of the excitement and flair of that very first one, in large part because our targets from then on out had all been more or less the same. Never again did we seek out very specific, very unusual Sudanese terrorists. Instead, our target descriptions mostly revolved around the ubiquitous, generic Arab male: "dark hair, dark skin, mustache or beard, medium height, medium build; age between twenty and fifty; may be named Mohammed or Muhamed; single-source intelligence ties him/his cousins to local insurgent groups." Perhaps one time out of every ten, we got grainy, photocopied pictures of the suspected targets. The pictures' usefulness was questionable at best and misleading at worst.

This morning was no different than usual, and Noriel and Leza were ploddingly rounding up suspects from two different houses when Bowen, leader of our cordon force, called me excitedly over the PRR. A fugitive had just slipped out of his cordon by jumping from one house roof to another. Startled, I looked up the street just in time to see a man emerge from an alleyway three blocks away and take off down the road at a dead run. Teague and I darted after him, but, weighed down by our gear as we were, the suspect quickly widened his lead on us. We were losing him. Teague called me, panting, on his PRR.

"Sir . . . Do you want . . . me to shoot him?"

"Negative . . . Let him go." I wasn't prepared to shoot a fleeing, unarmed man in the back when all that we had to go on were single-source suspicions that someone in the house from which he had emerged was, perhaps, connected with insurgents. If, back in America, some unknown force had come for me in the dead of night, I too would probably have fled. And in America, the police didn't have a long and storied history of torturing or disappearing those whom they snatched. Many Iraqis still didn't understand that American detentions weren't like those of Saddam, and most of them reasoned that if someone disappeared in the middle of the night, then it was a fair bet they'd never be seen again in this life.

Five seconds later, the man took a quick right down another dark alleyway, and we lost him. Winded, Teague and I returned to the compounds to find that Leza and Noriel had consolidated all of our military-age male detainees in a single room, zip-tied their hands, and checked them against our photographs. As always, the women and children remained free, but a few Marines kept a watchful eye on them nonetheless. No weapons, explosives, or insurgent propaganda had been found—the houses were clean, and no one could tell from the grainy pictures we had been given whether the men inside were definite matches with our targets. They did fit the written descriptions, but, then again, so did 70 percent of all Iraqi males. Also like 70 percent of all Iraqi males, none of our targets had proper *hawilah*, identification papers. I called the CO, explained the situation, and received an order to bring all detainees to the company consolidation point, a housing compound at the end of the block. Before I took all of the men away, I wanted to explain to the frightened women and children that their husbands and fathers would probably only be taken for a little while, but without a translator, it was useless. So I didn't say anything. I just moved out.

We moved quickly, and half an hour later, all detainees were sitting, blindfolded and with their hands bound behind them, in a circle in the middle of a large, fenced yard, the company collection point. No sooner had we settled the detainees than fierce gunfire broke out to our south. Porcupine and Weapons had hit a few insurgent ambushes, and they were slugging their way through them tenaciously. Half a mile north, though, Golf Company remained untouched. With the palm trees waving idly above our heads and the Euphrates burbling placidly fifty feet away, our sister companies' fighting seemed distant and unreal. Half a mile was a world away until Carson suddenly bellowed.

"Holy shit! That hurts like a sonofabitch." Every Marine inside the compound turned to look at him as he took off his helmet and turned it over, examining it closely. Then, proudly, Carson brandished it aloft, displaying a long, shallow furrow running along the length of the top right side. Somehow, someway, a stray round from the distant firefight had penetrated our world and smacked Carson's helmet.

"Check it out, I just got hit in the head! Man, that hurts." Grinning and shaking his head, the giant Carson put his helmet back on. Standing next to him, half a head shorter apiece, Niles and Ott stared up at their team leader with wide eyes and open mouths. Jarred out of my reverie, I walked outside the compound to find out if Joker One needed to press south into the fight.

As soon as I made it past the gates, a disturbing sight greeted my eyes. We had raided consecutive housing compounds all along a raised dirt road; now all the wives and daughters of the men we had just taken had assembled on that road, heedless of the gunfire to the south. At first they simply stood there, holding one another's hands and staring numbly at us. Then a large seven-ton truck pulled up, and headquarters Marines started loading the bound and blindfolded prisoners into the back like so many boxes.

Seeing this, the small circles of women erupted with one of the most piercing displays of despair I have ever witnessed. Ululating wails rent the air, and, as the fervor built, the adult women started bending down to pick up the dust of the road and rub it through their hair, on their faces, in their eyes. They slapped themselves across their cheeks, or beat themselves about their heads and necks with their fists. They ripped off pieces of their clothes and stomped on them. The little girls clung to their mothers' robes, either sobbing or simply standing with their heads buried amid the voluminous folds.

I was unnerved, and so were my Marines. Yebra and Leza darted quick glances at each other; Niles and Ott stopped watching their prisoners and honed in on the mourners, completely mesmerized. Carson chivied them back to their tasks, but even he had trouble keeping his eyes off the screaming women and the crying girls. Soon the seven-ton trundled off, and the mourners, watching it leave, finally started to calm a bit.

The truck had barely gone a hundred yards when it hit a ditch and flipped over on its side, spilling Marines and prisoners alike out of its bed, and rolling over a few of them. I ran to the accident site, as did Docs Smith and Camacho, and they immediately got to work triaging and treating both injured prisoners and Marines. The docs made no distinction—the most seriously injured, regardless of nationality, were treated first. Of our forces, a squad leader from fourth platoon had a badly broken arm, and a few other Marines had other major and minor cuts and bruises. One of my men had literally jumped out of the turret as the truck rolled over, and thus he had avoided being crushed to death.

Our bound prisoners, however, had no such recourse. Several of them had been crushed underneath the vehicle as it rolled, and both of my docs were working on a couple of the worst ones. I managed to catch Camacho's eye, and he glanced down at his patient, then looked up and shook his head at me. I turned away, saddened.

Behind us, the wailing redoubled. I looked over at the mourners; a few of the women were now lying motionless on the ground. Prior to the truck rollover, and in spite of my post–April 6 resolve, I had wanted to run up to them and explain that it was all right, that we weren't Saddam, that their husbands would probably be taken in for questioning and then returned unharmed. Abu Ghraib notwithstanding, no one in our company or battalion deliberately mistreated prisoners. I didn't really know whether our detainees were bad or good—for all I knew, they could have been notorious insurgent leaders—but none of our hearts were so hardened as to be totally untouched by the deep, very real grief standing there on that miserable, dusty road.

Now, with our vehicle lying pitifully on its side and some of our detainees bleeding in a filthy drainage ditch in the middle of nowhere, I wanted so badly to tell the weeping women that I was sorry, that we didn't mean to hurt any of our prisoners, that we made mistakes just like everybody else but that unlike everybody else, our mistakes were life and death — sometimes life for us and death for others, and sometimes death for us and life for others. Today an eighteen-year-old truck driver — a random young Marine from the battalion's truck detachment — had simply misjudged the steepness of the road when he made his turn, and death and wounding, on both sides, had been the result.

I wanted to bend down and tell the little girls that our people had also been badly hurt, that none of us really wanted to separate them from their dads, that somehow every decision that we made in this crazy country always seemed a difficult choice between bad and worse and that nothing ever turned out quite the way we hoped. I couldn't do anything to help them, though. I couldn't even speak to them in their language.

So I turned my back on the crowd and did the only thing I felt I could: I started talking to my nearby Marines. They felt as bad as, if not worse than, I did, and I tried to answer all of their questions as honestly as possible — "What just happened, sir?" "Are the prisoners gonna be okay?" "What do we do for their families?" More often than not, though, I found myself saying something along the lines of "I just don't know. I wish I did, but I don't, and I won't tell you that I do. All that I do know is that all we can do is our best. Keep your head up. I'm very proud of you."

Some eight hours later, we returned to the base. Although the projected fighting hadn't materialized for us, Echo and Weapons Company had seen heavy combat. Eventually, a fierce counterattack killed or dissipated the last remaining insurgent holdouts, but ten more of our comrades lost their lives in the firestorm of the initial ambushes. Yet again, more of our friends didn't return home from the mission.

That evening, I lay awake all night long. Insomnia had hit before, but usually it allowed at least a few hours of sleep before dawn.

TWENTY-THREE

After the intense combat of early April, the insurgent presence in Ramadi declined dramatically, partly because our enemies lost so many fighters during the fierce, toe-to-toe battles and partly because many of the most committed terrorists had relocated to Fallujah after the Marine offensive there was halted on April 9. That embattled, cordoned-off city had become the front line in the war against America, so a good deal of the most dedicated insurgents left Ramadi for her smaller sister thirty miles east. During the last two weeks of April, the attacks on Golf Company nearly ceased. Ramadi was eerily quiet.

I enjoyed the calm, but I suspected that it wouldn't last. We still had five months left in our deployment—five more months of constant fighting and five more months away from our wives and children. And all of the Joker platoon commanders had five more months of the lonely, ever-present burden of combat leadership, of the constant knowledge that forty lives rested on our every decision, of the wound-tight tension of never being able to really share our responsibilities with anyone, and of the sleepless nights that came with all these things.

So, during those few quiet weeks of late April, I visited the platoon's house as often as my duties and officer-enlisted propriety permitted. Judging how much time to spend around the men, especially in the place where they live, is always a tricky business for a young officer. Spend too much time with them and you risk descending into micromanagement, learning things that you just don't need to know, or convincing the men that you are their friend. Spend too much time away from them and you risk losing touch with their day-to-day concerns, becoming aloof and disconnected, and convincing the men that you don't really care because you don't sacrifice you own personal time. So I walked the thin line between too much and too little and checked on the men every time I could. Every time, I found something different, for, other than knowing that some would be watching movies and some would be writing letters, there was absolutely no way to predict what my Marines would be doing in their downtime. Nearly always, I loved the surprises.

One morning, I walked into the platoon's courtyard and found, to my immense surprise, that the entire 300-square-foot space was taken up by a plastic children's wading pool filled with water. Inside it were the extraordinarily pale and skinny Niles and Mahardy—with the exception of their sunburned faces and hands, they looked a lot like long, lean grubworms. Sitting around the pool, sunning themselves as if they were on the beach, were the stocky, tan or black Guzon, Bolding, and Raymond. Bared to the waist, Noriel was just walking out of his room when he spotted me and the obvious shock on my face. Of course, he started grinning from ear to ear.

I was speechless. We hadn't showered for at least a week, and somehow my Marines had scavenged not only a pool but also the precious water with which to fill it. As it turned out, George the translator had bought the pool at their request during his last foray into town, and Teague had simply pulled over the Iraqi water-delivery truck on its way out of our base and asked it to pump its remaining cargo into our courtyard. (By now, the Ox had engaged an Iraqi company to fill up the two plastic fifty-gallon water reservoirs installed by Achmed the contractor. Thus Golf Company could all take showers roughly once every week.) The scheme had succeeded brilliantly, and now I had multiple Marines crammed into a child's pool, brown faces and pale bodies pointed up at the sun.

For a minute I didn't know what to say. Having a wading pool in the courtyard was not only a gigantic waste of water but also a recipe for injury—

the more time the Marines spent without a solid roof over their heads, the higher the probability that they would be hit by one of the mortars that in mid-April had begun falling in and around the Outpost nearly every day. I looked at the men. Mahardy was trying to dunk another Marine, Lance Corporal Kepler. Niles was splashing Raymond, who was lying on his sleeping mat in the sun, trying to get a tan. I sighed. Maybe I should have made my Marines dump the water and ditch the pool, but I didn't have the heart. There were so few things that they could truly enjoy over here, and if the pool was one of them, then I figured I'd let them have their fun for at least a few hours. Once the water became intolerably unsanitary, we'd dump it.

The following day, I walked into the courtyard unexpectedly and found Corporal Walter parading around it wearing only a pair of pantyhose and the little green hot pants, which he had somehow turned into a thong. I immediately about-faced, walked back out, and hoped that no one had seen me. I had no idea how Walter had managed to get his hands on a pair of panty hose, and I had no plans to find out. I didn't need to know everything that the Marines were doing in their spare time.

Two days later, I warily peered around the courtyard's entrance. Inside, I saw nine Marines trooping back and forth, all shirtless and covered in blood. I nearly fainted. I rushed through the entrance with my head on a swivel, frantically trying to get a handle on the situation. Noticing my sudden arrival, Bowen ran over, grinning like the Cheshire cat, and I accosted him with nervous questions. Why was everyone bleeding so badly? Why were empty IV bags everywhere? Why did the Marines all look so happy? Why, damn it? Answer me!

As I wound anxiously down, Bowen simply widened his grin and explained that all of the blood, all of the ghastly mess inside our courtyard, was just a part of some IV training he had set up with the docs. It was getting hotter, he said, and everyone needed to be prepared to rehydrate everyone else in the quickest and most effective manner possible: electrolytes straight to the bloodstream. Hearing this explanation, I stared wordlessly at Bowen and at the rest of the Marines, and I marveled. They had spent the last two hours alternately insulting one another and then jabbing one another with needles until everyone bled from at least four different places, all so that they would be better prepared to keep one another alive during combat.

By the day's end, all of my men were covered in blood and smiling.

TWENTY-FOUR

A s it turned out, my absolute best day in Iraq happened during that fleeting late April calm. The events took place mainly in and around Joker One's house, although the day did begin somewhat inauspiciously outside the Combat Outpost. In fact, the day began with Joker One being blown up on a mission. It was April 28, and we had just completed the morning's route sweep and were heading back to the Outpost in five unarmored Humvees (after early April, ammunition, including much-needed grenades, equipment, and vehicles had been showered on us from above). About halfway through the Farouq district, the second one, Bolding's Humvee, disappeared in fire and smoke as an IED exploded directly underneath it.

When I glanced back, shocked at the explosion, I once again believed that I had just lost five men, but soon enough the wounded vehicle crawled forward out of the all-enveloping dust cloud. Despite being unable to feel his left arm, Bolding had managed to drive the vehicle out of the kill zone, and, half an hour later, the entire convoy made it back to the Outpost. As soon as we parked the vehicles, Bolding excused himself to go to the medical station. It was only then that I found out that the blast concussion had knocked out the feeling over much of the left half of his body. Later, in the doctor's room, I offered Bolding the rest of the day, or even the week off, but he tactfully refused. Smiling broadly, he informed me that he just wanted to get back to the squad—according to him, that would be all the healing he needed.

Shaking my head, I wandered out of the medical office, once again amazed by my Marines. Were I in Bolding's shoes, I probably would have taken the day off, and you could be damn sure that I wouldn't be smiling if I was still having trouble moving my arm.

A few hours later, I spotted Noriel walking by the hangar bay's entrance carrying two shovels and a pick. Very unusual. By now, I had learned the hard way that nearly all of the unusuals, no matter how small, needed to be at least cursorily checked lest weirdness run too rampant among Marines with too much downtime between missions. I called out to him.

"Hey, Noriel, what are you doing with those things?"

"Oh, hey, sir. Staff Sergeant says every Marines has got to fill twenty sandbags apiece. The ground, he is hard, sir, so I got the platoon some picks and shovels. It's hard to dig with our little e-tools."

"Every Marine in the platoon has to fill twenty bags?"

"Oh yes, sir."

"Okay, very well, make sure that you have twenty empty bags for me. I'll be over shortly to fill them."

Noriel smiled. "Roger that, sir," he said. Then he trooped back to the house with his armful of gear.

I hadn't really thought through the decision to dig with my men when I made it. In my mind, it was simple: The whole platoon had a dirty, menial task to perform, which meant that I had a dirty, menial task to perform with them. Maybe I should have considered the choice a bit more, though. Maybe the digging somehow diminished my status as an officer; maybe I should have had better things to do with my time than hack cursingly away at the rock-hard earth under the scorching desert sun. Maybe I violated an earlier admonition from the Gunny to be a lieutenant doing a lieutenant's work, not a lieutenant doing a lance corporal's work. There are a lot of maybes, things that might have happened had I decided to allocate my time somewhat differently on that day, but one thing remains certain: The decision to spend the afternoon sweating mindlessly with my Marines—getting blisters on my palms from the stupid shovel handle and a piercing dehydration headache from the stupid desert sun—gave me my best day in Iraq.

About twenty minutes after my conversation with Noriel, I walked over to the platoon's house and found my Marines already digging. Just five feet away from our courtyard, a large mound of soft, loose dirt had been piled high by some sort of construction vehicle. To my surprise, the Marines were completely ignoring this ready-made source of sandbag-filling material, instead laboriously chipping their own dirt out of the hard desert ground. Puzzled, I queried my platoon sergeant, who, when I arrived, had been smoking a cigarette and "supervising" the Marines' efforts.

"Hey, Staff Sergeant," I said. "Why are we bothering to scrape our own dirt out of the ground? Why not just scoop it out of this nice pile here and fill up as many sandbags as we can until it runs out? Then, if we need to, we can fill up the rest with the dirt we dig up ourselves."

"Oh no, sir," came the prompt reply. "That's the Gunny's dirt. We can't use it."

I stared blankly at Staff Sergeant for a few seconds. The connection between the Gunny and a pile of dirt escaped me, so he clarified.

"Sir, the Gunny told me a couple of days ago that that dirt is his and that he may use it for something in the future. We can't take it from him, sir. We just can't." Staff Sergeant looked horrified at the very thought of touching the Gunny's precious dirt.

By now, most of the Marines had either stopped digging altogether or were just going through the motions, looking at us out of the corners of their eyes and waiting to see how the conversation between Staff Sergeant and I played out. I thought briefly about the Gunny and his dirt, then decided to assume that he must certainly have been saving that dirt for us to use for sandbag filling. If I was wrong, the Gunny might correct me, respectfully, of course, but if he really didn't care that much (and I suspected that he didn't), then we could save maybe an hour or two of scraping away at the unyielding desert floor. Normally, I didn't like to go against Staff Sergeant in front of the Marines, but this time I didn't see any graceful way to change course.

I glanced around—the Gunny was nowhere in sight—so I turned back and smiled wryly at my platoon sergeant. "Well, Staff Sergeant, I didn't know that the Gunny was into real estate speculation in Iraq, so why don't we assume that he's been saving this dirt for us. If the Gunny asks you any questions, just tell him that I ordered the Marines to use it and send him my way."

Having made my little statement, I propped my M-16 up against the courtyard wall, pulled off my cammie blouse, and, dressed ridiculously in boots, pants, undershirt, and a floppy camouflage sombrero, I took a big scoop out of that beautiful, soft dirt mound. The Marines started cheering, really, and poor Staff Sergeant stared helplessly at me as everyone else attacked the dirt with gusto. Just a bit later, someone rustled up a pair of tinny little speakers and a CD player, and Niles assumed DJ duties and started blasting horrible punk music as loud as the pathetic speakers would allow. A digging party had begun.

Shovels and picks rose and fell in no particular rhythm as the Marines started arguing fiercely among one another as to which bands truly qualified as punk. Mahardy and his best friend, Lance Corporal Waters, fell into a heated discussion on the topic, but Waters cut the debate short by shouting "I'll show you punk" and then punching Mahardy squarely in his solar plexus. The whole platoon laughed uproariously at this clever rhetorical device. When, after at least half a minute, he finally straightened up, a hurt and embarrassed Mahardy announced, "God, Waters, you suck. I hate you so much. You're so stupid," before sulking his way back inside the house. The platoon cheered Waters's victorious debate. Ten minutes later, Mahardy reappeared, smoking, of course, and resumed chatting with Waters. With no words of apology exchanged, the two had seamlessly transitioned back to being best friends.

A few CDs later, everyone grew tired of Niles's happy punk music, and he was forced to abdicate the DJ throne amid universal protest featuring such delicate comments as "What the hell is wrong with you, Niles?" "You suck, Niles, and your music sucks, too," "I can't believe they let you be a Marine, punk-boy," and "Give up the CD player before I beat you" (Carson). I think the last one sealed it.

Ott quickly took his teammate's place and started booming out some hip-hop, much to the delight of most of the platoon. After a few songs, a fierce chant swelled among the Marines until it reached nearly the volume of a small roar. At first I had trouble understanding it, but the word soon became intelligible (if entirely unilluminating):

"*Gooch! Gooch! Gooch! Gooch! Gooch!*"

I had no idea what was going on. As I looked around for some explanation, I noticed that every one of my guys had stopped digging and was now staring expectantly at the exit from the house's courtyard. I leaned on my pick and waited. I had no idea what was coming, but I did know that whatever it was, it was bound to be interesting.

I wasn't disappointed. Within a few minutes, a filthy, dirt-covered, now Private Guzon strode out of the house, dressed in his full combat gear and carrying a liter bottle of water in the right cargo pocket of his pants. The whole platoon erupted into cheers. From his DJ's perch, Ott announced, "This song's for you, Gooch. Make it happen."

A smooth, heavy bass line started thumping out, and Guzon began slowly turning around, shimmying his shoulders, wiggling his butt, winking suggestively at the rapt crowd. The Marines howled. Off came the Kevlar helmet. Guzon twirled it above his head, then flung it into the crowd. Someone caught it on their chest with a loud thump. The flak jacket was next, shed oh-so-slowly off the back as Guzon looked over his right shoulder at us and gyrated his hips. By now the rest of the Marines had worked themselves into a frenzy of catcalls. If any of us had had dollar bills, we would have thrown them at him.

The camouflage blouse was next, and trousers and undershirt followed. Gleeful Marines caught each item of clothing as it was tossed into the crowd. Guzon was now wearing only the green hot pants and a pair of combat boots. I had never seen such a ridiculous sight in my life, but I was laughing so hard that my stomach had started hurting. The best, however, was yet to come. Just when I thought that he had to be finished, Guzon reached down and picked up the water bottle that he had carefully staged before beginning his little routine. The crowd went silent as Guzon unscrewed the cap, lifted the bottle high above his head, and proceeded to slowly pour the water over his face and onto his chest, running his free hand through his hair and sighing in mock ecstasy. The Marines exploded into cheers, applause, and unsolicited commentary.

"Damn, Guzon, that's the hottest thing I've ever seen. Do it again."

"You're a sick man, Guzon. You're sick. Sonofabitch, that was cool."

"I feel dirty. Somebody give me some water." And so on.

However, the act was apparently a one-show engagement, and no amount of peer pressure, enticement, or threat of imminent bodily harm could motivate Guzon to perform again. He put his pants back on, and I noticed that the dirt and dried sweat now ran in little tigerlike streaks all over his torso. It had been days since we had had any shower water.

A few hours later, all the required sandbags had been filled, and the Marines and I retired to our respective living quarters to escape the oppressive heat. I don't know exactly why, but for some reason, digging mindlessly until my hands were bloody, watching my Marines physically assault one another, and applauding wildly as a filthy, five-foot-four private performed a risqué striptease had all somehow combined to create the best day I ever had in Iraq. Maybe it had something to do with admiration and envy for the way a group of nineteen-year-olds pushed aside the fact that they had been blown up not four hours ago (and the fact that they had five more months of explosions to go) and took sheer, unadulterated joy in the moment they had been given. Maybe while I was digging with them, that joy had touched me, and I had, for a time, been able to forget about the weight of all of their lives on my shoulders.

That evening as I lay awake in bed, I was smiling contentedly.

TWENTY-FIVE

y joy didn't last.

On May 13, Niles was shot in the arm. After an all-night mission, second squad had left one of our breach kits—backpacks full of specialized, hard-to-replace tools—at their observation post, located in the middle of the city. We hadn't noticed the kit's absence until we returned to the Outpost, and, when we did, I was furious with Leza and determined to punish his squad. I sent them back into the city to retrieve the missing kit. On the way there, a group of armed men sprayed AK fire at the lone foot-mobile squad. Niles was shot right through the top of his M-16, which deflected the bullet away from his chest and across his arm. It wasn't much more than a flesh wound, and he was shaking the docs off him when I showed up with the medevac, but I was still upset with my men and myself. Our first wound, caused because we were forgetful and because I sent one squad into the city when I should have sent the platoon.

Five days later, the platoon was out on Michigan again, but this time we weren't protecting the road and hunting IEDs or their makers. Instead, we were executing Operation Devil Siphon, another of the many Coalition Provisional Authority–driven tasks that probably made sense to the twenty-six-year-old political appointee who drafted it in the safety of the Green Zone but that seemed completely illogical to those of us tasked with its execution. The theory behind Devil Siphon was fairly straightforward: The legitimacy of the provincial government was being undermined by a robust black market that had sprung up to distribute gasoline, so coalition forces needed to dismantle said market because the Iraqi police were incapable of doing it themselves. In Ramadi, control of all official fuel stations seemed to be firmly in the hands of the government, and the twin levers of fuel supply and gasoline prices were potent ones indeed. Anything that diminished the power of those levers or that made the appointed government look incompetent probably seemed to be a threat worth eliminating in the eyes of our overseers in Baghdad.

However, like everything else in Iraq, sweat-soaked, blood-soaked reality was more complex than disconnected theory composed neatly in air-conditioned rooms. The vast majority of downtown Ramadi was supplied by a single gas station with restricted hours, and whenever we patrolled past it, lines of cars stretched for hundreds of meters along Michigan, waiting for hours with their engines turned off for just a brief chance at the pump. In response to the overwhelming demand and sharply restricted supply, dozens of local entrepreneurs had set up shop along the highway, selling gasoline (cut with varying amounts of water) out of plastic jerry cans, empty glass Pepsi bottles, and any other container they could scavenge. Though the sales were technically illegal, these newly minted businessmen were serving a serious need, and, it could be argued, helping to keep the overall level of popular resentment down. To those of us routinely subjected to the glares of stranded motorists, the rationale behind eliminating what seemed a fairly robust safety valve was suspect, to say the least, and threatened to alienate the locals further. Besides, for every jerry can we slashed, five more took its place immediately. Nevertheless, we had our orders (and they weren't immoral or illegal, just illogical), so we were constantly trying to disrupt the operations of anyone selling substantial quantities of black-market gasoline.

On May 22, we spotted a particularly egregious offender. At the time, the whole platoon was rumbling east down Michigan after having inspected the one official fuel station in the heart of the souk. As the Ox was in charge of contracting and other inspection work for the company, he had come along with us, bringing with him George and a radio operator. Now the Ox was traveling in our second vehicle, along with Leza and Raymond. As the convoy neared the Saddam mosque, Leza called over the PRR.

"Sir, we just spotted a guy selling a lot of gas right in that little field next to the mosque. Do you want us to get him?"

"Yeah, have Raymond jump out and take care of business." Our Devil Siphon plan called for Raymond and his team to leap out of our vehicles, hustle over to whatever target we had spotted, and quickly slit or otherwise irreparably damage the fuel containers. The rest of us would wait near the Humvees—the idea was to be maximally time-efficient so that our stationary convoy didn't present too much of a target and so that the truly important missions, like patrolling, could continue with a minimum of Devil Siphon–imposed interruption.

The whole convoy screeched to a halt in a nearly five-hundred-meter-long line along the south side of Michigan, and Raymond's team launched themselves out of the back of their Humvee without bothering to wait for it to come to a halt. Unbeknownst to me, the Ox also decided to launch himself on the quick fuel-spill mission. As the convoy ground to a complete halt, Raymond's team, augmented by the Ox and his radio operator, sprinted as fast as possible across Michigan. Quickly, they closed the distance on the fuel salesman and his assistant, a male relative who appeared to be in his early teens, perhaps a son or a cousin. It didn't take long for both of them to catch sight of the six armed Marines charging across the busy four-lane highway, and it took even less time for the salesman to realize that he was the intended target. As Raymond's team jumped the concrete median divider, the salesman bolted for a nearby yellow-and-orange taxi that was parked near his enterprise, leaving the teenage male to fend for himself.

By the time the Ox and Raymond made it completely across the street, the salesman had already revved up his car. As the Marines closed, he suddenly bolted with it, nearly running them over as the taxi fishtailed out onto Michigan. However, the street was jam-packed with cars, and the fleeing salesman ground to a halt before traveling even one block. Raymond's team pursued on foot, so the salesman pulled his car up onto the sidewalk and started driving crazily along it at what must have been well over thirty miles per hour. Shouting civilians frantically dived left and right as the vehicle upended a few tea tables that had been set up on the sidewalk. The taxi may even have hit a few of the pedestrians, and as the vehicle continued its crazy course down the sidewalk, the driver gained at least a block of distance between himself and Raymond's team.

As the gap widened, the Ox yelled out an order, the substance of which we will never know. He (and his radio operator) claimed that he screamed out "Stop him!" to get the Marines at the back end of our convoy to take action, but, in all the confusion—the madly honking horns, the screaming citizens, the helmets flopping back and forth across the Marines' heads, the fogged glasses—Raymond and the other three Marines heard "Shoot him!" from their superior officer.

So they knelt and began firing at the rear window of the vehicle, imploding it. The car continued driving, and as it passed the last two vehicles of our convoy, the Marines there opened fire as well. They hadn't heard the order, but as soon as Raymond's gunshots rang out, they had reasonably assumed that this taxi, like so many other taxis in recent days, had just performed a drive-by shooting on our convoy. Staff Sergeant put three well-aimed rounds through the driver's side window as the car hurtled past him on the sidewalk. Others hammered the door with their SAWs. Just after it passed our final Humvee, the taxi veered off the sidewalk, cut across two lanes of traffic, and slammed head-on into the concrete median divider, where it came to an immediate, jarring halt. The driver's side window was spiderwebbed and spattered with darkness.

Nearly four hundred meters away, at the front of the column, I saw none of this. Instead, I heard a few quick M-16 pops, then the swelling roar of fully automatic weapons fire. Immediately, I assumed that our stationary convoy had just been ambushed—Flowers and fourth platoon had been hit at this exact same spot yesterday by roughly ten men armed with rockets and small arms. I started running along the convoy toward the sound of the fire, and I mentally braced myself for the horrible double explosions of armed RPGs.

They never came. Instead, silence descended as all the horns shut off and most of the pedestrians disappeared from the sidewalk. Bewildered, I arrived at the crash site to find the salesman dangling upside down out of the open driver's side door. Docs Smith and Camacho were tugging at him, trying to pull him out of the vehicle to provide first aid. The man's eyes were closed and his tongue hung out of the side of his mouth, clenched firmly between his teeth. Seeing him, my first thought was that the cabdriver looked just like the deer that we used to shoot back home. My next thought was, "What have we just done?"

At the time, I knew nothing of the Ox's order, and I had no idea why the platoon had opened fire. All I knew was that an apparently unarmed Iraqi was now hanging out of the door of his car, breathing shallowly with ropy streams of mucus, spittle, and blood dangling from his mouth and nose.

The docs wrestled the unconscious man out of the car and went to work, but he was bleeding pretty heavily from the midsection, and a dark pool quickly formed on the pavement beneath him. Meanwhile, I set the squad leaders, all of whom were as confused as I, to assembling a 360-degree cordon around the area. The pedestrians were returning, and they were eagerly gathering in large numbers around the macabre scene. As soon as the cordon was set, I moved back to the docs, and this time it was Smith who looked up at me and shook his head. I nodded back at him and instructed both docs to keep working nonetheless, to try keep the man alive until an ambulance showed up. We weren't allowed to medevac Iraqis ourselves — scarce American medical resources had to be husbanded carefully for American use — but Iraqi emergency care vehicles, we had learned, usually showed up quickly at the scene of any shooting.

I was still confused about what had caused us to open fire, so I started walking the platoon's perimeter to find Raymond and his team. Halfway through the circuit, an agitated Ox approached me and said something roughly approximating the following:

"Hey, One, I never told them to open fire. Someone gave an order to start shooting, but it wasn't me. You've gotta believe me. I have no idea why they started shooting. I never told them anything. It was someone else. Someone else told them to open fire."

I stared at the Ox uncomprehendingly. I still didn't know of his impromptu foray out with Raymond, and I had no idea why the company XO would have been ordering my men to be doing anything, let alone opening fire, from the back of the Humvee where I assumed he had been. Why was the Ox so vehemently defending himself? Puzzled, I blinked at him and moved on. He was interrupting me; I wanted to begin my investigation of the sequence of events with Raymond, not the Ox.

Just a little bit farther down, I found the Marine I was looking for and asked pointedly why he had started shooting. Taken aback, Raymond stared placidly at me for a second, then said simply, "Sir, Joker Five ordered us to."

"What? Why in the hell was Joker Five with you guys?"

"I don't know, sir. He just jumped out with us and started running. When the guy started getting away in that car, he told us to shoot him."

"Joker Five did?" I was incredulous. Now the Ox's bizarrely preemptive self-defense was starting to make some sense.

"Yes, sir."

I interviewed the other three Marines, and they all gave the same story. Joker Five told us to shoot, sir, so we did. You sure you heard right? Oh yes, sir, it was unmistakable. That's why we started shooting, sir. We wouldn't have otherwise, but he told us to.

Furious, I made a beeline back for the Ox, but my assault was checked in midstream by an outbreak of sharp, agonized wailing. The teenage relative had arrived on scene. Taking one look at the bloody mess that had been the fuel salesman, he started crying violently, and when I approached, the kid was trying to shoulder his way through the crowd and through our cordon. Seeing him, my anger at the Ox died, and in its place was born deep sadness with the whole messy situation. George managed to calm the kid enough to talk with him, and when they had finished up George informed me that the young man was the fuel salesman's son. We let him through our lines. Right at that time, the Iraqi ambulance finally arrived, and two stretcher bearers ran over to take our grisly cargo. Glad to quit the scene, I ordered the man transferred to them and the platoon to mount the Humvees. We headed back to the Outpost, silent.

I'll never know for certain what the Ox said during that one frantic moment, but I do know that ever thereafter, my Marines despised him with everything they had. For his part, the Ox began to treat me and my platoon with a bit more deference. Maybe it was because he knew that I knew that the first thing he had thought of after the shooting was absolving himself of any responsibility, a cardinal sin in our world. Or maybe it was because he really had issued the order to fire. Or maybe it was because he felt as bad as I did that Joker One had shot someone who almost certainly didn't deserve the death penalty for whatever crime he had committed. And at the end of the day, no matter who said what and no matter what orders were or were not given, it was my platoon that had shot, and thus my responsibility for the outcome. As a former platoon commander himself, the Ox understood this basic truth, and though I can't say for certain, I believe that a part of him knew that, like it or not, I had assumed responsibility for his decision.

I took two sedatives that evening, but sleep still came only fitfully.

A subsequent investigation cleared both my platoon and the Ox of any willful wrongdoing. My men testified truthfully as to the order they thought they had heard, and the Ox and his radio operator testified truthfully as to the order they thought he had given. In the end, the investigators concluded that no one had failed due to negligence, laziness, or malice. The Devil Siphon incident was just another of the tragedies that inevitably occur during the fog and the chaos of war, tragedies that affect anonymous individuals on all sides of the conflict.

Their stories are usually crushed out by the larger narrative of nations, and history doesn't even record their names. Their children still cry, though.

TWENTY-SIX

On May 27, I woke up to a horrible feeling of dread. I can't really properly put that heavy sense of impending doom into words, but the feeling meant that, for the first time, I was so scared about what the day held that I didn't want to leave my sleeping bag. I had been scared before other missions, of course, but never before had I felt such a deep certainty that something bad would happen to my men if they left the Outpost that day. I didn't want us to leave, but what I wanted was irrelevant. We had a mission, and, with or without me, my Marines were going to go out into the city and get it done. I forced myself out of bed and headed downstairs.

Our task that day was deterrence. General Jim Mattis, in charge of all USMC ground forces in Iraq, was hosting the second day of talks with dozens of tribal leaders and local officials at the Government Center. Such a concentrated host of important people from both sides made the center a very attractive insurgent target, so one Joker platoon was tasked to guard the building itself while another patrolled the environs to prevent mortar attacks. The day prior, Joker One had stood post on the Government Center's walls. Now it was our turn to leave them to patrol the city.

We planned to use five Humvees to zip unpredictably about the city, moving quickly from one foot patrol site to another as we investigated areas favorable for mortar launches. However, at the last minute, very typically, the CO threw an unexpected change at us. In consonance with his contracting duties, the Ox needed to inspect an elementary school that Golf Company had paid a local builder to repair. As long as Joker One was patrolling the area, the CO reasoned, the company could kill two birds with one stone by taking the Ox to the schoolhouse and guarding it while he performed the inspection. I protested mightily. After our last experience with Joker Five and his decision-making process, I didn't want the man coming within one mile of my Marines and a mission. Furthermore, inspections take time, and from numerous previous patrols I knew that the area around the school offered only minimal cover for vehicles. A lengthy wait in the middle of a densely populated area with our vehicles completely in the open was a recipe for disaster. I said as much to the CO.

However, he overruled me, and my sense of unease deepened. To limit the damage from this undesirable assignment, I made two demands of the Ox: 1) that he give no orders to my men and 2) that he take no more than five to ten minutes inside the schoolhouse. Ten minutes, I told him, was pushing it; any longer than that and we were almost certain to get attacked. The Ox, still humbled by the Devil Siphon debacle, agreed. Done with the COC, I finished readying myself, and sometime before 10 AM, Joker One left the Outpost in five Humvees to carry out our assigned mission. As usual, Bolding was right behind me, driving our second vehicle.

We started our foot patrols with a few open areas in the middle of the city, then we moved in the vehicles to the wide fields at Ramadi's southwestern tip. There we spent at least half an hour patrolling the lush rural area next to the Euphrates offshoot, hoping to focus the enemy's attention on that place before we mounted up and headed back into the city for the school inspection. Sometime shortly before noon, we abandoned the open fields for the densely packed butchers' district and the little nameless school it contained. Ten minutes later, we arrived.

The school was constructed somewhat strangely in that it was not the usual thickly walled compound with a squat building complex inside. Instead, four thin, one-story, wall-less buildings joined together to form a hollowed-out rectangle, with a small break on the northern side creating an entrance to the rectangle's center and the open courtyard it contained. To its north, west, and south, the school was surrounded by twenty to thirty meters of soft dirt field, and beyond them the dense housing complexes sprouted thickly again all around. To the east, though, there was no field, just the usual long line of housing compounds separated from the school it-self by a small, trash-lined north-south street. It was on this street that we pulled up sometime around noon.

Immediately upon arrival, the Ox hopped out of his vehicle and headed into the school with the translator, a radio operator, and one of my teams. Just before he stepped through the rectangle's northern break, I called the Ox on the PRR.

"Hey, Five, remember, no more than ten minutes. I don't like this area."

"Yeah, One-Actual, I got it. I'll be out shortly."

"Roger that. I'd better see you soon."

The rest of us dismounted and knelt next to our vehicles, taking what cover we could. The drivers, Waters, Bolding, Fyfe, Henderson, and Lance Corporal Moore, stayed close to the driver's side doors in case they were im-mediately needed. They were a bit more exposed, but it was a necessary trade-off. The Humvees ran in a long, evenly spaced line down the street, from the tip of the very northernmost school building to the end of the open field to the rectangle's south. If the stay extended any longer than ten min-utes, we would reposition the vehicles to form a rough 360-degree perime-ter around the school, but establishing that formation would take precious time, as would getting out of it. As long as the inspection finished quickly, we would stay well aligned, ready to mount up and head out in ten seconds or less.

Three blocks to our south we could see the busy east-west street, called Baseline Road by us, that marked the southern boundary of the butchers' district. I eyed the compounds lining it with hard suspicion, but nothing seemed amiss. Civilian foot and vehicle traffic was normal for the time of day. The weird little rhythms of commerce that marked the area seemed in sync, and all three squad leaders called in periodically. Nothing unusual to report, sir.

After five minutes, I started getting nervous, and I called the Ox to get a situation report. He was just finishing up, he said. He'd be right there. Five more minutes passed with no sign of the Ox. I called back, more forcefully this time, informing Joker Five that he either needed to leave the building immediately or let me know how much longer he was going to stay so that we could modify our defensive posture accordingly. Even with the heavy .50-cals mounted and manned on our first and last vehicles, sitting in a line along the road was only appropriate for a very short stop, I reminded him. His stay was starting to put us in danger. He'd be right out, the Ox replied.

Maybe three minutes later, the Ox and his entourage finally reappeared, trailing the usual crowd of twenty to thirty small children behind them. Designated Marines rapidly handed out the soccer balls and other small gifts that we had brought, and, vastly relieved, I gave the order to mount up. The drivers hopped back in first, and the rest of Joker One began loading the vehicles smoothly and quickly, just as we had done hundreds of times before.

I waited with my door open until the last of the Marines started mounting. The little kids stood in a tight knot on the sidewalk right next to our third vehicle, waving at us as we hopped in the Humvees, pleading for us to hand out more gifts. I smiled a bit—it was nice to be appreciated—and threw my left leg through the door as Noriel, Bowen, and Leza called out almost in unison that all squads were mounted and ready to head out.

Then a few things happened simultaneously, or maybe there was a timeline, but everything sort of runs together in my head as I try to remember it. A boom tore open the silence and an RPG hissed by, maybe a few feet over the top of my closing door. Small-arms fire rang out from our south, and from the .50-cal turret right above me, Brown started firing back with his heavy gun. My platoon sergeant flung himself out of the way of the rocket, twisting in the air, wrenching his back. Another explosion rang out, and the crowd of small children disintegrated into flame and smoke. From somewhere behind me, Marines started screaming out the worst words a platoon commander can hear: "Doc up! Doc up! Someone get a corpsman! Doc up!"

I jumped out of the Humvee and looked around. I can't give specifics of the scene—I was too busy scanning the whole area and sorting out the enemy threat in my head—only a general impression, and it was of a macabre tableau from hell. The rocket had missed us. Instead it had impacted squarely in the middle of the crowd of small children. Dead and wounded little ones were draped limply all over the sidewalk, severed body parts mixing in with whole bodies, or in some cases flung even farther, into the street. Blood, always the blood, streamed onto the sidewalk and into the dirt, where it settled darkly in pools or rivulets. Across the whole scene drifted smoke and dust. The Marines jumped out of the vehicles and ran helter-skelter among the children, collecting the wounded and their body parts, applying first aid where they could. The docs were working frantically. I noticed, strangely enough, that they hadn't bothered to put on their latex gloves.

Throughout it all, Brown continued hammering at the enemy firing position he had spotted in the housing compounds across Baseline Road. At some point in time, the AKs ceased chattering, and one of my Marines, Fyfe, shouted at me that he had seen the RPG gunners, that they had taken off to the east, that he could guide us there. All three squad leaders called in to report that none of our Marines had been wounded and that the only fire we appeared to be taking was coming from due south.

That information was what I needed to hear, so I started giving orders over the PRR:

"One-Three, you are the casualty squad. Stay here with the docs and set up a collection point for the kids inside the school. One-One, One-Two, mount up. We're heading south."

Three terse "Rogers" came back, and first and second squads flung themselves into the first three Humvees with abandon. When they were mounted, the first two vehicles screeched south in pursuit of the terrorists. My driver took a hard turn, skidding the Humvee sideways, and headed east. Behind us, Bolding took the turn more carefully, and his vehicle dropped back. Twisting around and not seeing his vehicle, I called back to Fyfe, sitting in the seat kitty-corner from me.

"Where'd they go, Fyfe? Where'd they go? Tell me!"

He was suddenly no longer sure, and I can't blame him for that, for as soon as we had made the eastern turn onto Baseline, the Humvee had been enveloped by the normal butchers' area crowd. Completely impervious to our private tragedy just three blocks away, the locals were carrying out business as usual. Foot traffic thronged the area, merchants hawked their wares, and more blood, animal this time, ran through the streets. Fyfe settled on a likely house, and my driver bounced the compound gate open with the Humvee. Five of us hit the house, but it was a dry hole. I came back out to find that our vehicle was still alone. We had left too quickly, and the other three Humvees were zipping about somewhere nearby. I tried raising them on the PRR, but had no success. With crowds everywhere and no sign of our attackers, I decided to head back to the schoolhouse and the misery and to regroup there. On the way, we caught Joker Five calling over the PRR, and I instructed him to rally the rest of the convoy with us at the school. Less than ten minutes after we had left hell, we were back.

While squads one and two had been hunting, Bowen and his men had been doctoring, emptying their first aid kits until they had no bandages left, then using whatever else came to hand—bandannas, T-shirts, anything to help the kids. At some point during the process, Brooks found a little huddled pink-and-red mass, blown almost ten feet from the site of the explosion. Leaving his weapon dangling across his chest (and himself completely defenseless), Brooks picked up the bundle with both of his arms to find a pale, badly wounded little girl, bleeding profusely from her neck and breathing shallowly. Later, Brooks told me that as he ran with her to the docs, all he could think of was his own daughter. She was the same age as the shredded thing that he now held so tenderly.

When I arrived back at the scene, a pale but composed Bowen ran up and reported in. I noticed that his first aid kit was open and that his sleeves were rolled up to mid-forearm. Both sleeves and forearms were streaked dark with blood. I could barely make out the tattoos.

"Sir, we've got most of the little kids back in the school, but that explosion blew them everywhere. We're still finding them in random places, sir. The docs are working as hard as they can, but we've lost some already, and we're gonna lose more if they can't get to a hospital or something. We've managed to keep some of the most badly wounded alive, sir, but we can only do so much. They need to get some professional help."

His report finished, Bowen waited expectantly for direction, and right at about that time the rest of the convoy pulled up.

I wish I could say, given what followed, that I thought for a bit then, that I carefully weighed the pros and the cons of the various available courses of action, that I made a well-reasoned decision based on an in-depth analysis of the varying outcomes of any action. I wish I could say that I stepped back and coolly and dispassionately evaluated the situation, but if said that, I would be lying. The fact of the matter is that as soon as I spotted my first and second squads, my decision was already made. We were United States Marines, and a bunch of dying children needed our help. It was just that simple. There were too many of them to medically evacuate all, and the U.S. doctors might not cooperate even if we did so, but damned if we couldn't remain there to protect and minister to the little ones until Iraqi help showed up. Of course, a protracted stay meant another attack, and I knew this fact even as I settled instinctively on my decision. But we had been hit dozens and dozens of times to date, and none had yet resulted in any serious casualties. With the decision made, I started issuing orders, and I began with Bowen.

"Okay, Bowen, we're gonna stay until these kids get some help. We're gonna form a solid defensive perimeter around the CCP [casualty collection point], so you've got the standard six to ten o'clock area. Keep the docs and whoever else you need working on 'em and get Anderson and his scope up on a house so we've got overwatch to the west. One-One'll take ten to two, and One-Two'll take two to six. Got it?"

Bowen nodded. "Yes, sir. We'll make it happen." Then he was off, hustling toward the school and shouting orders at his men. I relayed the defensive perimeter positions to Noriel and Leza over the PRR and got two "Roger that, sirs" in return. With the decision made and the orders issued, I paused for a second to watch my squad leaders in action. They were magnificent. To the north, Noriel had one hand on his weapon and another outstretched as he stormed fearlessly this way and that in the middle of the street, indicating exactly where he wanted his vehicles and their machine guns pointed. I could hear the distinctive Filipino voice ring out.

"No, damn it, I want him here!" He gesticulated forcefully. "Here! No, not Hendersizzle [Henderson's nickname], stupid, the vehicle, damn it, the vehicle. Right here. Two-forty this way. This way! Tig, where are you, Tig? Oh, good, get your team up in one of these building. Now, move it, damn it! Move it! Bolding, where are you? Oh right, by the Humvee. Okay. Good."

Then, over the PRR: "One-Two, where are you tying in?"

Leza called back. "I've got Raymond's team right in that building—see it?" I looked over to see him pointing. "No, not that one . . . Yeah, that one. I'll watch the street to our south. Make sure you get the one to our north. Hey, One-Three, where's your guys?"

In my left ear, Bowen spoke up. "Hey, we've got the kids inside the building and I've got some of my squad tied up with them. Can you guys take more of my sector? I think we're gonna have to put some guys on the top of the school to cover the west. One-Two, I need you tie in farther south. Oh, shit, I've found another kid. They're everywhere. Hey, if your men find them, bring them here inside the compound."

Everything was moving fluidly. Just north of the school, the docs were hustling around in the street, treating the kids who were hurt too badly to be moved inside the compound. I wanted to help, to reposition the vehicles and shape our perimeter as I saw fit, but my squad leaders were doing a much better job corporately than I could have done individually. For now, I reasoned, I was best off staying out of their way. Just then, the full impact of the moment hit me: My men didn't need me, they were doing just fine without me. I had done my job with my squad leaders. The feeling produced ten seconds of beauty inside a day of horror.

The Ox interrupted the reverie, but, for once, I was glad to see him—because, for once, he had a productive suggestion.

"Hey, One, George and I can bang on all of these houses to see if someone'll let us use their phone to call an ambulance? We've gotta get these kids some fucking help."

It was a good idea. I had no idea when or if the locals would take action, and we—and the children—couldn't afford to operate under the assumption that they would. I had already called the COC to inform them of the situation and to let them know that our battalion needed to call the Iraqi police liaison and get some help on scene. The Ox's idea, however, promised more immediate returns, so I nodded my agreement, and the Ox took off. Something like ten minutes later, though, he was still gone, and my pride in my men had been dispelled by the anxiety of remaining tethered to a fixed position. I called the Ox.

"Hey, Joker Five, where are you, what's taking so long?"

"Hey, One. These stupid Iraqis won't open their doors to us. I've got the translator screaming at them that we just need to use their phone to call an ambulance, but they don't care. They won't let us in. I hate these fucking people. Their own kids are lying wounded in the street and we're trying to help as best we can and they won't even let us in. Fucking cowards. Screw this, I'm kicking in a door."

The tirade over, the Ox signed off. I sympathized with his feelings. Five minutes later, he was back on the PRR. The hospital had been contacted. An ambulance was on its way. I breathed out my relief, then continued moving around the perimeter, keeping a watchful eye on my Marines and the surroundings for any signs of trouble, but it was Corporal Walter who spotted trouble first and called over the PRR.

"One-Actual! One-Actual! The people on that street three blocks west just started running."

"Roger that," I shouted back. "Everyone, stand by, we're about to get hit."

Later, Walter informed me that right after his transmission and during mine, he had started raising his SAW to his shoulder to take aim down the street over his open Humvee door. Halfway through the motion, two men dressed in head-to-toe black suddenly popped around the corner, one standing, armed with an AK, and the other kneeling, armed with an RPG. Walter fumbled with the SAW's safety for a second, then pushed it through the weapon and loosed off a few rounds. Maybe he hit the men, maybe not. It didn't really matter. Our attackers had managed to get the RPG off.

At the time, I was walking on the eastern side of the school, halfway down the long side of the rectangle. I heard the first boom and whipped my head north; then I heard the second. Gunfire rang out, and mixed with it came the horrifying cries of my first squad screaming, "Doc up! Doc up! Doc up!" My heart sank. I started running north, toward the sound of the explosion and the gunfire.

As soon as they heard the cries for the corpsman, Docs Smith and Camacho rose from where they had been taking cover and ran pell-mell down the street toward the second explosion, heedless of the tracers that clearly zipped all around them. I watched as together they sped across my field of vision, and then I continued my run toward the action. Over the PRR came Noriel's frantic voice: "Sir, sir, sir. Bolding's been hit, sir. His legs, they're gone, sir. They're gone, sir."

I heard the transmission, and some part of me howled out briefly, but the rest was so overwhelmed with trying to sort out the tactical situation that it didn't feel anything at all. Adding to the confusion, at just that time, despite all the fire, an ambulance trundled up to the school from our north. The drivers belatedly realized what they had gotten themselves into, and they dived out of the van, disappearing into the rectangle's interior. Still running, I reached the northern tip of the school and took cover behind some junk. Then I called breathlessly over the PRR to Noriel.

"One-One . . . Get ready to evac Bolding . . . You and the docs'll get him out of here . . . I'll be there in just a bit."

No reply came, and I started moving carefully toward Walter to get a visual on our enemies. As I ran across the street, it slowly dawned on me that the firing had ceased. By the time I made it over to Walter, all signs of combat had vanished. All signs save the screaming Bolding, of course.

The human body has a lot of blood, more than most of us realize. Cut some of the major veins that carry that blood and it starts spilling out everywhere. Cut some of the major arteries and it starts spurting out everywhere. Major veins and arteries run up and down the legs, and Bolding didn't have any of those anymore below his knees, so blood absolutely poured out of the lower half of his body. First squad, Staff Sergeant, the Ox, and Docs Smith and Camacho worked frantically to stop it.

As is often the case, Bolding was unaware of his missing appendages, perhaps because his nerve tissue had been badly burned. The RPG that took his legs had first hit a lightpost next to which he had been kneeling, as he faithfully stayed near his vehicle in case his services as driver were needed. The impact with the lightpost had caused the RPG's hot metal penetrator to detonate, and some combination of molten copper and sharp metal post fragments had gruesomely severed both of Bolding's legs at his knees. The Marines collected the separated pieces, and they gently placed them into an ice chest in the back of a Humvee. The legs were still wearing their boots.

The medical term for this type of injury is "traumatic amputation," and, like much of our shorthand, these two sterile words paper over a lot of gruesome reality, like, for example, the fact that Bolding was shouting, over and over, that his legs felt tangled. Would someone please untangle them, he asked. Or the fact that, for a second, the shouting stopped as Bolding gripped Walter, his best friend, by the collar and demanded to know if his nuts were still in place. I don't know whether Walter checked or not, but he did reassure Bolding that everything he needed was still intact. I'm told that Bolding was greatly relieved.

I'm told because I never saw the injury at close range. Once I realized that the firing had stopped, I moved out of cover and started walking to the street corner where I could see the docs hunched over, working on Bolding. I made it to within about ten feet of them when the Ox did a wonderful and magnificent thing. Seeing me approaching, he straightened up from where he crouched near Bolding, walked up to me, and held up his outstretched hand. Blood dripped from it.

"Hey, One. That's close enough. You don't need to see this, trust me. It'll just fuck you up. You need to fight the platoon with a clear head, and you're gonna have a hard time doing that if you see Bolding up close. We're doing everything we can. We'll get him out of here. Turn around. Fight your guys."

Over the Ox's shoulder I could see Bolding's torso jerking and twitching, and the docs working to hold him steady. I still felt nothing, and in my detached state I realized the truth of the Ox's words. I nodded and turned around to find a defiant Sergeant Noriel.

"Hey, sir," he said. "We're good here. We don't need to go. We need to stay and fight, sir. Get someone else to evac Bolding, sir. I want to fight."

Later, Noriel would tell me that at that exact moment he was furious and that he and the rest of his squad wanted only to fight and to kill, to exact some revenge in retaliation for what had just happened to their most beloved member. However, I sensed none of this bloodlust. As I stared at my angry squad leader, all I knew was that his squad was the casualty evacuation (casevac) squad that day—they were always the casevac squad—and that now they had to do their job. Whether they wanted to or not was, like everything else in our world, absolutely irrelevant. So I replied very simply to Noriel's demand: "One-One, you're the casualty squad. You know that, you've been that on every mission. It's because you've got the most drivers. You are evac'ing Bolding and you are doing it ASAP because he's bleeding out. Get going. Link up with us back at the Government Center when you're done."

I have no idea what happened to the children after our departure; the need to fight had yet again overtaken the need for compassion. I know that we saved a few of the kids, and I can only hope that some of the children survived who otherwise wouldn't have, because God knows we paid a terrible enough price for staying.

As my two squads pushed west, everybody we encountered fled as soon as they set eyes on us. It could have been that news of the fight traveled quickly, but I believe it was more likely that the civilians knew immediately by our faces, by our body language, by the way we moved in short, vicious spurts that we were on edge and looking for any excuse to take up a fight. None offered itself, and none of my men were so far gone that they made up their own, so we made it back to the relative safety of the Government Center without firing a shot. I have no idea how long our movement lasted or what time we made it back there, only that we did and that I was completely exhausted when we finally took off our helmets in a room inside the center. First squad may have been there by the time we returned, but they may also have arrived a bit after us. Again, time in these situations is very fluid.

As I sat there, vest on, forearms resting on my thighs, head hung down above my knees, weapon slung limply across my chest, I still felt nothing. My mind was fixed in tactical mode, trying to sort out which new problems were going to present themselves and how I should prioritize and respond to them. Slowly, it dawned on me that we weren't fighting anymore. I looked around at my Marines.

Some of them sat as I did, stunned and silent. Others gathered in huddled little knots, talking quietly to one another. Still others, like Teague, stood by themselves with hard eyes and stone faces, fingering their weapons. Over time, I watched as more of my Marines joined the latter category, and I knew what that group wanted. They wanted revenge on our faceless enemies and on the fearful civilians whose hesitance had prolonged our waiting and cost us one of our best men. They wanted revenge on the stupid, broken Iraqi public services whose ambulances had taken so long to respond to the wounded little children whom some of us had watched die. And they wanted revenge on the whole miserable city of Ramadi for forcing us to make horrible choices, day in and day out, until it seemed like no matter what path we took, we lost.

I knew that the hard ones were thinking these thoughts because I was thinking them myself. The numbness had worn off, and in its stead rose a dull rage at more or less everything in my world except for my Marines. But the rage was irrelevant. I was a lieutenant, and a leader, and no matter what I felt, I had to take care of my men and accomplish our mission, and, unfortunately, revenge wasn't our mission.

After some time sitting there, I sorted myself out enough to figure that my job hadn't ended just yet. My Marines still needed caring for. So I found the squad leaders and told them to gather our men. When they were ready, I spoke words to the platoon that I didn't feel but that needed to be spoken nonetheless because they were true and because they would help us.

I started by telling Joker One that I wanted to kill very, very badly, and that a part of me didn't really care what it was that I killed as long as I got to do so. I fixed my eyes on Teague as I said this, and he nodded back. I told the Marines that a lot them probably wanted something similar. Teague nodded again. Then I told everyone that what we wanted didn't matter because we were United States Marines, and since our Corps had been founded, we had kept our honor clean and that Joker One was going to be no exception to this rule. We knew our mission and what we had come to do and it was still worthwhile, and we knew that as well. Something horrible had just happened, but it didn't change the mission and it didn't change how we got it done, and they knew this, I told them.

Some of the Marines nodded, but most just stared blankly at me.

So here's what we're gonna do, I continued. We're gonna go out there tomorrow and we're gonna try to make life a little bit better for the people we can. (Teague's face was immobile at this.) And if anyone attacks us while we're doing this, God help them because we're going to kill as many of them as best as we possibly can. And when we're finished fighting, we're going to get back to the business of rebuilding. (Teague's face was still blank.)

At about this time, I noticed that the CO and the Gunny had somehow appeared at the back of our room and that they were watching me. I ignored them because I wasn't talking to them, and I continued the little speech to my Marines:

Here's what we're not going to do. We're not going to kill everyone we feel like. We're not going to shoot indiscriminately at random civilians every time the fire breaks out. We've worked too hard to quit on the mission now. (At this, more Marines started nodding. Some were still silent, tears running down their young faces. Teague's dry eyes, though, bored back at me, his face still emotionless.) And you know what? I continued. Bolding wouldn't want us to start killing everyone randomly. You know Bolding, you know this is true. If he were here, you know that he would tell us to never mind him, to keep doing what we were doing because it's the right thing to do. You know this. You know this.

Now almost every one of my Marines was nodding. Some were still crying and some were still dry-eyed, but they were nodding along with the words. I looked at Teague. He was nodding, too, and I knew that I had gotten through.

As soon as I knew this, though, the mantle of leadership crumbled, and the full weight of what had happened finally overwhelmed the tactical numbness. The dull rage died, and in its place I felt only tremendous sadness and the crushing feeling of failure. Because of my decisions, one of my Marines had lost both of his legs. It may not have been my fault, but it was certainly my responsibility because everything that happened to my Marines was my responsibility. That's one of the first things you learn as an officer, and if you're a leader who's any good at all, then as you go on you know that you always err on the side of taking too much responsibility until the weight crushes you, and then your men pick you up, and then you take still more responsibility until they need to pick you up again.

Staring at the Marines, I started getting crushed, and I started losing it. Tears welled up, and I choked them back and probably finished up the talk with a few inane, meaningless sentences. Then I literally turned on my heels and fled the room, helmet in hand, for the filthy, excrement-encrusted, piss-stained Iraqi bathroom down the hall and to the right. I arrived there blind from tears and banged open the door with my shoulder. Then I sank to the ground, curled up on myself, and cried and cried and cried.

I didn't know it, but the Gunny had noticed my abrupt departure. Maybe ten seconds after I crashed through the door, he opened it very gently and looked in on me. I didn't see him then, and in fact I didn't notice the Gunny's presence at all until he sat down next to me and wrapped his arms around me. Instinctively, I hugged him back, buried my face into the rough Kevlar of his shoulder, and sobbed. He told me that it was all right, and then he didn't say anything at all.

TWENTY-SEVEN

Bolding made it as far as Germany, but once there he succumbed to acute respiratory distress syndrome (I'll never forget that sterile phrase) brought on by massive blood loss. We heard that his doctors had been amazed that he had even made it that far, given the nature and severity of his injuries. He must have been very strong, they said. He was.

Bolding's death came as a severe shock—prior to it we had all assumed that his recovery was assured. I had been checking with our doctors and corpsmen every day to find out anything that they knew (they had a direct line over the radio to the other doctors throughout the theater), and together the Marines and I tracked Bolding's progress from Baghdad to Kuwait to Ramstein, Germany. When we heard that he had arrived there, all of our conversation suddenly shifted away from questions surrounding the probability of Bolding's survival and toward debates on the extent of his healing. In my hope, I told my men that today's prosthetics were excellent and that there was even a very slim chance that Bolding's own legs would be reattached.

On June 3, though, I assembled Joker One at the house, and, trying desperately to maintain my composure, told them that Bolding was dead. It was horrible, and I didn't want to do it. After leading my men to believe that Bolding would be just fine, I now had to reverse course completely and shatter the expectations I had helped to set. As much as I didn't want to face the men with the tragic news, I didn't have a choice. It was my responsibility to keep them informed. So I did, and I don't remember much else about it, just a hazy picture of the men kneeling and me trying not to cry as I told them what had happened. And, to be honest, I don't really want to remember much about that moment. I do know that once I finished, I fled the courtyard to be alone in my room.

There I found that my hope, built so painstakingly over the past eight months, had been ruthlessly extinguished in one terrible moment in a nameless, dirty Iraqi street in a city that most people will never hear of. Having that hope crushed out was (and still is) a difficult, difficult thing, and, on the day I told my men that Bolding was dead, I fell into a deep depression. For a week, I didn't want to eat, and I didn't want to leave my bed, even though I found no respite in sleep. Instead of sleeping, I spent my time endlessly replaying the scene of Bolding's injury in my head, wondering where I had gone wrong, selfishly second-guessing myself with constant rounds of "What if I had . . ."

So I was tired all of the time, physically and psychologically. Tired of making myself do pull-ups and push-ups when there was no guarantee that I would even come home with both arms attached. Tired of carefully planning each mission as well as we could in order to protect our Marines, only to have the inevitable last-minute changes of combat throw off all our careful preparation. Tired of having to make life-and-death decisions every day, tired of having unexpected things go wrong no matter how hard we tried, tired of my Marines paying the price for my shortcomings, tired of my responsibility as a leader. And I was tired of trying to help the ungrateful Iraqis who seemed completely unappreciative of our efforts and our sacrifices on their behalf—we later found out that local residents blamed not the RPG-firing terrorists for the death of their children, but us for precipitating the attack.

But the mission continued with no regard for one small lieutenant and his loss of hope. And why should it regard him? All over Iraq, that same loss of hope was repeated for other lieutenants every single day, and all over Iraq, the Iraqis themselves were dying in scores in terrorist or sectarian violence.

The mission couldn't afford to pause and feel sorry for individual pain and grief, even if it wanted to; it was too important, and far bigger than any individual. No matter what, the mission needed to continue unabated.

Fortunately, my Marines understood this basic truth much better than I did. The enemy and the missions left us no time for a respite after Bolding's death, so my men strapped on their gear daily and headed back out into the city, still trying to make life a little bit better for the people we were there to protect. They weren't bitter, they weren't angry, and, unlike me, they weren't trapped in a selfish spiral of recrimination and angst. On some level, my men still retained a beautiful, simple, powerful faith: There was a mission to help a brutalized people, that mission was worth doing, and if someone had to do it, then it might as well be them. And if anyone tried to stop my Marines in pursuit of that mission, then God help them, because my men would do their utmost to kill our enemies stone dead.

My Marines were magnificent, and they saved me that time. Fortunately, I wasn't so far gone in my self-destructive spiral that I couldn't go out on Joker One's missions. I hadn't laid down my responsibility altogether—I wasn't worth very much as a decision maker for a week, but at least I was physically present with my men, sharing the hardship and the danger. As I shared, I watched them, and I noticed, perhaps more intently than ever before (probably because I needed my men more than ever before), all the small, wonderful things that made my Marines the best. I noticed their perseverance and their ability to pick themselves up and move on with some joy in their hearts. I noticed their tenderness toward one another, their selfless service even as the barbed teasings and the practical jokes continued unabated.

I noticed Noriel, Leza, and Bowen all pick up the leadership ball that I had dropped, talking to one another, planning their missions in absence of guidance from me, walking the lines, talking to the men, touching each on his shoulders. I listened to Mahardy and Waters fight like cat and dog one minute, only to have one offer the other the last of his water on a long, hot patrol the next. I listened to Niles relentlessly goad Ott, and Ott stolidly respond. I watched Guzon volunteer to carry the SAW, adding another twenty pounds to his combat load even as the temperature soared well above 120 degrees. I watched Docs Smith and Camacho bending over my Marines' horrific feet, lancing boils and dispensing medical advice like nervous mothers. I noticed Bowen patiently teaching his men during nearly every spare minute of downtime, making himself less so that his squad might become greater.

All these things and more that I can't put into words I noticed, but noticing prepared me to finally receive some sort of absolution in the form of the skinny, filthy, wonderful Private First Class Gabriel Henderson. For whatever reason, Henderson's tender heart kept a close watch on me, and one day, roughly two weeks after Bolding's death, he walked up to me and said out of the blue:

"Hey, sir, you know that none of the platoon blames you for what happened to Bolding. It's okay, sir."

I didn't know what to say to that.

Henderson broke into a big smile. "Bolding's in heaven now, sir, and I know that he's smiling down at us right now, just like he always smiled at us when he was here. He's okay, sir. Don't worry, sir. He's okay. And someday you will get to see him again, sir."

I had to turn away to keep from crying.

I think that Henderson's profound, simple faith was what finally allowed me to pick myself back up, and, in some very real sense, regain my own faith. Despite the anguish, and the self-doubt, and all the questions, I wasn't ready to give up on God just yet. I didn't understand the tragedy of Bolding's death, and I still don't and I won't pretend to, but seeing the simple faith of my Marines made me realize that, as a leader, I had a very basic choice to make: 1) I could throw in the towel on God—in other words, rationalize away my inability to understand and comprehend the infinite by stating that He didn't exist; or 2) I could accept the fact that this life is painful, and tragic, and messy, and that God's designs often don't coincide with my plans and that many times I won't, and will never, understand why they don't, but that none of this means that God doesn't exist or that He isn't ultimately good. The first choice, as I saw it, offered me no hope. Without God, then Bolding's life and death were meaningless—he served no ultimate purpose, he worked for no greater good, and now that he was gone he had no hope for the future. With God, though, Bolding's life and death were in service of the infinite, of a personal deity who cared and who intended the best for His people, even if they didn't see it or didn't want it. The second choice offered me hope, and I reached for it and strapped myself back into the responsibility of leadership.

But even as one hope kindled, another died. Prior to Bolding's death, I had assumed that I would survive Iraq. In the aftermath, I wished fervently that I had died in Bolding's stead, but since I hadn't, for a time I clung to the belief that God somehow owed it to me to bring me home alive. With acceptance of the second choice and of God's unqualified sovereignty, though, I finally realized that, no matter how hard I prayed, God didn't owe me anything, not even life. With that realization came an acceptance of death and even more than that. Finally, I had gotten to where I needed to be as an infantry lieutenant. Finally, I considered myself already dead, with each day a precious gift that I didn't deserve.

The mind-set shift didn't make life easier going forward, and it didn't remove the responsibility of combat leadership in any way, but it did help me to make decisions with less consideration of my personal welfare. And for a time, it helped me to take joy in the day we had been given with no expectation for more, with no expectation that God would grant me another tomorrow.

Part 4
GRIM

TWENTY-EIGHT

A s June moved slowly along, the daily temperature climbed rapidly, making us long for the breezy hundred-degree days of May, and to amuse myself I would occasionally hang my Suunto digital wrist-top compass/watch/thermometer off my flak jacket and watch the degrees Fahrenheit skyrocket throughout the day. A few times, during the heat of the early afternoon, the Suunto reached 135 degrees, but mostly the temps hovered between 115 and 125. Of course, these were only numbers, and the full impact of the heat didn't hit me until I walked into the house's courtyard one midafternoon and saw a whole line of our aluminum canteen cups arrayed along one wall. When I asked Carson why the strange arrangement, he told me simply that it was quicker to use the desert sun to heat ramen noodles than it was to use our portable stoves.

No matter what adjustments we made, walking in these temperatures was grueling. Luckily, the local Iraqi government was supposed to take control of Ramadi sometime in late June, and their national guard and policemen were expected to start performing a large share of the day-in, day-out patrolling. I, for one, was happy for a chance to step back and let the local security forces do their jobs, as they were the only ones who could truly identify the terrorists in their midst.

This Ramadi changeover was planned as part of a larger, countrywide Turnover of Authority (TOA) from the CPA to an appointed interim Iraqi government. On June 30, it was announced, Ambassador L. Paul Bremer would hand over control of Iraq to an Iraqi prime minister and disband the CPA forever (not a minute too soon, as far as I was concerned). The Iraqis would have their country back—their future would be in their hands, at least theoretically—and U.S. forces all across the country would take a less active role in day-to-day operations as the Iraqi army and police began to step up to a leading role in their own security. For our part, 2/4 planned to curtail its patrols and searches deep inside the city in the hope that a re-duced presence would prove less onerous to the locals. The Army even set up an official liaison office in Junction City, its huge base just across the river from Ramadi, to help the infantry companies coordinate joint action with their Iraqi counterparts. If we ever needed anything, just call, they said.

So I hoped that our unrelenting mission pace would calm down during the weeks leading up to June 30, but, as with so many other things I hoped for, I was soon disappointed. Halfway through June, a new, more time-consuming mission took the place of our scaled-back patrolling schedule. Because of the increasing number of IED attacks along the main highway through Ramadi, the battalion tasked Golf Company with a new twenty-four-hours-a-day, seven-days-a-week mission: Keep Route Michigan clear of bombs. The only way to accomplish this was for us to man our own obser-vation positions (OPs) in the heart of Ramadi—in essence setting up little squad- and platoon-sized firmbases well outside the Combat Outpost.

The CO anticipated that this round-the-clock responsibility on top of all our other round-the-clock responsibilities (securing the Government Cen-ter, raids, and so on) might very well break his men. So he negotiated hard with his superiors for a reprieve, and he got one: We were only to secure Michigan for the eastern half of the city, and going forward, Fox Company, one of 2/4's other infantry companies, based on the west side of Ramadi, would split the Government Center protection responsibilities with us. The second piece meant a welcome break from short patrols through the teem-ing, cramped alleyways of the market area, but the first piece was even bet-ter. If we could just find the right building with the right view of the highway, then we might need to set up only one mini-firmbase inside Ramadi.

After a few trial-and-error experiments, we found our candidate: a tall building just west of the al-Haq mosque, on the southern side of Route Michigan with an excellent view of both the highway to the north and the Farouq district to the south. We called the building "the Ag Center," short for "the Agricultural Center," in the mistaken belief that it housed an agricultural training facility. As it turned out, that facility was actually two hundred meters east of the Ag Center. The building that we selected for full-time occupation was, in reality, an Islamic library and a religious training center. Unable to read the Arabic titles of the books that lined the building's two cavernous front rooms, it took us roughly three weeks to discover our mistake, but by then it was too late. All the students and teachers left after week two of our occupation in spite of our attempts to set them at ease and avoid disturbing their lectures. We had the building all to ourselves, and, even though we had tried to avoid that situation, the isolation probably made our immediate situation a little safer. Of course, arbitrarily confiscating a center of Islamic learning did little for the long-term counterinsurgency mission of winning hearts and minds.

At least the Ag Center was nearly perfect from a security standpoint. The facility itself was a wide four-story building with a flat roof big enough to accommodate at least two Marine squads. A small, three-foot-high parapet ran the entire length of the roof, giving whoever was up there decent cover from incoming small-arms fire. The main walls of the building itself provided even better cover, as they were composed of thick cinder blocks reinforced with iron rebar. Most Iraqi machine guns never penetrated them, and even the RPGs could only tear small holes through the solid concrete.

The first floor of the Ag Center was by far the biggest, and it was separated into two halves. The front, Michigan-facing half contained two identical rooms, each with volumes and volumes of religious literature stacked high on tall wooden bookcases. The rear, Farouq-facing half comprised one gigantic room with a blackboard on one end and ten or so rows of desks and chairs facing the blackboard. There was one main entrance to the building in between the two book rooms, and another, smaller side entrance opened up at the rear corner of the schoolroom.

The other three floors of the building rose out of the first one like a thin rectangle placed on top of a squat square base. Floors two and three were each bisected by a corridor running east and west that separated the front and rear halves. Ten-foot-tall windows, each with a good view of Michigan and the buildings along it, lined the northern wall. On the southern side were five small rooms, each with a narrow view of the Farouq area, which sprung up just fifty feet to the Ag Center's south. Though these rooms each had toilets and sinks, the building itself had no running water or electricity, so early attempts to use the facilities (both the toilets and the sinks) to relieve ourselves quickly turned each room into a stinking, fetid mess that just got worse with every passing day. When we could, we relieved ourselves into water bottles or in the corners of the building's courtyard. The fourth "floor" consisted solely of one tiny, north-facing room built into a small box nestled on the wide roof. Finally, an open courtyard surrounded the entire Ag Center, and around the courtyard ran the center's thick outer compound walls. The walls had front and rear gated entrances, but only the former was large enough to admit a determined suicide car bomber, something that hadn't yet become common, but which we all thoroughly feared. Someone who's determined to trade their life for yours is very hard to stop, and is usually the smartest weapon on the battlefield.

Though the Ag Center's thick inner and outer walls provided a good bit of security on their own merits, we quickly took steps to improve our home away from home. We built sandbagged machine gun bunkers at the building's southeastern and southwestern corners, and in front of the main gate we strung a long line of metal barriers and triple-stranded concertina wire. No suicide bomber would be driving his vehicle through that opening if we could help it. Furthermore, after a bit of experimentation, we placed a medium machine gun and several thousand rounds of ammunition on the roof. In the event of a decent-sized attack, a predesignated Marine would move out of the room on the fourth floor, grab that prestaged machine gun, and quickly move it around the roof to where it could best be employed to stem the enemy's assault. For that same reason, we also placed on the roof our one shoulder-fired rocket launcher armed with the standard high-explosive rounds and the newest rocket in the Marine Corps arsenal: the thermobaric NE ("Novel Explosive") round. No one in the company had ever fired one of these before, but the effects were supposedly devastating.

Each NE round contained four pounds of PBXN-113, an explosive that cre-
ates huge shock waves when detonated inside a building, sucking all the air
out of it and more often than not collapsing the entire thing. We were curious about our new toy in the way that men often are about any kind of new
and cutting-edge gadget, so we wanted to see the NE round in action.

Even as we hardened and armed our mini-firmbase, the OP missions
began in earnest. Starting the first week of June, Golf Company manned the
Ag Center around the clock. A typical day would start at about six in the
morning, with the Day Ops platoon sending one squad out of the Outpost
on a foot patrol through either the industrial or the Farouq area en route to
the OP. If the patrol wasn't attacked, then the squad usually made it to the
center in under half an hour. If it was, then the squad sometimes took a bit
longer depending on the intensity of the enemy fire and/or the casualties
sustained during the engagement.

During the night, the Ag Center was manned by the Night Ops platoon,
so once the day patrol made it safely inside the building, the Day Ops squad
leader or platoon commander would conduct a turnover with his Night Ops
counterpart while individual squad members peeled off to relieve the Night
Ops Marines at each fighting position. After all the necessary information—
How was the patrol in? Anything weird happen last night? What's the shop
activity like this morning? Are the kids going to school?—had been passed
back and forth between individuals, the Night Ops squad would patrol out
of the Ag Center, heading back to the Outpost via a different route than the
one just used.

A typical shift could be as short as six hours and as long as twelve, but
shorter was better for a number of reasons. First, sitting and staring for hours
at a narrow, predesignated sector is incredibly boring, and it is easy for minds
to wander and attention spans to shorten. Even though the higher-level
brain knows that an attack could be imminent, it takes only an hour or two
of relative quiet to become episodically distracted from the task at hand, and
though your eyes might be trained on the road, your mind wanders: I wonder what Christy's doing right now. Probably sleeping. I hope she's not too
worried about me. Maybe I'll buy a new car when I get back. I can smell
myself. I wonder when we'll have shower water. I hope those clowns in the
other platoons save some of the good food for us tonight, if the log (logistics)

train even brings it today. I'm tired of eating MREs for dinner. Is that stupid donkey still tied up across the street? Man, how many firefights can that thing live through . . .

Second, as the day heated up so did the building, transforming itself into a giant concrete oven as the hours wore on. Swaddled in our thick layers of nonbreathing Kevlar, we slowly cooked inside. Even without moving, even hidden from the brutal desert sun, the heat wore us down, making us more and more sluggish in responding to enemy attacks even as it made us less and less likely to see them coming.

And come they did—an immobile outpost in the middle of the city made a very attractive target, and within a week the enemy was hitting the Ag Center nearly every day. For a brief period, the insurgents contented themselves with hit-and-run, spray-and-pray small-arms attacks directed in the general area of the building, but when those proved ineffective, the enemy became creative. RPG soon followed RPG in quick volleys, and on at least one occasion the insurgents staged a diversionary small-arms attack that allowed them to get off a shot with a heavy antitank rocket. Chunks of concrete blown out from the wall shattered dozens of desks and chairs, and the school's chalkboard cracked all the way down one side. The following morning, the last Iraqi holdout—the building's caretaker—took one look at the devastation inside and immediately turned on his heel and walked away. We never saw another local inside the Ag Center again, but we probably wouldn't have let them in even if we had. If we could have found the owners of the building, we would have compensated them for its loss, but we couldn't, so we didn't.

Throughout June, the small-unit attacks on the Ag Center continued apace. With the third week of the month came a new tactic: stand and fight. On at least three separate occasions, groups of ten to twenty men moved in from the north and staged just out of sight in the industrial area across the street. When they had screwed up their courage enough, they would launch suddenly out of their hidden redoubt with sustained bursts of rocket and small-arms fire. The attacks always came from the same place, a little taxi stand just across the road, and the short battles always shaped up the same way. A heavily armed, well-fortified U.S. force squared off against tenacious but lightly armed, poorly protected insurgents who eschewed their normal hit-and-run tactics. During each fight, delighted Marines enthusiastically fired every weapon in the arsenal, to include all of the thermobaric SMAW rounds. The results were devastating. In one case, the taxi stand was completely destroyed; in another, a nearby garage had its doors, its windows, and its rolling steel front blown out. In all cases, the enemy died in place almost to a man and Golf Company emerged unscathed. We relieved fourth platoon shortly after one of these battles, and one of their Marines, Corporal Stephanovich, ran up to me, pumped his fist wildly, and related the attack to me in animatedly excited tones.

As crazy as it seems in retrospect, at the time seeing Steph's unbounded joy made me wish that the enemy had attacked my platoon. Every time the insurgents decided to stand and fight instead of hit and run, the normal roles switched: We became the hunters, and our enemies became the hunted. Despite all the attacks lately, it had become a rare thing to be able to bite back cleanly and fiercely, and I was jealous. Why was fourth always the lucky ones? Couldn't the enemy have waited just one hour? Then we'd have been the ones firing the thermobaric SMAW rounds.

TWENTY-NINE

The regular assaults on the Ag Center were just a piece, albeit a large one, of a pattern of widespread hit-and-run attacks that developed slowly throughout Ramadi during the month of June. After the powers that be brought the first Marine invasion of Fallujah to a screeching halt, that city became a regionwide magnet for willing *jihadin*. In fact, it even began to export its own battle-hardened insurgents. A mere half hour to the west, Ramadi became a favorite destination for the newly mobile fighters, and through these and other methods our enemies slowly rebuilt the combat power they had lost in the widespread fighting of April. By the end of June, 2/4 was averaging three or more enemy contacts a day—whether small arms, RPGs, IEDs, or whatever—making it one of the most heavily engaged units in all of Iraq.

The Combat Outpost, our home away from home, would become one of their favorite targets. Although our walls and watchtowers prevented all-out assaults on the base, the enemy began using distance weapons—rockets and mortars—with greater effectiveness and frequency throughout the month, and the thin illusion of safety that we clung to inside the base's walls slowly eroded in the face of the explosions that constantly shook the buildings. Our lives inside the Outpost became increasingly difficult.

During the first week of June, a 120mm mortar round, the largest made by the former Soviets, landed in the middle of the courtyard of the platoon's house. It destroyed half the outer wall, tossing the heavy cinder blocks about like so many matchsticks, and it gouged a four-foot-wide crater out of the solid brick floor. Back in the COC, the massive explosions rocked the entire hangar bay, and I ran to my platoon's house, nearly frantic with worry at the reports of casualties in Joker One. But, amazingly, only two of my Marines were wounded—small bits of shrapnel in their hands and faces. Had the mortar round landed literally one minute earlier, it would have been a very different story, because the courtyard would have been packed full of my Marines. For a variety of different reasons, everyone had decided to go back inside their rooms just seconds before the mortars launched; thus, the courtyard was empty when the 120mm rounds devastated it. If any of my men had been in it, I would have had at least one fire team, and maybe an entire squad, KIA.

A few days later, we had another scare. Sergeant Noriel and I were walking back to the COC after a long patrol in from the Ag Center when a loud explosion rang out and a rocket zipped across our field of vision. It tore into the side of the hangar bay. We sprinted the rest of the way to the building, and there we found a white-faced and shaken second squad clustered outside the entrance to the QRF room. The rocket warhead, as it turned out, had ripped its way into their room. There, it had hit the ground in the very middle of my second squad, where the explosive device began spinning slowly. After a stunned pause, Leza, Carson, and the others had piled out of the room as quickly as possible, with some diving out the door in their haste to escape an imminent explosion. However, it never came—the deformed warhead simply sat there on the concrete, slowly spinning to a stop in an empty room. Standing outside, I marveled at our good fortune and thanked God for small mercies like a defective fuse in an antitank rocket.

However, the law of averages was working against us, and we couldn't stay lucky forever. On June 13, after yet another mortar attack, PFC Boren walked into the hangar bay, bleeding from his thigh and hand, shaking his head and grinning. He had been using the restroom when a mortar attack began, and one of the rounds had landed four feet away from the end of a long row of portable toilets. Fortunately, Boren was on the other end, and only a few fragments penetrated to where he sat, doing his business with renewed urgency. Prior to that day, I never would have guessed that survival might hinge on choosing the right toilet. But the news wasn't all good: Boren was evacuated to the States—shrapnel had lodged right next to the bones of his hip and hand, making it impossible for the doctors to remove. To this day, he hasn't fully recovered.

With all of the exploding going on inside the Outpost, Joker One and I spent less and less time in the open air and more and more time with at least two feet of cinder block between us and the shrapnel. Still, there were exceptions, like the time I climbed onto the huge hundred-gallon plastic water tank that normally held our shower and laundry water and spent about five minutes staring down into it. I had left the sanctuary of the hangar bay for the trip to the tank shortly after noon, when one of my men, PFC Williams, had run into the COC and planted himself in front of me. That was unusual, so I looked up from my map to see Williams quaking with excitement, hopping happily from one foot to the other.

"Hi, Williams. What is it?" I said.

He broke into a gigantic, full-out smile. "Sir, sir, sir," he said breathlessly. "There's a *catfish* in our water tank! Come see, sir, come see!"

A catfish in the tank that supplied our supposedly purified shower and laundry water—this was indeed worth seeing, and besides, I was bored stiff. Nothing was exploding at just that minute. We headed off to the shower area, taking care to avoid the swamp along the way.

Williams led the way to our red plastic reservoir, where a good chunk of my platoon stood chatting animatedly. As soon as I arrived, Williams and another Marine helped boost me to the lip of the giant plastic tank. I grabbed the opening and stifled a shout—it was scorching hot. More carefully this time, I leaned over the top and glanced inside. Sure enough, at the very bottom of the tank, a catfish swam lazily in a small circle. First I laughed, then I sighed, and then I asked the Marines to please put me back down.

Up until now, our water service had been sporadic at best, but we had assumed that what little water we had gotten had at least been pure. Apparently, that was not the case. A subsequent investigation established that the contractors had been driving their trucks to the nearby Euphrates, filling their gigantic tanks with water straight from the river, and driving directly over to the Outpost to supply us. We had been given several lectures back in the States on the life-threatening parasites that dwelt in the rivers, and the doctors had told us to avoid submersing ourselves in its waters at any cost. Unwittingly, we had now been bathing in the Euphrates for at least two months.

For the next hour, the Marines took turns boosting one another to the top of the tank. Their joy was contagious, and for the rest of the day, I smiled every time I thought of our new friend, the catfish. He even took front and center in that night's e-mail to Christy.

Shortly thereafter, I tempted fate again by spending nearly an entire hour in the platoon courtyard smoking cigars with my squad leaders. The moment came about because a few days after June 15, Sergeant Leza ran up to me with a satellite cellphone in his hand and a huge smile spread across his round face. "Sir, sir! The baby came, sir! Martha's had a boy and they're both doing just fine, sir! We're gonna call him Royce, sir! I'm a dad again!" He was beaming, and I threw my arm around his shoulders.

"Congratulations, Leza. Get the other squad leaders. I'll be back in ten minutes. We're gonna celebrate."

"Roger that, sir." He disappeared inside the squad leader's room, and I left the platoon's courtyard and headed back to the COC. Someone had just sent Hes a package of cigars, and he had promised me four of them when Leza had his baby. Now I went to collect.

Ten minutes later, I was back, and the squad leaders were waiting in the courtyard with four plastic chairs that they had dug up from parts unknown. Staff Sergeant wasn't there, as he had been evacuated to Baghdad one week earlier due to a noncombat knee injury that only he could have inflicted on himself. It had happened during a cordon-and-search mission when my platoon sergeant had been trying to help pry a lock off a suspicious auto repair shop. The crowbar had slipped, and Staff Sergeant had pirouetted wildly, arms akimbo and gear flying all across his body. The wild balance dance had ended with Staff Sergeant falling ass-first through the open hood of a car with no engine. There he had sat, folded neatly in half like a kid stuffed into a trash can by a lunchroom bully, until the Marines had recovered from their astonishment and unwedged him. Calling in the medevac, I hadn't known whether to laugh or cry.

So, on the day of the birth of Leza's second son, Joker One's leadership consisted of only the three squad leaders and I, which was exactly the way I preferred it. I passed out the cigars, and we used our bayonets to cut off the ends. Then Bowen lit up each of us in turn, and we sat in a small circle, quietly smoking, completely oblivious to the world around us. For a brief time, rank disappeared. There were no titles and no sirs; we were simply the four combat leaders of Joker One sharing a companionable moment together. It was wonderful.

THIRTY

To our surprise, the Turnover of Authority went two days earlier than announced, on June 28 instead of June 30. Ambassador Bremer, former head of the now-defunct CPA, flew home, anticlimactically, the very next day. We, however, stayed and dealt with the aftermath of the CPA's regime: a splintered and ineffectual Shia-dominated central government that couldn't provide even the most basic services—water, electricity, a functioning police force—for its citizens in the predominantly Sunni province of Anbar.

As a result, the much-anticipated turnover brought us nothing but more of the same: more OP missions at the oft-attacked Ag Center, more twenty-four-hour postings at the extremely vulnerable Government Center, and more frustration and disappointment with the complete failure of Ramadi's Iraqi security forces. Even worse, the attacks on us increased sharply after we turned over security responsibilities to the Iraqi police and army. The enemy activity grew in ferocity and frequency throughout July, and by the end of the month, Golf Company found itself fighting large-scale, citywide battles at least once a week.

The first of these fights occurred on Wednesday, July 14. A group of insurgents attacked Weapons Company just west of the Saddam mosque, and, after about ten minutes of exchanging rifle and rocket fire, it became apparent that the enemy's numbers were sufficiently large to warrant reinforcements. Our platoon, along with third and fourth, launched out of the Combat Outpost on foot, with two Humvees mounting medium machine guns in support. After fighting our way west through the city for an hour or so, Joker One received orders to hit a building "just north of the Saddam mosque minaret, at the very middle of the city."

Immediately, the Ox's voice crackled over the radio. "Roger, Bastard Five, will do. Be advised, what's a minaret? Over."

A long silence followed, then the radio barked back: "Joker Five, the minaret is the large tower that every single mosque in the city has next to it. Looks like a big dick. Over."

Even in the middle of a firefight, the sheer magnitude of the Ox's lack of knowledge brought me up short for a bit, but the moment didn't last for long. Less than five minutes after receiving the order, we stormed across an open field, weapons at the ready, and hit the designated building. Weapons Company had received heavy fire from its top floors, so we expected to have to fight our way up to the roof. However, on entering we encountered no resistance—the building was eerily quiet. Soon we found out why: Every one of Weapons's ambushers had been wounded during the company's fierce counterattack. When we made our way carefully to the building's second floor, we found four bearded men, surrounded by spent bullet casings and bleeding from their chests, stomachs, and legs. They were shrieking and groaning and rolling slowly over the floor. Smith and Camacho immediately got to work.

The wounded weren't all that we discovered inside the building. Shortly after the docs had stabilized the enemy fighters, Noriel motioned me over to a door that was barely hanging off its hinges. As my squad leader ushered me inside, I found a large room lined with storage lockers and brown crates. Noriel's men had smashed open the crates, and each of them contained dozens of RPGs. Ten or so AK-47s littered the room, stacked up against the wall or scattered on the floor. Propped up in the corners were several RPG launchers, and assorted ammunition crates, knives, swords, machetes, and machine gun bandoliers rounded out the room. Even for Iraq, it was an impressive display of hardware.

A few minutes later, Carson and Noriel began kicking at closed storage lockers. Very few things that the Iraqis had constructed could resist Carson, so after about the fourth blow, the doors buckled inward to reveal their contents. More RPG rockets. Dragunov sniper rifles. Crates of mines and hand grenades. Mortar rounds. In our five months in-country, Joker One had yet to find a weapons cache of this magnitude. For the next ten minutes, Noriel and I moved from room to room on the second floor, discovering more of the same in each. Once our survey was complete, I headed back down to the first floor, out into the compound courtyard to report our findings. On the way out of the building, the white sign we had noticed coming in caught my eye. The English letters ANC stood out from the Arabic lettering all around, and I finally realized why they seemed familiar. The ANC was a legitimate political party, one that was supposedly cooperating with our battalion's efforts to build a peaceful political process in Ramadi. I shook my head in disgust.

We radioed our find in to an incredulous battalion headquarters, and after three recitations of our cache's contents, they finally believed me. Five minutes later, Lieutenant Colonel Kennedy showed up with a TV news crew in tow. Kennedy took a quick survey through the upper rooms and then ordered us to move the cache from the building's second floor to its courtyard. Properly arranged, the weapons would make a nice picture for the cameras.

So, as the fighting all around us began to peter off, we slung our weapons across our backs and started passing the rockets, mortars, swords, and other assorted instruments of death down to the first floor. In the courtyard, Bowen and I supervised the arrangement of the weapons under the battalion CO's watchful eye. I felt like a perverse florist. Halfway through this process, the ANC party leader showed up at the compound, brandishing an English-language letter from an Army colonel who, he claimed, had allowed him to keep these weapons for "defense." On the CO's orders, we arrested the party leader, zip-tied his hands behind his back, and placed him in the back of a truck. Then we continued the unloading.

Twenty minutes later, we had brought down all the weapons and were preparing for the photo shoot when the battalion CO stopped us. He wanted the ANC sign placed in the middle of our layout, so we pulled it off the wall and propped it up behind the water-cooled machine gun. It was a bizarre sight — "Iraqi National Unity Party" was written in English and Arabic below the letters ANC, but surrounding the sign were all the implements of national discord. Staring at the weapons and the sign among them, I lost most of my hope that local city leaders would be able to use the political process to build a more stable, more peaceful Ramadi anytime in the near future. If they were anything like the so-called "National Unity Party," these politicians probably didn't want to. Across the city, there were almost certainly political-party arms caches such as this one, all of them just waiting for the day when the U.S. forces would leave and the real political process — a winner-take-all fight to the finish — would begin. Given the short occupation time frame predicted by our civilian leadership before the war, I didn't know whether the U.S. military would be allowed to remain in Iraq long enough to convince the people that political reconciliation was the best, and only, way to resolve their differences. That sort of change has historically taken roughly a decade, but we were furiously engaged in it nonetheless. Apparently, the citizens of Ramadi didn't know whether we'd stay long enough, and they were definitely hedging their bets.

I'm told that our little weapons arrangement made the evening news back home. Even if we had had access to network TV at that point, I wouldn't have watched it. I hated being reminded that the world outside Ramadi still existed.

THIRTY-ONE

xactly one week later, Ramadi exploded into violence yet again. It took us a bit by surprise—after the citywide fighting of the week before, we didn't expect our enemies to recover for quite some time. Additionally, the day had started out fairly quietly, with Bowen and his men spending six uneventful hours at the Ag Center, and Noriel's squad spending eight at another OP to our east. However, on the patrol back to base, first squad had been caught in the middle of a mortar attack, forcing them to take cover in a few abandoned buildings nearby. By the time the explosions ceased and the COC allowed the men back into the base, my first squad had spent close to ten hours baking in the 130-degree heat. So, when second squad and I relieved Bowen at the Ag Center around noon, nearly two-thirds of my platoon were exhausted and thoroughly dehydrated.

Still, for the next hour or so the city remained completely quiet, and I had just started to relax when a massive explosion and small-arms fire rang out to our west. A few minutes later, the COC squawked over the radio that Weapons had been hit by an IED and a follow-on rocket attack. Third platoon was about to launch in support, and we needed to be ready to cover their movement.

Less than two minutes later, Leza's entire second squad was on top of the Ag Center. From the middle of the roof, I surveyed their arrangement. Niles had a 240 Golf, our medium machine gun, propped up in the very northwestern corner, ready to hose down Michigan and the buildings to our north. His partner, Lance Corporal Ott, stood just three feet away, busily laying out long strings of linked machine gun ammo. When Niles ran out of ammo for the 240, Ott would slap one of these belts on the gun to get it up and running again. Across the roof were Carson and Pelton's fire team, covering the large open area to our south, and hovering over everything was Sergeant Leza. He moved from position to position, making small changes here, speaking words of encouragement there, preparing his Marines for the inevitable fight to come.

Just as we had finished settling in, third platoon rumbled by, driving down the wrong side of the road as fast as the street allowed. Ten seconds after their last vehicle passed us, all hell broke loose. A massive explosion, closer now, rocked the Ag Center, and streams of tracers lanced out of the buildings west and north of us as the enemy triggered another ambush. The double booms of RPGs started ringing out, and several of them slammed into the front of the first vehicle of third platoon's convoy, completely disabling it and stopping the Humvees behind it dead in their tracks. Trapped in the middle of the kill zone, Hes screamed orders to his men as he took cover behind the open door of his Humvee.

Under withering enemy fire, the Marines of third platoon jumped out of their vehicles, pointed themselves south, and ran straight into the teeth of the enemy's ambush. Behind them, the gunners in the backs and tops of the Humvees remained in their positions, motionless and completely exposed to the enemy but pouring out fire so that the assaulting infantry would have cover. The quick thinking worked—the insurgents hadn't fully set in their ambush position by the time third platoon rolled by, and most of the running Marines were able to slam through the gates of nearby housing compounds without taking major casualties. Those manning the guns behind them spotted a small civilian car unloading RPGs and RPG gunners. The Marines laced it with their guns, and the car caught fire. For the next twenty minutes, explosions rang out as the dozens of RPGs inside cooked off from the heat.

Up on the roof of the Ag Center, we were under heavy fire as well. Insurgents popped out of the buildings to our north and south and started pumping round after round of automatic weapons fire at us, and the bullets snapped and cracked all around as they passed. We took cover as best we could below the parapet. Two huge antitank missiles, launched from an alleyway just to our south, ripped through the floor below us, tearing huge chunks out of the wall, shaking the building like a tree in a violent wind. Every Marine in second squad started firing back at the tracers that lashed our position. To our south, Carson alternately shouted orders and popped off rounds from his grenade launcher. Across the roof, Niles screamed and fired the machine gun like a man possessed. Next to him, Ott lifted ammo belt after ammo belt and slapped them down on the gun when it ran dry. Together, the two of them were a sight to behold. A skinny but fearless Niles dashed from position to position on the roof, slamming the machine gun down on the wall wherever he could find the best firing position to engage newly emerging threats. Ott shadowed his every movement, carrying yards and yards of belted machine gun rounds across his shoulders and two cans of additional ammo in each hand. If I hadn't know better, I would've thought the two were a trained machine gun team, and for a brief second, I marveled as I watched them work.

My quick reverie was interrupted by Leza, who, nearly tackling me as he ran across the fire-swept roof, announced in breathless tones that one of our men had just shot an Iraqi policeman. I was stunned, but Leza continued. The policeman had apparently driven his patrol car nearly all the way up to the Ag Center, and our men had refrained from shooting—after all, the police were supposedly our friends. When the driver jumped out of his car, however, he had a beefed-up AK-47 in his hand, and he immediately proceeded to let loose at us on the roof. After about twenty seconds of stunned observation, Lance Corporal Pepitone shot the man dead. Shaking my head, I told Leza to tell Pepitone good job. Very little surprised me anymore. Then I grabbed the radio and asked the COC to send out the rest of my platoon. We were going to need them in this fight against all comers.

ack at the Outpost, the recovered Staff Sergeant began furiously rounding up the rest of Joker One. Upon hearing the call for reinforcements, he bounded into the platoon's house and screamed at the Marines to put their gear on and head out. Midway through the rant, Noriel reminded him that first and third squads had just recently returned from the action and that they were still filling up their water bottles. He also pointed out that no one had eaten yet that day, because, without me knowing, Staff Sergeant had forbidden Joker One from taking any food to our OPs—the Gunny was concerned about the trash buildup, and Staff Sergeant was apparently taking no chances.

In reply, Staff Sergeant simply tossed Noriel a bottle of water and screamed at him to get the men moving. My first-squad leader sighed, and, shaking off their lethargy, he and Bowen started shouting, getting their sluggish, bone-weary squads moving. Marines with empty canteens and Camel-Baks crammed bottled water into their cargo pockets as they hustled out of the platoon's courtyard. Dehydrated from their long hours in the sun and having eaten nothing all day long, first and third squads threw their heavy combat loads back on and ran through the Outpost's northwestern entrance, back into the fight. Against orders, Yebra attached himself to the reduced platoon as it moved out. I had left him back at the Outpost that day because of severe dehydration brought on by a horrible case of dysentery, but, as Yebra later told me, "Sir, with all due respect, there's no way I was going to lay inside the base while the platoon was out fighting." Despite his weakness, our radio operator armored up and headed out with everyone else.

After nearly two hundred meters of sprinting through houses and alleyways, all the water bottles so hastily stuffed into cargo pockets had fallen out. After three hundred meters, Bowen's squad moved out of the cover of the houses and into the open area surrounding the Racetrack, the large road that branched north off Michigan. As the first team sprinted across the road, an enemy machine gun to their north opened up on them. Rounds skipped and sparked off the pavement, and the squad dived for cover, but there wasn't much available. Bowen and his men were more or less trapped in the open.

Behind them, still sheltered by the houses, first squad froze. The Marines in front of them had halted their advance under heavy fire, and Teague's point team paused to work out their next move. Seeing the hesitation, Noriel lost his temper. He ran to the head of the squad, into the open area, and started doing a dance of frustration, completely ignoring the fire kicking off the pavement behind him. A stream of absolutely unintelligible curse words and orders issued from his mouth.

The rest of the squad stared back, amazed. Teague later told me that their hesitation wasn't from fear or disobedience—it was simply that, worked up as Noriel was, no one could understand the garbled English. However, the failure to immediately comply only further enraged my feisty first-squad leader. He moved closer to the road and started firing his weapon into the dirt, still dancing his jig of anger. Now the message was clearer: If his squad didn't move, Noriel's bullets might well join the ones the enemy aimed at his men.

The tactic worked. First squad broke cover and started moving, firing up the Racetrack as they ran. Nearly simultaneously, third squad crossed the road, heading to the cover of the northern soccer stadium. Meanwhile, back on top of the Ag Center, Niles spotted the flashes from the machine gun position nearly seven hundred meters away, directly north of us. He opened up on it, and the gun's tracers made a great target designator for the Cobra attack helicopters that had just arrived on the scene. Coming out of their holding pattern, they dived close to the rooftops and hit the house hard with rockets and 20mm chain guns. Watching the incredible firepower unleashed on the enemy's house, I felt a great deal of satisfaction.

It didn't last long—I needed to get off the roof and to my first and third squads, by now holed up under fire in the northern stadium. Grabbing Ott, the nearest Marine, I headed down the stairs, out of the Ag Center, and to the gates of the compound. Together we squeezed through the entrance and moved through the tangled concertina wire to the open sidewalk. There we both paused briefly, then sprinted across Michigan, stopping only to struggle clumsily over the waist-high concrete median. Ten seconds later, we reached the stadium and ran inside.

The first thing that I saw was Mahardy, nearly doubled over, his butt and thighs against the stadium's wall. He was clearly having difficulty standing, but immediately upon seeing me he tried to straighten up, and, failing, he began apologizing profusely about his weakened condition. Absently, I reassured my RO that he was fine, grabbed his pack, and slung the radio across my back. Then I climbed the stairs to join Sergeant Noriel.

Together we surveyed the area to our north. The smooth patch of empty dirt normally used as a second soccer field stretched out for nearly two hundred meters. There was no cover there. However, if we moved west from the stadium, and then north, we could use the housing compound Noriel had spotted to shield us from some of the heavy fire. Moving that way would allow us to cross less than fifty feet of open field before we got to the Racetrack and the cover of the housing compounds across it. It was the only way we could see to move against the attackers to our north, so, after a few minutes of assembly, we headed out at a quick jog.

The first team reached the intended cover without incident and edged carefully along a set of compound walls until they ended, making room for the rest of the platoon to find shelter. Both squads stacked up along the fifty short feet of concrete, Marines pressed nearly back to back against one another. At the front of the column, Corporal Walter and I carefully peered around the edge of the wall, trying to get some sense of the enemy's firing positions. Nearly immediately, a machine gun started up again, firing down the Racetrack from the north. The rounds cracked all around us, and Walter and I whipped back around the corner to safety.

Walter immediately turned backward and yelled down the column for Feldmeir and his grenade launcher to move up and lay down some smoke to cover our movement across the road. Running clumsily up the line, Feldmeir arrived, and without warning, pulled up his grenade launcher, placed the muzzle right next to Walter's leaning head, and fired off a smoke round. Walter stumbled backward, reeling and flailing his arms. When he had recovered, he launched himself at Feldmeir and swatted him across the head. Somehow, though, Feldmeir had managed to put the round in almost exactly the right place, and now a disappointingly small cloud of purple smoke was kicking up from where it landed.

Walter noticed the smoke and took off at a dead sprint across the street, screaming for his men to follow. Behind them, Ott and I moved from the cover of the wall, took a knee, and started firing furiously at windows we suspected housed enemy machine gun positions. It didn't do much good. When Walter's team reached the road, the guns opened up again, but the Marines moved quickly through the smoke and made it unscathed to the steel-gated entrance of a housing compound.

As the team began kicking in the door, Ott and I hurled ourselves out from the wall, moving quickly across the field as Noriel and his men covered us from the rear. Firing, I moved across the road in a crouch. Ott followed, and soon we were running through the gates that Walter's team had kicked open. As I passed through the entrance, something snagged, and I snapped backward, nearly falling. The radio antenna sticking out of the pack on my back had caught on the top beam of the entrance—unused to carrying the radio, I had forgotten to duck as I passed the threshold. Cursing, I recovered my balance and moved into the courtyard.

Team by team, the platoon crossed over the Racetrack, and within three minutes first squad had occupied Walter's housing compound, and third was flooding into an adjacent one to our north. Marines raced up the stairs to reach the roof, where they would have better observation and fields of fire. I was moving into the house itself when Flowers's voice came over the radio.

"All units, be advised, Cobras are doing armed reconnaissance in the area. They're about to start looking for targets. Break. They need all squads to mark their positions with smoke right now. I repeat, all squads mark their positions with smoke right now. Over."

I stopped in my tracks and yelled into the PRR for all squads to mark their positions and move to cover. With me, Noriel complied immediately, but from the next compound over, Bowen didn't reply. As the sounds of the helicopter blades came ominously closer, I grew increasingly nervous. Suddenly, Bowen's strained voice came across the PRR.

"Sir, we can't get to the roof to pop smoke. They've welded the doors shut up here. We're trying to pry 'em open, sir. We're all in the house but we can't mark our pos!"

I could hear the Cobra gunships approaching, and I started panicking. I pulled out my GPS and consulted the coordinates quickly. Then I called Flowers over the radio and yelled at him to inform the Cobras of our exact location. No reply came, so I tried again. This time, Flowers's voice responded nearly immediately:

"All Joker units, be advised, the Cobras are starting their gun runs. Mark your pos now. I say again, mark your pos now. Over."

He hadn't heard me at all—something was horribly wrong. I knelt in the courtyard and tore the radio off of my back, frantically trying to roll the radio to the frequency of the Cobras so that I could talk to them directly. Suddenly Yebra was at my side. He knelt, grabbed the radio, and silently began fixing it. I was momentarily nonplussed. I knew Yebra shouldn't be out here because he should have been confined to his bunk, recovering from dysentery and on bed rest. However, my worry about friendly fire was too great, so I shoved my concerns aside. Straightening, I stood back and let my RO start punching buttons. Suddenly, the distinctive pilots' voices rang out from the handset, crystal clear.

"Joker COC, this is Cobra One. We have one Marine position below us, marked with red smoke. Looks like there's enemy in the house next door. We're beginning a gun run now. Over."

I grabbed the handset back from Yebra, truly panicked now. "Cobra One, this is Joker One. Abort, again, I say abort! That is my third squad to our north. They can't pop smoke right now. Abort! Abort!"

It was like I was talking to myself. The pilots called again, completely unfazed. "Joker COC, this is Cobra Two. We've got the enemy below us. We're about to engage with twenty mike-mike, over." I could hear the rotors getting closer and closer now. I looked up, scanning the sky. Just to my east, I could see the first Cobra, maybe two hundred yards distant.

I dropped the radio handset and screamed back into the PRR. "Bowen, the Cobras are coming. You're gonna get hit. Pop smoke now, damn it! Pop it now!"

"I can't sir. We're still beating at this door!"

"Damn it! Move down! Take cover on—"

I was cut off. The Cobras above me opened up on my third squad. Two helicopters swooped down, their 20mm cannons blazing, tearing the air with the sound of ripping paper amplified fifty times over. It was one of the worst things I have ever heard, and all that I could do was look helplessly up at the helicopter underside as it flew overhead, wreaking devastation on Bowen and his men.

Unknown to me, inside the squad's house, seconds before the gun run began, Bowen had left off beating at the locked steel door and screamed at his men to start running down the stairs. As the bullets tore through the top-floor walls, all the third-squad Marines were diving down the stairs, Bowen bringing up the rear. The 20mm tank-killing rounds shredded the upstairs, and the squad lay huddled on the first floor, arms over their heads as bits of concrete and plaster rained down on them. Then, suddenly, everything was over. The Cobras had finished the run.

As soon as the helos banked off to the north, I heard their voices over the radio again. "Joker COC, this is Cobra One. We hit that insurgent position but we're circling back around for another run. Over."

My heart sank. I immediately called Bowen, praying that he was still alive.

"One-Three, this is One-Actual. Are you there? How many casualties do you have?"

Immediately his voice came back. "We've got no casualties, sir. We're all on the first floor now, sir."

"Stay there! The Cobras are coming back around. Stay there! Take cover. I'll try to call them again."

"Roger, sir."

Yebra was still fiddling with the radio. He had the handset off the radio body now, and he was wiping down the connections between the handset's cord and the radio's plug-in. I knelt back down and reached for the device as he carefully put the two together again.

"Cobra One, Cobra Two, this is Joker One. Abort mission! Abort mission! You are hitting my squad. I say again, abort mission!"

Nothing happened for a few seconds, but then the pilot's voice came back, calm and unruffled. "Joker COC, this is Cobra One. We have completed our turn and are approaching the house again. We're going to hit it with another run. Over."

Flowers came back on. "Roger, Cobra One. There should still be no friendlies in that area. Over."

I called Bowen again. "Take cover now, One-Three! The helos're comin' back! They're going to hit us again. Take cover, I repeat, take cover."

"Roger, sir." Inside his house, Bowen turned to his squad and gave the order. They flung themselves back onto the floor. As the rotor sounds came closer, though, one of his men had had enough. Rising from where he lay on the ground, Lance Corporal Kepler screamed "Fuck this" and began searching for a smoke grenade. As the rest of the squad watched, hunched under whatever cover they could find, Kepler ripped a smoke marker off the nearest Marine and ran back up the stairs to the second floor. As the helos made their final approach, he smashed out a window with the barrel of his rifle, carefully raking the glass from the edges of the window frame. Then, as the guns opened up on the house, Kepler climbed out, up the outside wall until he was close enough to its top to throw the grenade to the roof.

Even as the bricks next to him ripped apart in a solid line from floor to ceiling, he popped the tab on the marker and tossed it to the roof.

Suddenly, I heard the pilots talking animatedly. "Cobra One, I've got smoke on that roof we're hitting. Abort, Cobra One! Abort! There are friendlies down there!" The fire broke off immediately, and the helos banked steeply off to our east again. Back in my house, I had no idea why or how the miraculous smoke had suddenly appeared, but I was thrilled. I called Bowen.

A weak voice came back. "Sir. We're all good. We're gonna move to your pos now. Be there shortly."

I almost collapsed with the news, and, encouraging Yebra to keep working on the radio, I headed up to the roof of my house to get a better idea of the situation surrounding us. Upstairs, Noriel quickly filled me in on the battle situation as he saw it and showed me how he had arrayed his men. I took it in and surveyed the surrounding houses—no immediate signs of any enemies. Then I headed back downstairs. I needed to get on the radio to coordinate our next move with the rest of the company.

When I got to the first-floor living room, I nearly fell over. There, on a pile of Iraqi rugs, lay Yebra, naked and spread-eagled. Doc Camacho crouched over him, working furiously to insert an IV as Yebra's body twitched spasmodically. Several other Marines frantically ransacked the rest of the house, obviously looking for something. I ran over to figure out just how my Marine had gone from alert and clothed to unconscious and naked.

Without looking up from his work, Doc tersely informed me that Yebra's disease-induced dehydration had done him in. Our RO's core body temperature had shot up to 106 degrees Fahrenheit, and his brain was beginning to be affected—hence the seizures. Unless he received medical care at the Outpost within the next half hour, Yebra would die of heatstroke. The Marines were searching the house for ice in which to pack him, but we needed an immediate evacuation if we wanted to keep Yebra alive. Hearing the news, my shock quickly turned to terror—we had no vehicles, and without them, I had no way of getting Yebra back to the Outpost in time to save his life. Making matters worse, more and more of my exhausted first and third squads were beginning to show serious signs of heat exhaustion. If we couldn't get them out of the fight, they too might end up like Yebra, naked and twitching on a bare concrete floor.

I turned away from Yebra and considered the options. We could try and call in for a medevac, but with the radio still not working and no guarantee that we'd be able to fix it, we'd probably only waste precious time on a useless course of action. Or we could try a mad dash back to the northern soccer stadium. Echo Company had staged there with four or five vehicles. Maybe we could borrow one or two to use for medevacs. Of course, to do this, someone would have to run back across the machine-gun-raked soccer field. Neither option seemed all that great, but only the latter offered any real hope of saving Yebra in time. I decided to make the run.

Without any more thought, I placed Bowen in charge of first and third squads until I returned, grabbed my two nearest Marines—PFCs Phelps and Meyers—and dashed out of the compound gate with them in tow. As we neared the Racetrack, I absently noticed that the machine gun to our north had kicked up again. As the bullets cracked around us, we made it across the street and sped up—there was still a long way to go. There was nothing tactical about our movement—no bounds, no cover, nothing. It was just a straight-out footrace between us and the machine gunner to our north; us to see if we could reach cover, he to see if he could figure out the appropriate lead before we did so. Halfway through the field, I glanced to my right. Huddled against the same wall we had used for cover not twenty minutes earlier, a long line of Echo Marines watched our progress across the field incredulously—they weren't covering us because they couldn't. It's funny, the things you notice while running for your life.

What I didn't notice, though, were the rounds impacting all around us as we ran. Others did, and they later told me that watching that run across the open dirt field was like watching a scene from a movie. Marines ran, and behind them a long line of exploding dirt snaked up out of the ground as the gunner swiveled to catch up. He never did, and the three of us made it safely to the shelter of the stadium. There I managed to grab two Humvees from an Echo staff sergeant. Phelps and Meyers leaped into the rear one while I threw myself into the lead one and prepared to zoom off.

As I stared at the unfamiliar dials above the driver's wheel, however, I soon realized that I had no idea how to operate a Humvee, for, as an officer, I had never driven one of them before. Behind me, Meyers knew exactly what he was doing—he was one of our trained drivers—but without a PRR I had no way to talk to him. Momentarily nonplussed, I studied the instrument panel for a few seconds, then looked down at where the stick shift on a normal car would be. There was only a lever there. I hesitated, then pulled it up one notch and stamped on the accelerator. Nothing happened. I swore, then reached back down and pulled the lever up another notch. I punched the gas and the vehicle lurched forward. Yes! Whipping the wheel around, I pointed the Humvee's front at the dirt field to our north and sped up. The vehicle rocketed out of the stadium and hit the sloping concrete curb that separated the stadium from the surrounding dirt. I hadn't realized it was there, and the Humvee launched off it. All four wheels left the ground.

A few feet later, the vehicle crashed back down. The impact threw me chest-first into the steering wheel, and my Kevlar helmet smashed into the windshield (we never wore seat belts—it took too much time to unbuckle them when we needed to exit the vehicles quickly during an ambush). The Humvee nearly ground to a halt as my foot left the accelerator, but I recovered quickly enough and started moving again. Perhaps this time we were fired at as well, but, as before, I didn't notice, and within twenty seconds Meyers and I had made it into the shelter of the alleyway just outside first and third squads' house.

I jumped out of the Humvee and headed inside to give more orders, but Bowen already had the men moving. Four of them were carrying the naked Yebra as Doc Camacho trotted alongside, holding up a bag full of IV fluid. Tenderly, they placed the unconscious Yebra in the vehicle. As the loading finished up, a long line of Marines staggered out of the house, some carrying others with their arms flung around their shoulders. There were at least twelve suffering from varying degrees of heatstroke—a full squad. I had no idea the temperature had taken such a toll, but it made sense given the length of time that first and third had been out earlier in the morning. Staggering drunkenly past me, Mahardy again apologized furiously to me for his weakness. Again I reassured him.

Five minutes later, the convoy full of heat casualties roared out of our house, and I headed back up to the roof to get a better sense of the shape of the fight. On my way up, Bowen bumped into me—he had fixed the radio by replacing its antenna. I thanked him, slung the heavy pack across my shoulders, and headed up to the roof. Around us, sporadic rifle and rocket fire could be heard as second and third platoons continued to press the enemy, but the CO ordered us through the now-working radio to stay put. The fighting was dying down.

While most of the Marines waited on the roof, Teague's reduced team secured the compound's entrance and the house's first floor. As he moved around, checking his men, Teague noticed a small, huddled form lying on the sidewalk next to the Racetrack. He looked closer. It was an Iraqi child, maybe ten years old, and he appeared badly wounded. Teague pulled Doc Camacho aside and told him to be prepared—Teague was going to run out and retrieve the wounded boy.

Hearing the plan, Camacho shook his head. "Corporal, you're gonna get shot doing that. Let me help." Then, without warning, Doc sprinted out of the compound, into the middle of the Racetrack. Dancing back and forth, waving his arms, Doc Camacho started screaming along the lines of the following:

"Look at me! Look at me! Start shooting, you assholes! Look at me! I'm right here! Shoot at me!"

The machine gunner to our north obliged, and, nearly immediately, rounds started snapping all around our little corpsman, kicking sparks off the pavement where they impacted. Taking advantage of Doc's distraction, Teague ran out to the sidewalk where the little kid lay. As quickly as he could, Teague scooped up the child in his arms and staggered back to the house. Once they had both made it inside, Doc broke off his dance and ran headlong for the compound's entrance. The bullets chased him as far as the alleyway.

Safely inside the compound walls, Doc and Teague rolled the little boy onto his back. He was unconscious and breathing shallowly, suffering from a sucking chest wound. A bullet, likely from the trigger-happy machine gunner to our north, had torn open the bottom left side of the child's ribcage. Quickly, Doc applied a plastic bandage to the hole to seal the wound. Then he rolled the boy onto his left side so that the fluid draining out of his damaged lung wouldn't impair the functioning right one.

With the boy stabilized, Teague called me on the PRR and told me what had happened. Without a medevac soon, he said, the boy would almost certainly die. Two minutes later, I was down from the roof and bending over the child. It was clear that his condition was worsening by the minute. He was turning pale, and his breathing had faded to the point of near-nonexistence.

I was at a loss—with fighting still fierce in pockets throughout the city, there was no way we could arrange a U.S. medevac, but Teague had an idea.

"Sir, there are still cars driving on the Racetrack right now. I think we could maybe stop one and load the kid in there."

It was as good a plan as any, and we moved to execute it. Teague bent down and picked up the child again. Once he was ready, Doc, Teague, and I moved to and through the compound's entrance, back out onto the street. The enemy guns stayed silent, but I was in a hurry to get the child loaded and my men back to safety. One car whizzed by as I ran toward it waving my arms, so, as soon as I made it onto the Racetrack, I stepped directly into the path of the next oncoming car and raised my rifle to my shoulder, pointing the muzzle at the driver. The car screeched to a halt, and Teague and Doc loaded the child into the backseat, repeating, "Hospital, hospital" until the driver got the picture. Teague slammed the door, and the car sped off. Our mission of mercy complete, we moved out of the street, back to the house.

For the next half hour, we held our positions, waiting for orders to move out. Finally, the CO called me. The fight was more or less over, he said. Bowen and Noriel headed back to the Outpost with the remnants of their men, and Ott and I ran back to the Ag Center to rejoin second squad. When I got there, I sat down heavily on the floor, my back up against the wall, completely exhausted and unable to think. Ott sat down as well, then collapsed onto his side. Carson and Doc Smith quickly started him on an IV, and, slowly, Ott revived.

Ten minutes later, the walls of the Ag Center started spinning around me. Something about my hands seemed strange, so I looked down at them. They were shaking uncontrollably, and I realized that I had forgotten to eat anything since my sprint across Michigan several hours ago. I needed electrolytes, quickly—the water I drank had kept me hydrated, but I needed to replace the huge amount of body salts I had lost over the past few hours. I lurched to my feet and staggered over to the trash can that had been set up on the first floor. Marines sometimes threw away the parts of the MREs that they didn't want, and I had, unfortunately, eaten all of my own food before my run out of the OP.

I pawed through the disgusting mess inside the trash can, throwing out spit cups, used toilet paper, and half-eaten, slippery bits of food until I found a few unwrapped MRE items. Grateful, I sat down next to the trash can and tore into my treasures. Soon enough, the spinning stopped and my hands quieted. After ten minutes more rest, I finally felt well enough to rise, and, once I confirmed that I could walk in a more or less straight line, I headed up to the third floor to confer with Leza.

The fight had broken off completely, and he had moved his Marines off the roof, out of the direct sun and into the standard third-floor fighting positions. Two hours later, the CO sent a squad from second platoon to relieve us. By that time, we had been out at the Ag Center for well over ten hours.

When I got back inside the wire, Noriel and Bowen explained to me how, behind my back, Staff Sergeant had countermanded my orders that every Marine have at least half of an MRE (and preferably a full one) on them at all times. I was furious, yet again amazed by my platoon sergeant's lack of common sense and his unhesitating willingness to sacrifice the welfare of his men to his own fear of the Gunny. I headed back to the COC, intent on confronting him, but before I got there, the CO intercepted me.

"Hey, One," he said. "Did you realize you had sixteen fucking heat casualties? Sixteen? You know that I consider every heat casualty a leadership failure!"

I deflated. I felt exhausted and beaten, and I barely had the energy to reply. So I began a halting explanation of why my men had gone down — ten hours out in the sun, not enough time to fill up their water, and so on — but the CO wasn't interested. He cut me off less than halfway through, repeating again that my platoon's heat casualties were directly attributable to my leadership failure. I shut up for the rest of the tirade. It was clearly a waste of time to try to explain the difficulties of occupying an OP for eight hours in 130-degree heat to a man who had been to one of them only once, and then for less than three hours.

THIRTY-TWO

On Wednesday, July 28, the insurgents would stage yet another large-scale attack, once again exactly seven days after their previous one. This time, however, they didn't target U.S. forces; instead, they kidnapped the provincial governor's children. Hes and third platoon responded to the attack, but they were too late. By the time the Marines arrived, the terrorists had snatched the children and set the governor's house on fire. A few minutes before the attack, every single member of the Iraqi police force tasked to guard the governor's family walked away from their posts. Shortly after the attack, the governor appeared on national television, sobbing and apologizing for his role in assisting the infidel occupiers. At least now we knew, without any doubt, that the governor had previously been on our side.

Shortly thereafter, multiple intelligence sources confirmed what the battalion now suspected—that Anbar province's police chief was not only corrupt (he had hundreds of nonexistent employees on the payroll) but also was actively assisting the insurgents. In a strange irony, Weapons Company arrested the man in his own police station and shipped him off to prison. As we waited for a replacement, we decided that we would abandon our OP at the Ag Center and move to another, less optimal building across the street. As it turned out, that building was the same abandoned hotel that Niles had poured several thousand rounds into not twenty days previously. Walking up the stairs for the first time, our eyes traced the path of our own bullets back and forth across the abandoned hotel's walls. The signs of our attack were everywhere: huge chunks ripped out of every window frame, irregular blocks of mortar scattered throughout the hallways, shattered glass littering the floors of every room. It felt strange to make a home out of the same place we had earlier attacked so viciously.

The reason for our change seemed relatively straightforward to the battalion. Local sheiks had told our intelligence shop that the Ag Center was so often attacked because the Western presence in it desecrated a holy Islamic library, inflaming religious passion and provoking everyone from extremists to moderate fence-sitters to attack the unbelieving defilers. The CO argued against moving, stating that the original OP was the best building for the mission we had been assigned and that the main reason for the attacks was simply that we were there. Nevertheless, Colonel Kennedy, our battalion's commander, overruled him. With all the political turmoil in the city, most of which its inhabitants blamed on us, a gesture of goodwill seemed in order. We moved across the street and began the hard work of fortifying all over again.

Unsurprisingly, just a few days after the move, three antitank rockets ripped their way into the Hotel OP, as it became known, filling the place with dust, partially deafening those of us inside, and signaling that no matter where we went, the enemy would follow. At least one thing in Ramadi was predictable. As the disappointing, grueling month of July came to an end, we braced ourselves for a disappointing, grueling August. It wasn't long in coming. In response to the citywide battles of July, in August the battalion initiated a series of vast cordon-and-search operations throughout Ramadi. To preempt and disrupt the enemy's bold, if predictable, Wednesday offensives, 2/4 decided to launch its own pushes on Mondays and Tuesdays. Each week began with a 2 AM wakeup followed by a 4 AM mission kickoff and ten to fourteen hours of hot, exhausting house searching.

Thus, August 11 found us walking across the peninsula south of the Hurricane Point base, an area just to the northwest of Ramadi's marketplace. By noon, we had been walking for ten hours, and I was looking forward to the mission's end. At one o'clock, it finally came, and Joker One and I stopped our searching and headed back on foot to the marketplace's outskirts to meet vehicles that would take us back to the Outpost. Ten minutes later, we found them, and, walking between the long lines of Humvees with their mounted machine guns, I started to relax.

I should have known better. Not more than ten seconds after our last man made it to the vehicles, the double boom of an RPG split the air, and, somewhere behind me, the heavy .50-cal opened up with its methodical thumping. Leza's voice came screaming in my ear. Carson and Williams had both been hit, and they were seriously wounded. On autopilot yet again, I turned in place and ran down a long line of crouching Marines, toward the gunfire and the horrible cries of "Doc up." When I got to the scene of the explosion, I saw something amazing. Lance Corporal Carson had one of his sleeves cut off, one of his arms bandaged, and two Marines wrapped around his torso, trying to drag him to cover. They weren't getting anywhere. Carson was resisting with all of his might, kicking his legs and thrashing himself forward against the restraining arms like a man possessed, which, in some sense, he was. His injured arm dangled limply at his side, but with his good one he held his M-16 with its attached grenade launcher straight out, pointed at a clump of houses two hundred meters away, across an open field. Carson was alternately shouting at his enemies to come get him and firing his weapon in the general direction of the attack. Carson, apparently, didn't do combat shock.

Williams wasn't nearly as animated, probably because he could no longer stand on his own. The RPG shrapnel had dug a huge chunk out of his thigh, and he had his arms thrown around two Marines as Doc Smith, having already cut off his pant leg, applied a rapidly reddening pressure bandage. Ten minutes later, the Ox medevaced both of them back to Hurricane Point, cutting an Iraqi vehicle in half in the process. Both of them came back to us two days later, but shortly thereafter we had to send Carson away for the rest of the deployment. The massive hole in the meat of his shoulder had to heal from the inside out, and our filthy living conditions wouldn't allow that process to happen. Watching one of my best team leaders and strongest men struggle to climb into the back of the seven-ton that would take him to Hurricane Point with his crippled left arm nearly killed me. I consoled myself by telling myself that Carson, at least, would make it out of Ramadi alive, that we had managed to bring him home safe, if not entirely whole.

Williams, however, eventually recovered, and he rejoined the platoon two weeks later, just in time to be caught in the middle of a mortar barrage. This time, he escaped the shrapnel, but Sergeant Leza didn't. As my second-squad leader ran with his men across the massive garbage dump just north of the Hotel OP, he tripped and fell into one of the many small pits that dotted the trash. His right leg, however, stayed immobile, trapped in the junk. The resulting torque snapped both his tibia and fibula, and by the time Leza's upper body hit the ground, his lower half had stopped working.

I rode out to the site of the injury with third platoon's medevac convoy. When I got there, I stood forlornly next to Yebra, watching Hes's Marines load up a splinted and screaming Leza, the man who had been everything to his eleven men, the man who had become one of my pillars. As the stretcher headed for the back of the military ambulance, I walked with it, trying to calm my agitated squad leader, but I couldn't help. Leza barely noticed me—he was in too much pain to notice much of anything, and he rolled from side to side on the stretcher, alternately groaning and screaming. Our thoughtful, cool tactician had been reduced to agony on green canvas. I turned away and headed into the Hotel OP. Leza or not, the mission still needed to continue, so I took over second squad in the absence of its leader. Sitting there in the shattered hotel, staring at the quiet street below me, I was sure that Leza was never coming back to us. We would have to come to him, and, even more heavily now, I understood that there was no guarantee that that would happen, that we would all make it out alive.

I was right about Leza. He had been medevaced to Hurricane Point while his squad manned the Hotel OP, and from there he was flown to Germany and then to the States. As August wore slowly on, it seemed that no matter how hard we tried, no matter how well we prepared, and no matter how quickly we innovated to stay ahead of the enemy, Joker One couldn't escape the steady stream of our own casualties. Pepitone took shrapnel from a mortar through his back, an IED lacerated Noriel's finger, Brooks collapsed from exhaustion and sickness. The missions kept getting longer, the temperatures kept getting hotter, and my men kept spilling their blood in the dirty Ramadi streets. Each day, it became more and more difficult to get out of bed and lead. Each day, it became more and more difficult to give the orders that I knew, with absolute certainty now, would result in the wounding or death of my men.

THIRTY-THREE

ugust 20 found Joker One outside the Outpost with three Iraqi special forces members, called "Shawanies," in tow. The day prior there had been twelve of them, but a drive-by shooting on a patrol with us had killed their squad leader and disabled eight others. On the twentieth, 2/4 was out on yet another neighborhood cordon-and-search, this time deep in the southern Farouq district, and by 6 AM all platoons had their hands full with their respective sectors. Our Shawanies had helped us out a bit by occasionally talking with and calming down particularly fearful families, but, for the most part, the middle-aged Iraqi soldiers preferred riding in one of our accompanying Humvees and smoking.

After four hours of wandering through houses and coming up dry, Staff Sergeant and third squad found a massive arms cache buried in the front yard of an empty housing compound. Initially, I was ecstatic. The large plastic-lined cave that they discovered contained dozens of mortar and artillery shells, several Dragunov sniper rifles, thousands of rounds of machine gun ammunition, and, the pièces de résistance, two complete 82mm mortar systems. An hour later, around noon, I was more tired and less enamored with our success. We had indeed found several hundred pounds of explosives, but in a country awash in hundreds of millions of tons of unsecured ordnance, our find didn't even qualify as a drop in the bucket.

Still, Golf Company had completed searching its assigned area, and, as best I could tell, the battalion's mission was nearly finished as well. We had been walking now for almost seven hours, and I was eagerly awaiting the command to mount the nearby vehicles and head back to the Outpost. Instead, a different set of orders came down.

"Joker One-Actual. This is Joker Six. Are those Shawanies still with you? Over."

I glanced back at our Humvees. Sure enough, inside one of them sat the Shawanies with their helmets off, talking and smoking.

"Six, One. Yes, sir, I've got them. They're in a vehicle next to me. Over."

"One, battalion wants you to head a few blocks north and cordon off the Farouq mosque. Break. Then, they want you to use the Shawanies to search the mosque. We've been getting reports of weapons being stored inside. The Shawanies might be able to confirm that for us. Use them to search the Farouq mosque. Over."

My heart sank, and the same feeling of inescapable dread that had hit me on the morning of Bolding's death crashed down yet again. We had just been ordered to search the most anti-American mosque in the most anti-American part of town in the very middle of the day. Cordoning the mosque meant cordoning the entire block it sat on, which meant standing outside on the sidewalk running the length of the block, which meant putting on a show for the locals. Plenty of touchy residents were certain to be watching the foreign presence violating their sacred site, and the sidewalk offered little cover from a hostile response. I wished battalion had thought of the mission at 4 AM, when we had been raiding a house not fifty meters south of the Farouq mosque. We could have searched it quickly and quietly with no one the wiser.

I pushed my dread aside and asked for some flank cover—without it, we'd be completely exposed on all sides as we sat in our cordon around the mosque. Golf would see what it could do, came the reply. Sighing, I put down the radio handset and explained the mission to the squad leaders. They'd all have their usual cordon sectors, I said. Suddenly, my brand-new second-squad leader, Sergeant Nez, came on the PRR and asked me tentatively what his usual sector was. I sighed. Nez wasn't bad, but he was no Leza, and he didn't have the time to become one. At that moment, it hit me hard that our platoon was missing one of its mainstays. All those months of training, of missions together, of implicit coordination built through mutual dependence—gone in one random mortar strike. Skill and teamwork meant something out here, but not enough, I thought.

Bowen's voice broke the short reverie. "One-Actual, do I understand right? They want us to search the mosque in the middle of the day? The hajjis are gonna see us and get real pissed, sir."

"Yeah, I know, One-Three. But we've got our orders, and we're gonna search that mosque, end of story. So, be prepared to get hit. Now, everyone let me know when you're ready to move."

Three "Rogers" came back. As I waited for the squads to collect themselves, I sidled over to the Shawany Humvee and explained the mission to Snake, the Iraqi translator who had replaced George. Snake, in turn, explained it to the Shawanies. The unintelligible Arabic conversation quickly became animated, and, once it ended, Snake turned to me. "Sir, this is bad mission, they say. It is great disrespect to search a mosque." I nodded and walked off. Apparently the Shawanies shared our lack of enthusiasm.

Five minutes later, the platoon headed north. Once our point element spotted the mosque, I pumped my fist twice in the air, and Joker One broke into a quick jog. The three squads streamed into position to set the cordon quickly—the longer we took, the more time suspected hideaways had to flee. In less than a minute, a strung-out line of Marines stood posted in a large rectangle around the mosque. Where sudden jags in the walls or small mounds of dirt and trash offered bits of cover, we took it, but for the most part we stood on the sidewalk, completely exposed. At the north, south, and east corners of the rectangle, two-man teams made their way to the tops of the tallest houses in their sectors to give us overhead observation. In rapid succession, my three squad leaders called me.

"One-One is set."

"One-Two is set."

"One-Three is set."

I turned to the Humvee carrying Snake and motioned him and the Shawanies out. Reluctantly, they dismounted, and the three of them, Snake, Mahardy, and I headed over to the entrance to the mosque compound. The *kelidar*, the mosque's caretaker, met us at the gate. He and the Shawanies exchanged a few terse sentences. Then all fell silent and Snake turned to me.

"Sir, they say they cannot search the mosque. It is bad. It is disrespect. They will not do it."

Damn it. "Snake, tell them they have to. Tell them we're not leaving here until they search this thing. Tell them we'll sit here outside the entrance to the mosque all day if we have to." Snake looked reluctant, but he translated the instructions nonetheless. The Shawanies replied. "Sir, they still say they not search the mosque. Disrespect too great. Everyone here"—Snake gestured at the surrounding houses—"get angry at us."

Well, at least nothing would change if that happened. Still, the Shawanies had called my bluff. I looked at their new leader. He shook his head at me and then stared pointedly at the ground.

I was at a loss. For a moment, I considered putting the Iraqis at gunpoint and forcing them into the mosque, but that seemed a last resort. Stories like that spread quickly through the populace, and the last thing I wanted was a provincewide rumor about a rogue American officer who threatened to kill our Iraqi partners if they didn't violate a holy site. I didn't know how badly battalion wanted the Farouq mosque searched or how solid the intelligence really was. Perhaps if they heard of the Shawany refusal to enter, they would reconsider the mission. I decided to defer my decision and instead called the CO, who deferred his decision and instead called Battalion, which was tied up with something else at the time.

So we waited in front of the mosque for further instructions. After a minute or so with no response from higher up, I called the squad leaders on the PRR and explained the situation to them. Then Mahardy and I knelt down behind a chest-high mound of dirt piled next to the mosque's courtyard entrance. The Shawanies and Snake remained standing, exchanging occasional tense Arabic sentences with the *kelidar*. Ten more minutes passed without any communication from the CO. Meanwhile, my anxiety level skyrocketed. Hanging out on the sidewalk, motionless and completely exposed, was a tactical mess during a normal mission, let alone one that involved openly surrounding a highly sensitive holy site in the most anti-American part of town. I called the CO, but battalion still hadn't gotten back to him. He'd let me know as soon as he heard anything, he promised.

Putting down the radio, I shook my head and started thinking about other ways to handle the Shawanies if battalion didn't get back to me quickly. Another five minutes passed; then it finally dawned on me that I needed to reassess the safety of my men—the initial cordon positions had been based on a ten- to fifteen-minute-long mission, not a twenty- to thirty-minute one. We needed to find better cover even if it meant a less robust cordon. Quickly, I hit the PRR and gave my squad leaders orders to move their men inside the nearest housing compounds.

Sergeant Nez radioed back immediately. "Uh . . . sir, this is One-Two. We all already started doing that. I've got about half my squad in one compound now, sir. I'm moving the rest of my squad into the one just to its south. We'll all be covered soon, sir."

I looked up the street, to the northwest. One by one, Marines were peeling out from their cordon positions and running into an open compound door guarded by Niles and Ott. I looked southeast—third squad was doing the same thing. Silently, I breathed a prayer of relief that my team was picking up my slack. I looked back up the street—second squad was nearly entirely inside their compounds—and then turned my attention to the Shawanies.

No sooner had I taken my eyes off my squad than a long string of gunfire erupted to the north. Immediately, I looked back up the street, trying to get a bead on the attacker but instead I saw Niles hopping across the sidewalk on one leg, fifty meters away. He reached the entrance to the compound he had been guarding. Then he collapsed limply onto the sidewalk, still exposed to the fire coming from the north.

I pulled up my M-16 and returned fire at the very edge of a wall, at the very end of the block, some two hundred meters away. Behind me, Mahardy did the same, shooting over my shoulder. I couldn't see our attacker, but I could see his tracers, and I hoped that maybe my bullets would punch through the concrete and hit him.

Then, without making any conscious decision to move, I suddenly found myself running toward Niles, shouting, for the first time, the words I hated so much to hear.

"Doc up! Doc up! Doc up!"

Before I got to Niles, Doc Smith darted out of the compound and, heedless of his exposure to the enemy, began cutting off the downed Marine's pant leg. By the time I reached the scene, the wound had been clearly exposed, and it was nasty. One of the machine gun bullets had ripped right through Niles's lower left leg, taking out a good chunk of his tibia and fibula along the way. Blood seeped through the white gauze bandage Doc pressed against the leg with both hands. Niles lay silent and pale, shaking slightly. I turned behind me and nearly knocked over Mahardy. Silently, he handed me the radio handset, and I called in the medevac.

Lance Corporal Niles. Gunshot wound to left leg. Bleeding badly, no arteries cut. Priority medevac. Over.

That one got battalion's attention. Within two minutes, an entire headquarters convoy arrived on the scene and somehow crammed itself into a small two-hundred-meter front just outside the mosque's entrance. Within another two minutes, an Army convoy sporting two Bradley fighting vehicles and two armored ambulances rolled up to our position. The street became a wall-to-wall parking lot.

I was disgusted by the lack of dispersion, but I had better things to do than supervise the tactical array of units over which I had no control. Four stretcher bearers from the Army ambulances came running toward us, and, together with Doc, I helped them load Niles onto the ubiquitous green canvas. As they moved carefully with their burden back to the ambulance, I moved with them. Niles had held his hand up to me as they lifted the stretcher, and I had taken it. Now we moved, hand in hand, to the ambulance's yawning entrance.

Throughout the short trip, Niles didn't say anything. He just looked at me. He was still shaking, and he was growing continually paler from the blood loss. I knew that I should say something, but I didn't know what. We continued to move. He continued to stare. Finally, I spoke.

"Niles, you're gonna be fine. I promise. We'll get you out of here. Don't worry. You'll be fine. I'm here. Don't worry. I'll make them take good care of you. I promise. Don't worry."

Niles never said anything back, but his hand stayed firmly clenched in mine until the stretcher bearers carried him up the ramp to the ambulance. I held on for as high as my arm could reach, but eventually I had to let go. I had a different destination. For a brief second, though, I wanted to leave it all, to go with them, to hold Niles's hand the whole way to Junction City, to tell him that he'd be okay until the doctors could get to him, to tell him that

I was there for him and that he didn't need to worry anymore. I wanted to leave that dirty street, the scene of yet another of my failures, and the whole mixed-up situation behind, but I couldn't.

So I watched Niles until the slowly rising back hatch of the ambulance shut him off from me for good. Then I forced myself to forget him altogether, and I turned my attention back to my primary responsibility—sorting out the tactical situation at hand.

It was even messier than when I had detached from it. Vehicle after vehicle had piled into the street directly in front of the mosque, until that short segment of pavement became an unending sea of steel. It gave the enemy a nice, fat target to hit. Behind me, second platoon had stormed their way past the Shawanies, through the mosque courtyard, and into the building itself. Part of the squad fanned out to search the building while the rest headed up to the roof. Now I could see Marines running along the mosque's roof to covered fighting positions, watching over the close-packed vehicles below them and getting ready to get hit again.

It didn't take long for the new battle to materialize. This time, two RPGs slammed into the brand-new vehicle depot in front of the mosque. The enemy probably didn't even aim—they didn't have to—but the explosion killed two Army soldiers immediately and wounded another three. A short but intense firefight broke out. In the midst of all the gunshots, I glanced to my south and saw one of the younger Shawanies standing on the sidewalk with his machine gun held at his hip, its barrel pointing into the air at a sixty-degree angle. Wide-eyed, the man frantically swiveled his head back and forth and then decided to get into the action by ripping off burst after burst of completely unaimed machine gun fire.

The enemy quickly melted away into the surrounding neighborhoods, and as soon as the fight died down, second platoon moved out of the mosque itself and searched the buildings immediately adjacent, buildings that the locals considered to be part of the mosque complex. There they found two huge weapons caches including, among other things, antipersonnel mines and suicide vests. The search lasted for thirty minutes. The vehicle cluster in front of the mosque thinned out a bit as the drivers finally grasped the meaning of dispersion, but it didn't matter. The enemy hit us again, this time from the south. Running across a street to warn third squad of the potential attack, Teague was blown off his feet by an RPG. Both of his eardrums ruptured, and the blast drove small bits of dirt and shrapnel into his forearms. He got back up and continued running.

Shortly thereafter, battalion decided to move out, and two hours later, Golf Company and the three Shawanies were back at the Outpost. We never worked with them again. Our search had netted two huge weapons caches, both of which would likely be replenished within the next several weeks out of the billions of tons of high explosive still unaccounted for in Iraq. Joker One had lost one of our best Marines. If we were to stay another six months, and if we got lucky with our combat replacements, perhaps we could train up a new platoon member to Niles's level.

As night fell, I realized that Ott was the only member left from his fire team. I disbanded the team and gave Ott to Teague.

What a miserable day.

THIRTY-FOUR

The high casualty rate that Joker One had sustained over the past two weeks was par for the course for everyone in the battalion during the late summer of 2004. Throughout August, while most people in America took vacations, injured Marines poured into the Combat Outpost at least thrice weekly. Every time four stretcher bearers and their wounded cargo ran out to the medevac helicopter that touched down at the north end of our base, I wondered whether the young man staining the canvas dark with his blood would ever fully recover, whether his dreams had died in the middle of fire and smoke. I wondered when it would again be one of my men who took his place. And I wondered how many of us would eventually make it back whole to the States.

No longer did I think that just being good at our jobs would be enough to protect us, or that my own decisions under fire could in some way prevent harm from befalling my men. After Bolding's death, I had accepted the fact that I might not make it back. Now, every time we left the base I simply assumed that someone would come back wounded. It was a grim place to be, but it was freeing in some ways, for I wasn't carrying the weight of every injured man on my shoulders anymore. Not everything was my fault—

sometimes it was fair to blame the enemy, or ill fortune, or stupid missions for our wounded.

Though this mind-set shift made it easier to lead outside the base, it didn't make it any easier to see the wounded lying in their litters inside it. Some casualties hit us particularly hard, like the time Sergeant Longoria, leader of the sniper squad attached to Golf, had his left hand nearly severed by an IED. The litter bearers carried him semiconscious into the aid station. Little streams of blood dangled off the sides of the litter's poles. A few hours later, Doctor Crickard, the Navy physician at the Outpost, walked out of the aid station and told us that Longoria would almost certainly never regain full use of his hand again. Everyone looked downcast; all he'd ever wanted to be was a Marine scout-sniper. Another dream, dead.

Some casualties were particularly bad, like the one Duke Wells, the Weapons Platoon executive officer, brought in a few days after Longoria's injury. His convoy had just been hit by an IED, and when a few of the corpsmen threw open the tailgate of his casualty vehicle, a river of blood sluiced out and splattered all over our hangar bay floor. It created a dark, wide pool on the slick concrete. The corpsmen unloaded casualties and carried them to the aid station, and where they walked they left thick swaths of blood behind.

All of the injured looked terrible, but one was worse than most. Where his eyes used to be were two dark red gauze pads, held to his head by an elastic bandage. I had never seen an eyeless casualty before.

An hour later, the wounded had been carried out to the medevac helicopter, but the blood pool and the blood trails all over the hangar bay remained. Staff Sergeant and one other Marine wordlessly started mopping them up. The wet stuff came out, but the dark stains stayed. Staring at them later, I couldn't think of much worse than losing my vision. I hoped that if or when I got wounded, I'd keep my eyes. And my genitals, for that matter. I hoped the same for my men, and that night, I couldn't stop thinking about the young man whose eyes had been replaced by dark wells of blood.

Apparently, neither could Doc Crickard, because sometime toward the end of August he left the Outpost and was replaced by a new doctor whom we had never seen before. I bumped into the large soft-looking man and asked him casually what had happened to Doc Crickard. The new guy sort of shuffled his feet, and an embarrassed reply came back. "Oh, Doc

Crickard was rotated back to Hurricane Point. He was, uh, pretty burnt out from taking care of all the casualties."

I bit back my sarcastic reply and walked off. I was furious. The doctors got rotated, but the infantrymen were the ones fighting and dying out in the city, and there was no such thing as a day off the lines for us. The wounded and the dead continued to wear at my heart and mind, and it seemed that no matter where I turned, I couldn't escape the sight of them. Strangely enough, being outside the base had in some ways become easier than being inside it. At least out in the city you were focused, constantly busy evaluating the situation, making decisions, and keeping track of your men. When the casualties happened, they happened, and there wasn't much to be done about it.

Inside the base, though, there was nothing to do but brood on who'd be hurt next. Every time the booms rang out, or someone slammed a door, you jumped and the adrenaline started and you wondered who'd be brought inside in a litter, or if you'd have to go outside with litters of your own. You thought of all the things that had happened that you couldn't change, and you watched the bleeding young men brought in one at a time and wondered if they'd ever fully recover. Worst of all, you never, ever forgot, even for an instant, the inescapable truth that man is indeed mortal.

By late August, even the Gunny's hands had started ceaselessly shaking. The casualties got to everyone; there was little hope of rising above them. So, each night that I wasn't out in the city, I debated the probability of being called out on a mission before dawn. If I came down on the side of improbable, then I took two or three sleeping pills. If I came down on the side of probable, then I lay awake and consoled myself by telling myself that at least things couldn't get much worse for us than they were at the end of August.

THIRTY-FIVE

O f course, like nearly every other time I've challenged worse, I was wrong.

August 23, 3:30 AM found me in the COC, going over routine last-minute preparations with Hes, the current watch officer. We had a straightforward mission to protect the Government Center. Just outside, my Marines were assembling for the normal pre-mission inspection, and I could hear the quiet but insistent voices of my three squad leaders chivying them along. Together, Staff Sergeant and I quickly reviewed the position of all friendly units outside the Outpost. A squad from fourth platoon had just left the base on foot, en route to relieve the snipers at the Hotel OP. Their little pin put them a short two hundred meters outside the gates, and their patrol overlay indicated that they would continue straight down Michigan—the fastest way to the OP—until they hit the Hotel. Yesterday, an IED had exploded along Michigan, so it wasn't the route I would have chosen, but it was early enough in the morning to justify the decision. Other than that, no other units were out. Everything seemed normal. Hes gave me permission to leave, and Staff Sergeant and I hurried outside for the quick final inspection.

I was in a bit of a rush—we were running about twenty minutes behind schedule—so the inspection was somewhat perfunctory. Once it finished, the platoon mounted up, and sometime between 4:30 and 5:00, we roared out of the Outpost gates. Behind me, I heard Mahardy call it in.

"COC, be advised, Joker One has just left the Outpost en route to the Government Center in five Humvees."

Just as planned, the vehicles cut across all four lanes of Michigan at the median break in front of the Outpost. In the lead Humvee, I turned around as soon as we straightened out on the southern side of the road. Behind me, the other four vehicles carefully negotiated the median break. As soon I saw that they had all made it through, we would gun the engines and accelerate from a dangerously slow ten miles per hour to a much greater IED-defying speed. We were going against traffic, because there wasn't too much at that time of night, and anyway, I was more afraid of IEDs than collisions. In the driver's seat, Lance Corporal Waters suddenly fidgeted with something. The movement was unusual, and I turned to look at him. He had taken off his night vision goggles and placed them in his lap. For a driver, that move was a strict no-no. My night vision gear, a monocular device, remained tightly clamped to my left eye.

"Waters," I said, "what the hell are you doing? Why did you just put your goggles in your lap?"

"Look, sir. Streetlights're working up ahead. Goggles'll white out there and I won't be able to see. Plus, sir, you see those lights on the horizon? It looks like one of those trucker convoys that the hajjis run sometimes at night is heading our way. If the streetlights don't do it, those headlights'll white out my goggles for sure. I've only got the Seven-Bravos [an older generation of goggles that cover both eyes instead of just one]. I can't afford to be whited out. I'll put 'em back on once we're in the backstreets and there's no light and I don't need to worry about it anymore."

It made sense to me, and, anyway, Bowen had just called from the last vehicle to let me know that his Humvees were through the median and ready to roll. I gave the order.

"Waters, punch it. Let's do this."

"Roger that, sir." He accelerated rapidly, and within a few seconds all five vehicles were speeding the wrong way down Michigan. We traveled for a few blocks and began approaching a bend, one that started at the exact site of the IED attack the day before. I clenched up. As Waters slowed a bit to negotiate the curve, bright pink halogen lights suddenly flared in our eyes. The oncoming trucker convoy was a scant hundred meters away and approaching fast.

Waters shouted at me. "Which side of the road do you want me on, sir?" It was a critical question—when playing chicken with a tractor-trailer, we had learned through earlier experience that the best way of getting them to swerve was to pick a lane early, stay in it tenaciously, and force the oncoming traffic to adjust to us. Through a few near misses, we had learned that if you failed to clearly telegraph your intent, then you wound up with the same problem that people on foot have when approaching someone in a crowd: You move to your right, they move to their left, which puts you on collision course again and you almost hit each other, so you both move back to your original courses and almost hit each other again—the little age-old dance that you do in crowds all the time. Now we were doing it at fifty miles an hour with a convoy of semis.

I shouted back—they were almost on us, and the roar was deafening. "Stick close to the median. Don't pull up on the sidewalk—fourth's got a squad somewhere around here."

"Roger that!" Waters pulled our Humvee as far north as he could, almost scraping against the concrete lane divider. Then the trucks were on us. My night vision goggles whited out. My uncovered right eye went blind. I couldn't hear anything, just the roar of the passing convoy.

However, I could feel, and sometime during the passage of the last few trucks I felt a gut-wrenching double thump.

Thump-thump.

Just like that, with a mere split second's pause between the two. The Humvee jigged, then scraped up against the median. Waters slammed on the brakes.

I was irate. "Waters, what the hell? Did you just run over the median?"

'll never forget a single word of the reply. Wide-eyed, Waters turned to look at me as our vehicle literally screeched to a halt. I could only barely see him out of my right eye—the goggles over my left weren't working.

"No, sir!" he screamed at me. "I think we just hit a fucking Marine!"

My anger evaporated. Time slowed down. The vehicle behind, carrying the rest of first squad, slammed into our rear as Waters brought us to a complete stop, but I didn't even notice. Somehow, I was out of the Humvee before it fully stopped, running back along the slowing convoy to where I had heard that horrible thump. I was so confused—I had no idea whom we had hit or even who could possibly be out in the middle of the highway at 5 AM. It didn't dawn on me that fourth platoon might have been walking down the middle of Michigan rather than on the sidewalks, but it didn't take me long to locate the sprawled body of a Marine lying on the north side of Michigan. Our impact had flung him across the median.

I hurdled the little wall at a sprint and ran up to the still form. He had no helmet and his head was swelling. I don't want to describe it, so I won't. Suffice to say, the injury looked bad, and the Marine wasn't conscious. I immediately screamed into the PRR for my docs. Then I turned to Mahardy, faithfully behind me as always. I still wish that he hadn't had to share that sight with me. I called in the medevac.

"COC, this is One-Actual. Be advised, we have just run over a Marine west of the Michigan-Racetrack traffic circle. Break." Through the swelling, I could recognize the Marine, and what had happened suddenly struck me. "It's Lance Corporal Aldrich. He has a severe head injury. Medevac is urgent surgical. He will need a helo to Baghdad ASAP." As I spoke, Docs Smith and Camacho ran up. They were carrying a stretcher. "I've got the vehicles right here, so I'll stabilize Aldrich and get him back to the Outpost ASAP. Over."

Hes's voice came back. "Roger, One, I copy all. I'll arrange the medevac. Three out." Unlike the Ox, Hes knew better than to ask clarifying questions in the middle of a crisis.

I put down the radio handset and turned to Staff Sergeant. He had overheard the whole thing, and as my eyes met his, he nodded and went into action, screaming at the Marines to turn the vehicles around immediately. Noriel got into the action shortly thereafter, and all five of my Humvees backed up, performing quick three-point turns in the middle of the highway.

Meanwhile, the fourth platoon squad leader, Sergeant Ford, made his way back to Aldrich's position. We talked quickly for a bit, and he explained to me that he had moved the northern half of his squad off Michigan's north sidewalk because of the IED that had just yesterday exploded at the traffic circle. Fearing another of the same sort, he had instead had his men walk on the southern side of Michigan, just inside the median. If another IED were to go off, at least the bottom halves of his men would be protected by the thick concrete. It made sense, but I had assumed that fourth would have been traveling down the sidewalks like almost every other squad. Now my assumption was lying unconscious in the street.

Ford also explained to me that, like us, his squad had been completely blinded and deafened by the convoy. Aldrich had been rear security for the squad, and even after our Humvee struck him, the front of the patrol, oblivious to what had happened, continued walking for a few minutes until somehow the command to stop was communicated up to them. I offered to take the entire squad back with us to the Outpost, but Ford shook his head.

"Sir, we've still got a mission. We're going to continue it. You just get Aldrich back to the Outpost." Then he stood up and turned around. The rest of the squad was dispersed along the two sidewalks, kneeling and waiting for direction. I don't know how many of them fully grasped what had happened, but every man that I could see seemed relatively calm. Ford gave the signal to move out, and the squad picked up and resumed the patrol. I was stunned by the professionalism.

Just a few minutes later, the docs fitted a cervical collar around Aldrich, and, together with most of first squad, they loaded him into our second Humvee. We roared back into the Outpost, where the Navy doctor was waiting to take Aldrich from us. We unloaded him quickly. Back in the rear two vehicles of the convoy, third squad remained bewildered. The whole thing had taken place so quickly that they had no idea why we had inexplicably turned around mid-mission and headed back to base. Such is the fog of war.

Once Aldrich had been unloaded, I told the squad leaders to hold fast while I explained to the COC what had happened. There, I found the CO awake and clued in. I was terrified—we had just severely wounded one of our own men, and I had no idea what he would say to me. I was worried that he would start an interrogation rather than asking me for a detailed explanation, or, worse, that he would begin a lecture before I had a chance to explain myself.

I needn't have been. Quietly, the CO pulled me aside and asked simply for my story. For at least ten minutes, I spoke and he listened. When my words were exhausted, the CO nodded and calmly answered my unspoken question.

"One, it looks like the perfect storm hit us. I know your prep was good and I know that fourth was doing the right thing. I don't think this was the result of laziness or sloppiness. I don't think this was anyone's fault. I don't think it was your fault. Like I said before, no matter how good you are, sometimes shit happens to us. Now, you need to get back out there and relieve second platoon. Let me worry about the stuff here—we'll do an investigation and I know that it will show that all of us were doing the right thing. Like I said earlier, even when you're good, bad things sometimes just happen. Now you go. I need you out in that city."

At the time, I couldn't properly express my gratitude for his calm leadership, so I left wordlessly and continued the mission. An hour later, we were at the Government Center, and I was trying to explain to Quist what had happened, but I couldn't really get the words out, so I told him to ask the CO when he got back.

Halfway through the day, the Weapons Company XO showed up with a Weapons Company convoy, and he told me what the COC didn't want to, despite my repeated inquiries.

Aldrich was dead.

Though multiple investigations went exactly as the CO predicted, to this day I still think about how it could have been different if I had told Waters to go left instead of right, if I had dragged our precombat inspection out only two minutes longer, if I had spent a little less time in the COC before the mission. On that day, up on the roof of the Government Center, I played these same mind games all night long, as did Waters. Neither of us slept for the entire thirty-hour mission, and, sometime during the night, it occurred to me that Bolding and Aldrich had been best friends. The two of them had planned to room together in college down in Houston when they got out of the Corps. I had failed them both.

By the time the platoon finally got back to the Outpost early the next morning, I was mentally broken. Soon after the vehicles entered the gates, the world started spinning around me, and I barely made it to the aid station before I collapsed on one of the green canvas cots. The sympathetic Navy doctors gave me a shot of Phenergan to stop the nausea, and then they sedated me through an IV drip. I remained unconscious for hours, and during that time, I missed my first, and only, mission day with Joker One.

Part 5

TIRED

THIRTY-SIX

While we lost Carson and Leza and Niles and Aldrich and too many others all throughout August, America focused on something completely incomprehensible to us—the 2004 Summer Olympics, held in Greece. Apparently, the games began sometime in mid-August and continued through the month's end. Even as we patrolled the dirty, violent streets of Ramadi, competing grimly in the ultimate game, much of the rest of the world watched genteel athletic events in the comfort of their own homes, athletic events, by the way, that had their earliest origins in our world. For us, though, these watered-down games and their associated watered-down medals seemed so distant from our lives, so totally irrelevant to the unglamorous, messy fighting playing out every day in the alleys and buildings of Ramadi, that we couldn't be bothered to keep up with them.

But they managed to creep into our lives anyway. During the second week of the games, the soccer portion of them began, and when this event kicked off, the Iraqi national team took the field. They may very well have been the only true heroes to grace the Olympic screen that summer, for despite a horrendous training environment, terrible funding, and the uncertain future of the land they called home, this mixed-ethnicity team had nevertheless managed to qualify for the Olympics. During each game, every citizen of Ramadi, it seemed, sat glued to their satellite televisions. As they watched, their national team inevitably scored a goal or two, and when each goal was scored, the rapt people of Ramadi celebrated as only they could—by walking outside and firing their machine guns in unison into the air.

The first time this new phenomenon occurred, Marine units throughout the city took cover and called in terse reports of massive enemy ambushes. When the citywide gunfire cut off nearly as suddenly as it started, the entire battalion was perplexed, but eventually someone put two and two together and ferreted out the connection between Olympic soccer goals and widespread random gunfire. From that day forward, before each patrol left the wire, it received an Olympic soccer schedule update along with its regular intelligence briefing. So, those of us in Ramadi shared something in common with the folks back home after all: an intense preoccupation with international athletic competition. But while the Iraqi soccer team, the Cinderella story of the 2004 games, brought entertainment and maybe some hope to Iraq and America alike, to us each of its unlikely victories simply meant a greater chance of being killed by random, pointless gunfire.

At the very end of August, Joker One was itself caught in one of these insanely dangerous celebrations. Unsurprisingly, we were securing the Government Center at the time, and midnight found me, as usual, dozing on the roof of the compound, lying on my back next to a waist-high pile of sandbags sheltering a radio. Suddenly the city erupted in gunfire, and a few seconds later one of my Marines, Lance Corporal Anderson, was shaking me awake.

"Sir, sir, sir. There's shooting all around, sir. You'd better take a look, sir."

I didn't bother to sit up. Instead I simply opened my eyes, and, still lying on my back, I looked up at the sky. Sure enough, the tracer laser light show streaked straight up into the air all around us. Without moving, I asked Anderson the straightforward follow-up question.

"Is the shooting at us?"

Anderson looked puzzled for a moment, and he paused and cocked his head, listening for the unmistakable sounds of bullets cracking nearby. He didn't hear any.

"No, sir. I don't think it's at us."

I nodded. "Well, Anderson, just wake me up then when they start shooting at us," I replied. Then I closed my eyes again and focused on getting back to sleep. The gunfire and the light show continued for a few moments, and Anderson walked unconcernedly back to his bunker while I slowly slipped back into my light doze. We had come a long way from those first skittish days in Ramadi.

When September opened, Corporal Brooks came down with a weeklong case of dysentery from which he recovered exceptionally slowly—too slowly. When I finally asked him about the malingering, his excuse was honest and surprising: My team leader couldn't get the image of the injured little girl from May 27 out of his head. Again and again, he pictured his own daughter in her place—they were roughly the same age—and as the days passed, that macabre mental picture loomed larger and larger in his head until he felt that he couldn't continue without some sort of rest.

Just a few days later, Noriel snapped and threw a light machine gun at one of Bowen's Marines. The fury was out of proportion to the minor offense, and a large portion of the platoon was stunned by the outburst. Noriel later apologized, but it was too late. The incident had cost him some hard-won credibility, and it temporarily strained relations between my first- and third-squad leaders.

Even Bowen was affected by the strain—the very next day, I noticed him half jogging out of the hangar bay. When I intercepted him, he was openly weeping. Being Bowen, he apologized for his unmanly display, and, still crying, he turned to leave, promising me that the next time he saw me, he'd be fine. Without thinking, I grabbed my squad leader and wrapped my arms around him. He pushed me away for a bit, but soon enough the sobs got louder, and Bowen stopped pushing. There we stood, chest to chest for who knows how long, hugging each other through weapons and body armor and grenades and all the other bits of gear hanging off our chests. When the sobs slowed and he was finally able to speak again, Bowen told me how every day Staff Sergeant and the Gunny took advantage of his competence (he didn't say exactly that, but I read between the lines). Every day, he found himself overtasked because every task he did, he performed to near perfection. And every time he fell a little short, Staff Sergeant or the Gunny chewed him out with no regard for his constant commitment to go above and beyond his regular duties, ones that were weighty enough for two men.

Hearing the story, I realized that I had failed him—Bowen was my squad leader, my responsibility, and it was my job to protect him from everyone who would misuse him. Once again, I didn't know how to respond, so I simply asked Bowen to come to me every time someone other than me tasked him with something. Then I told him that I thought he was the best Marine in the whole damned battalion.

Leza probably would have been affected as well, but in early September he was in a stateside hospital having a metal rod put into his snapped lower leg. His absence hit me hard sometimes—when I walked into the platoon house and didn't see him, or when I turned to find him on a mission and he wasn't there, or when I issued an order only to hear a strange voice reply, "Roger that, sir."

All of the absences hit me hard by now, and it had become nearly impossible to sleep. During the days, I obsessed about the insomnia. During the nights, I obsessed about the missing, especially Bolding and Aldrich. To my dismay, the CO eventually had to pull me aside and refocus my attention on doing my job, not on avoiding casualties, for my men were starting to be affected by my reluctance to leave the base. As September continued, I became less and less effective as a combat leader.

THIRTY-SEVEN

ortunately, the rest of Joker One picked up the slack as we approached our final two weeks in Ramadi. In spite of their weariness, in spite of the ever-increasing strain, Bowen, Noriel, Teague, and all my other team leaders made one last push to the finish. They inspected their men with care, planned their missions in detail, and gently corrected me when I made mistakes. They held themselves together, and, watching them lead, I started a slow recovery, although I didn't know it at the time.

Their men were even more amazing. The Mahardys and the Hendersons and the Guzons—the ones who'd deployed with barely two months of training and who'd kept me awake with worry on the plane flight over—had been transformed from wide-eyed recruits into slit-eyed combat veterans. They'd seen all the horrors of war firsthand, again and again, but somehow they retained their faith in each other and in their mission. They knew with unshakable certainty that the Corps was strong and that Joker One was strong and that given enough time, we'd prevail no matter what the circumstances.

They loved one another and their mission—the people of Ramadi—in a way that I didn't fully appreciate until just a few days before we left the city, during the second week of September. I'd run into Mahardy, smoking outside the hangar bay as usual, and I'd asked him the standard throwaway question: Was he excited to go home? The response shocked me.

On the one hand, Mahardy said, he was excited to see his family, but on the other, he was sad to leave before the job in Ramadi was finished. We'd worked hard, and we'd come a long way, and Mahardy was worried that our replacements would just screw things up, would treat the people harshly and erase whatever small gains we had made in winning them over. Furthermore, going home meant that his new family, Joker One, wouldn't be around all the time like they were now. Mahardy loved the guys, he said, and he wasn't sure what he'd do without them there.

As I asked more of my Marines the same question I'd asked Mahardy, more of them gave me the same answer he had. The consistency of the responses shocked me. I couldn't in any way relate to wanting to stay in Ramadi. A good portion of the city's residents hated us just for being American, and a smaller but still sizable chunk of them actively tried to kill us every day. Why would anyone want to risk his life to help these people? How could anyone love them? What does it really mean to love?

It has taken time and distance from it all for me to understand fully what my Marines had been telling me then, but now I think that I get it. Now I think that I understand a bit more about what it means to truly love, because for my men, love was something much more than emotion. For them, love was expressed in the only currency that mattered in combat: action—a consistent pattern running throughout the large and the small, a pattern of sacrifice that reinforced the idea that we all cared more for the other than we did for ourselves. For them, love was about deeds, not words, and as I reflected that day on the love of my men, a thousand small acts came to mind.

Love was why Waters gave Mahardy his last cigarette.

It was why Mahardy said, "Fuck you, I'm not taking your last one," and gave it back.

It was why Docs Smith and Camacho chose to live in Joker One's compound when they could have had much nicer rooms with the other corpsmen in the hangar bay: why they forced the Marines to take off their boots every day so that they could inspect their disgusting feet.

Love was why Bowen taught classes on patrol overlays instead of sleeping: why Noriel cursed unintelligibly at his men when they practiced patrolling without their heavy body armor; why Teague walked point every day so that if something bad happened, it would happen first to him.

And love was why Brooks walked backward every day, guarding our vulnerable rear as we moved.

As time went by, these small acts—so many of which I either failed to notice or simply took for granted—created something in Joker One that was more than just the sum of all of us. In fact, these acts gave Joker One a life of its own, a life that wove all of us inextricably into itself, until the pain and the joy felt by one were the pain and the joy felt by all. And that life grew so vibrant, and so powerful, that my men practiced the ultimate extension of love—laying down their lives for one another—nearly every single day.

So Joker One was why Raymond and his team formed a wall in front of me when I was caught in that tangle of concertina wire. Joker One was why Yebra ran into the middle of a citywide firefight despite his horribly weakened condition; why he fixed a radio until his brain boiled and he passed out, convulsing.

Joker One was why Williams patrolled with a limp.

Joker One was why Kepler climbed into a helicopter gun run while everyone else took cover; why Doc Camacho ran into the middle of a fire-swept street, waving his arms, asking the enemy to please shoot at him.

Joker One was why Niles guarded a compound entrance until everyone else had made it safely inside.

For me, then, loving Joker One—something I so desperately hoped that I did—meant much more than simply feeling that I cared. It meant patience when explaining something for the fifth time to a nineteen-year-old who just didn't get it. It meant kindness when dealing with a Marine who had made an honest mistake while trying his hardest; mercy when deciding the appropriate punishment. It meant dispensing justice and then forgetting that it had been dispensed, punishing wrong and then wiping the slate clean.

Love was joy at the growth of my men, even when it diminished my own authority. It was giving the credit for our successes to the team while assuming all the responsibility for our failures on myself. It was constantly teaching my men, sharing everything with them until I had nothing left to give, with the expectation and the hope that they would become greater than me. It was making myself less so that they might become more.

Love accepted the Marines for exactly who they were and never believed that it was all they ever would be. Love demanded more, demanded their best, every single day; it cut through all rationalizations and excuses. It constantly celebrated the good in my men and refused to condone the natural selfishness that dwelt within us all.

Love told the honest truth when lying would have been much easier or would have made me look much better; it admitted to the men that sometimes I had no answers. It confessed my mistakes and asked for forgiveness when I had wronged, and it moved past those mistakes when forgiveness had been granted.

Love hoped that things would be better someday, maybe in this life or maybe in the next, but it didn't deny the reality of the pain and suffering that surrounded us day in and day out; it didn't dishonestly rationalize them or explain them away. Love didn't try to make sense of the senseless; it simply offered a light to run to.

But, like now, that light grew dim sometimes. So, sometimes, love meant just getting out of bed in the morning when everything inside screamed to rest, just for one day. Sometimes it meant simply putting one foot in front of the other on patrol. And sometimes it meant continuing the mission when you didn't see any progress, meant protecting the defenseless, refraining from pulling the trigger, putting yourself at greater risk, doing what you knew to be right even though you didn't really want to.

So that was how we loved those who hated us; blessed those who persecuted us; daily laid down our lives for our neighbors. No matter what we felt, we tried to demonstrate love through our daily actions. Now I understand more about what it means to truly love, and what it means to love your neighbor—how you can do it even when your neighbor literally tries to kill you.

And now I understand the true magnitude of what Bolding did.

At the time of the attack that took his life, I thought that Bolding had died for us. Now I know that, as much as he laid down his life for his brothers, Bolding also laid down his life for a group of small, badly wounded Iraqi children, trading his legs, his blood, and his future so that they might have a chance for a future of their own. More than any of us, Bolding had lived out the greater-love principle to its fullest possible extent.

On September 9, 2004, Joker One loaded up into trucks and prepared to head out of the Outpost for Junction City en route to the United States and home. We were leaving with fewer than we came, and the knowledge sat heavy on me as I hopped into the cab of my vehicle. However, we had done our very best, and we loved one another with everything we had. In the platoon, we had created something much greater than any of us, something that I hoped we would take with us for the rest of our lives. In Ramadi, we had made mistakes and paid the price, but to the fullest extent possible we had cared for those whom war always traps between bad and worse.

Looking back through the window at my men, seeing them smiling and pushing one another and slapping magazines into their weapons for the last time, I understood how much we had accomplished and how hard we had tried. After Aldrich, faith and hope had left me, and I despaired, but now I realized that love somehow remained. Slowly, it began to restore the other two.

THIRTY-EIGHT

After two weeks of waiting for a plane to become available, Joker One finally flew to Kuwait and from there back to the States. On September 25, 2004, we formed up with the rest of the company at the armory in Camp Pendleton, California. It was late there, around ten o'clock, but that hadn't stopped our loved ones from gathering to greet us. We could hear their cheers, just a few hundred yards away, up on top of a hill where they couldn't quite see us down at the armory. Once the company had assembled in a rough column of four squares, we set off up the hill, the CO marching at our head, Joker One and I following just behind him.

When the CO and the flag bearer preceding him crested the hill, the crowd erupted. The company marched toward them, eyes straight forward, hands swinging stiffly by our sides, heads held high. I don't know what the rest of the men were thinking then, but I, for one, felt proud. Ramadi hadn't become a bastion of security and stability on our watch, but it hadn't completely fallen to the insurgents, either. To prevent that, we had fought every day, street by street and house by house, bringing only what we could carry on our backs. We had fought hard, and we had persevered, and maybe the city was a little bit better for having had us there.

However, we had taken a tremendous beating in the process. The battalion had suffered thirty-four killed and over ten times that number wounded in seven and a half months. Across 2/4, those numbers worked out to be a little less than one out of every three men. In Golf Company, the ratio was even higher: Roughly one out of every two of us had been wounded. However, our sister company, Echo, had suffered the worst: They had suffered twenty-two killed, about one out of every eight men. They had quite literally been decimated. Later, we were told that when we returned to the States, we had taken more casualties than any battalion—Marine or Army—since Vietnam.

These thoughts flitted briefly through my mind as the company stopped its march directly in front of the gathered crowd. As one man, the battalion turned left and faced our shouting loved ones, and, staring at them as I saluted our CO and our flag, I was reminded of the tremendous price we had paid to march back with our heads held high. There in front of me, waving his right arm only, was Carson. His left was bound up in a sling. Leza and Niles stood next to him, both on crutches, and Boren was there with his wife and his cane. When the CO dismissed us, and the Marines of Joker One flooded out of the ranks to run into the arms of their crying wives, to hug their mothers and fathers, to have their little ones jump into their arms, I couldn't help but think that our joy was incomplete. One of our families was missing. One of us hadn't made it back, and his wife and parents had no reason to come to California to greet us. Even as I kissed Christy, and even as I watched my men tearfully reunite with those who loved them, I thought about the one family to whom I hadn't been able to keep my promise.

Four days later, the entire battalion went on a month of leave. It was wonderful to be back in America—and what better place to be than Southern California—but everywhere I went, I felt a little naked. I was used to being armed to the teeth, used to having an entire squad around me everywhere I traveled. Without the knowledge that twelve men were watching over one another and me, I felt nervous around crowds, and I avoided them. Loud noises scared me, and I jumped every time a door slammed or a car backfired. I still had trouble sleeping.

Still, each day was a little bit better than its predecessor, and, slowly, I eased my way back into America. By the time sleeping in my own bed felt more or less normal, everyone had returned from their leave and their respective homes. It was wonderful to be around the men again. One month later, though, I found out that I was being replaced as Joker One's platoon commander. It wasn't a surprise—with only five months of active duty left for me, I had to turn my men over to a new leader sometime. However, it was one of the hardest things I have ever done, giving the men who had been the center of my world over to someone else who didn't know them as I did. I let them go all the same. Keeping the Marines any longer would have been selfish—they needed time and training with their new leader, and the longer I kept them, the less well they would all work together.

Shortly before I left, Joker One threw a platoon beach party, and at it the men gave me a surprise. Just as we were preparing to leave, Noriel gathered the men and walked them and me over to a pickup truck that had been backed up to the beach. I hadn't noticed it before. As we assembled around the tailgate, Noriel announced to me that the platoon had gotten together to give their departing leader a little something. Then he dropped the tailgate and revealed my present.

Stood on its side so I could look clearly into its glass front was a custommade hardwood case lined with red velvet. Inside it were mounted an officer's sword and sheath. To my surprise, the sword fit me exactly. I looked up at Noriel on discovering this, and he was grinning from ear to ear.

"Now you know why I asked your inseams, sir." He paused and looked at me expectantly. Still dumbfounded, I looked back. Noriel spoke up again. "Damn, sir, you're dry-eyed still. I was hoping you'd cry when you saw this." Then he walked over and handed me something small and jangling. I looked down. It was a whole host of dog tags, all strung together one after the other along the standard beaded metal chain. They were bent and dented. Some were still covered in sand.

Noriel spoke again, serious now. "Sir, those are all of us, sir. So you can remember us when you're gone." He paused, then. "Sir, we even got Bolding's dog tag for you."

Hearing that, I nearly did cry.

I left the platoon the next week, and I thought that it would be the last time I would see them together, but I was wrong. Three weeks later, we held a memorial service for the battalion's dead, and the CO called me to make sure that I would come. Up until the day of the service, I couldn't decide whether I wanted to be there—Bolding's family was coming, the CO had told me, and I didn't know how I could face them. But when the afternoon finally arrived, I pushed my fear aside and walked down to the event. Standing at the back, in the very last row of a crowd of Marines, I had a difficult time maintaining my composure as the chaplain honored our dead for the last time. At the front of the crowd, I could see Joker One, assembled together with their new leader at their head. Some time passed, more words were spoken by the company commanders, and eventually the service ended. My Marines broke up and formed a long line—they were paying their respects to Bolding's mother and sisters.

Supremely nervous, I walked over to the line and waited my turn. I don't know how long the waiting lasted—it seemed forever but too short—and the entire time I practiced the words that I wanted to say to Bolding's mother about her son. Her son was a hero, I wanted to tell her, and he died defending others, children who couldn't defend themselves. He was one of the best of all of us, and he never quit on his team. He lifted us all with his smile and his cheerful nature. We missed him.

Then, suddenly, I was there, in front of her, and I couldn't say anything at all. For a time, I looked at her, and she at me, and then I broke down sobbing. It was the first time I had cried about Bolding since we lost him, since the Gunny had held me in that miserable bathroom in Iraq. I couldn't speak coherently, and the only thing I said, over and over again through my sobs, was this:

"I'm sorry. I'm so sorry."

Then, though I couldn't see, so I can't describe exactly what happened, Bolding's mom was hugging me. Just like the Gunny had, she pulled me down into her chest, and I wrapped my arms around her and cried and cried until I couldn't cry anymore.

I don't remember if she said anything to me, but when the moment passed, I felt some measure of absolution. Life continued, and so would I. Some things I will never understand, but I accept that now, and I no longer demand full comprehension as the price of the pursuit of excellence. So I'll keep putting one foot in front of the other as best as I possibly can until my mission on earth ends and God takes me home.

AFTERWORD

I didn't write *Joker One* thinking that it would ever become a book, much less a bestseller. In fact, I never thought that anyone other than my men and their families would ever read our story, a story I wrote because I felt that it was the final thing I had to do as the leader of Joker One. You see, while I was a combat platoon commander, I failed to write enough awards for my men. I didn't realize that what we were doing in Ramadi was unique. I thought that everyone in Iraq was fighting as hard as we were, that everyone was suffering one-half to one-third wounded as they battled for months without ceasing. But they weren't. What we did was special, even for the bloody summer of 2004. Because I thought it was normal, though, I demanded nearly superhuman feats from my men before I wrote them up for awards. For what they did and what they endured, nearly all of my Marines deserved medals. I didn't do enough to ensure that they got them.

Also, as a young lieutenant, I didn't realize the supreme importance of martial decorations. It wasn't until I left the military (the first time) and saw how people were rewarded in the civilian world that I finally got it. In the military, the only thing that we can do to show our appreciation for above-and-beyond performance, performance that often demands a limb or a life as its toll, is to take a little bit of ribbon, and wrap it around a little bit of metal, and pin it on a man's camouflage fatigues. If he's dead, then we present the decoration to his widow, or his mother. Junior officers can't hand out extra vacation, or a cash bonus, or a desirable duty location, or a promotion. All of those rewards are out of our hands. All that we can do is take the time to tell the Marine Corps the story of our men in a format it understands and hope that the awards boards agree with us. Sometimes they do and sometimes they don't, but it doesn't matter; we can't control the boards. All we can do is make the effort, and I didn't do enough of that. My Marines don't have all of the medals they deserve.

I thought about my oversight as I progressed through my first year of business school nearly a year after returning from Iraq. Throughout my studies, I kept in touch with some of my men. To a man, they told me the same thing: "Sir, we don't really tell anyone else what happened overseas. Not even our families. They just don't get it. It's like trying to explain red to a blind man: no matter how hard you try, they'll never fully understand, so you just stop trying eventually, you know?"

I did know, but the fact that the parents and the wives of my men had no real idea of what their sons and their husbands had endured didn't sit well with me. My Marines had performed magnificently in an environment that demanded more than they should have been able to give. Undermanned and underequipped, these nineteen- and twenty-year-olds had never given up, had never succumbed to the pressure, the heat, or their own worst natures. They had fought hard, kept the faith, and finished their mission with honor. And their parents knew none of it.

So, knowing that I had stories left to tell and knowing that my men hadn't told them, I determined that I would write down what we had done. That way, my men could give the finished product to their families and say, "Here's what I did. Now you can read about it. I don't have to tell it." From there, one thing led to another, and now the stories are a book, and many people know what my Marines did. It doesn't make up for the lack of medals, I know, but it was the last unfinished thing I had to do. Having done it, I felt a sense of completion that I lacked earlier.

Now I'm writing this afterword nearly five years after the events of that fateful 2004 deployment. Since then, I've completed business school, had two daughters, and been recalled for yet another tour in Afghanistan. In fact, I finished *Joker One* while in Kabul, Afghanistan's capital. I'm willing to bet that it was the first time my editor and friend, Tim Bartlett, had worked with an author in a war zone—perhaps there should have been a clause in our contract that specified exactly what happened in the event that the author was exploded by a suicide car bomb.

At any rate, it feels somewhat strange now to be finally writing in the comfort of my own home. The first chapter of the book feels even more true today than when I penned it back at school: the events in Ramadi seem like they happened to someone else, somewhere else, in a different life maybe. Now I have my own house in a city where all the streetlights work, and the trash gets picked up, and the roads don't explode when you drive on them. I see my wife every day, and my daughters don't age in stop-motion photography. I can drive down the streets without scanning the rooftops. I can go to sleep at night without having to keep my boots on. I don't have to worry about someone trying their best tomorrow to kill everyone I love.

But everything in Ramadi really did happen, even though it seems like it didn't now. For me, it hits hard, and sometimes all at once. I'll see a half-finished parking garage, and it'll remind me of one of our observation posts in Iraq, and I'll think of the time that Philips fell off of a wall while trying to climb into the garage, and how we had to medevac him and how funny it was later but how amateurish it felt at the time. Then I'll think of other medevacs, like Niles or Leza, and nothing will be funny for a while. But our good friend the catfish always makes me smile, and I always seem to remember the good times with the bad.

From everything that I've heard from my men since the book came out, good mixed with bad seems to be a pervasive theme. The good was people sacrificing for each other: Teague walking point, Doc Camacho running through fire to treat our wounded, random taxis stopping during firefights to pick up hurt civilians. The bad was all of the evil that we saw: the children who exploded in front of us, the trash that never got picked up, Leza—screaming—on that damn green canvas stretcher. I remember them both, but for some reason it's the good that mainly sticks with me.

That's been the case for most, but not all, of the Marines I've talked with since the book came out. Noriel has gone back to college, gotten his bachelor's degree, and is now applying to nursing school. He wants to work at the VA. Going there was like coming home, he told me. Teague joined a reserve unit and spent time teaching other Marines to get ready to head to Iraq. Walter just rejoined the Corps after a stint as a civilian. Mahardy is back with his family in New York State, attending college. Leza is a policeman in El Paso. Waters is one somewhere else. Brown is a firefighter. Bowen, as far as I know, is still in the Corps. He was voted Marine of the Year for the entire 1st Marine Division in 2004, and he has a bright future ahead of him as one of the USMC's finest.

Others have struggled a bit more. One of them thanked me for telling our story, because it reminded him of all the good we did in Iraq and all of the good times we had over there. Prior to the book, it seemed that all he remembered was the bad. Feldmeir deserted shortly after returning from Iraq. He rejoined the platoon sometime later, but he didn't last much longer before he was discharged. Carson achieved his goal in the Corps—he made it through sniper school to earn the coveted sniper specialty—but he eventually had to be medically discharged because his shoulder never fully healed.

To a man, though, every one of my men who has contacted me has been thrilled that their story has been told. They say that they appreciate the honesty and the reality, although I never set out be particularly good at either. Indeed, some have told me that they remember their roles in some incidents a bit differently than I do, and their points are fair. It's a nearly impossible thing, to put together a single firefight completely and accurately. It's even harder to string together a whole series of them; I have no doubt that I left out some notable deeds that should have been included, and that I included some things that should have been left out. When it comes to the overall story, though, everyone who's talked to me is in agreement: *Joker One* faithfully represents what happened to us during our bloody 2004 deployment, for better and for worse.

As for me, well, I like to think that I've come out of war a better young man than I was when I went into it. There are some things I'll struggle with for a long time, like why Bolding died, and why a lot of my men got hurt, and why I came through unscathed. But I've got life in front of me when so many don't, and it's my responsibility to live as best as I can for all of those who cannot. Every time I'm tempted to quit something worth doing because it's hard, or every time that I begin to feel sorry for myself and my circumstances, I think of all of my friends who are dead and how they'd love to have my problems. I think of everyone I know who's come out so wounded that just getting out of bed is a supreme obstacle, and I get instant perspective on my own problems.

Every time my daughter asks the same question for the fourteenth time, I remind myself of how painful life was separated from her, how I would have given anything for her to drive me batty with repeated "Why?" questions. Every time work goes poorly, I remind myself that no one died today. I'm more patient with my wife because I no longer take her for granted (as much), and I'm more patient with the small inconveniences of life in America because I no longer take her for granted, either.

So, one day at a time, I shoulder my load and do my small part to fight to keep our country great. I'm no longer in the service, but that doesn't mean I can't serve. I owe it to Bolding, to Wroblowski, to Winchester, and to everyone else who never came home to do my best every day. In so doing, I hope that I can bring honor to my God, my country, and my Corps. Life is good, and I now know that I don't live it for myself. And I finally understand why the "always" is so important in our motto.

Semper Fidelis.

ACKNOWLEDGMENTS

First, I would like to thank my wife, undoubtedly my better half (as everyone who has ever met both of us says), for her courage, strength, and unfailing support throughout three combat deployments, one involuntary recall, and six years of marriage. I could never have written a short story, let alone this book, without her. Throughout the entire process, she served as my editor, cheerleader, confidante, and counselor. I am a blessed man.

I must also thank Professor Nitin Nohria and Scott Snook of Harvard Business School for 1) their friendship, 2) their insight, and 3) making my dream a reality. They took the time out of their busy schedules to sponsor a veteran's writing project as a full-credit business school class. This book is the result of them pushing me to turn my chapters in on time. I also owe a great deal of thanks to my Harvard classmates, all of whom gave very generously of their time and advice in order to help a rough-around-the-edges infantryman adapt to the business world. I could not have asked for better friends and better people to help ease the reintegration into civilian life.

My agent, first editor, and dear friend Eve Bridburg also deserves more than I can give her. She took a bet on a complete unknown and then worked amazingly hard to turn a loose collection of war stories into a coherent narrative fit to give to publishing-house editors. Though she's been wonderful as an agent, it's her friendship that I value most of all. And speaking of friends, Craig Perry, one of my closest friends on this earth, took his very limited time to read all of my earliest work and give invaluable insight and advice.

Nate Fick—writer, friend, and Marine officer extraordinaire—helped make this book possible. Not only did he give excellent advice along the way, but he also read the entire finished product and gave indispensable critical insight. After I was recalled (and before this book caught the attention of any editors), Phil Kapusta, my boss at Special Operations Command Central, did the same thing Nate did, only Phil did it from an active-duty SEAL's perspective. He didn't have the time, but somehow he made it because he is a terrific leader.

Of course, my editor at Random House, Tim Bartlett, warrants great thanks for all the hard work he put into making this book as good as it could possibly be. Any shortcomings in the work have everything to do with me and nothing to do with him. Lindsey Schwoeri, Tim's assistant, has been wonderful as well.

PepsiCo as an organization also gets special mention. Without its unflinching support for my family and me, my third combat deployment would have been much more diffcult than it was. I am very lucky to work for such a terrific company staffed by such terrific people.

My amazing parents, Polly and Donovan Jr., are responsible for all of my success and none of my shortcomings. They have sacrificed quite a bit and done a wonderful job raising my four brothers and me. My greatest hope is that I can make them proud all of the days of their lives.

Others who deserve special mention are Brendan O'Donohoe, David Perpich, Arthur Golden, Ayan Mandal, Michael Stern, and Luke Eddinger, for all their help, wisdom, and friendship.

I thank all the men of Joker One. You taught me more than I can put into words. Hopefully, by the time you get to this part of the book, you know how much you mean to me.

Finally, I thank God, from whom all blessings flow.

GLOSSARY OF MILITARY TERMS

AK-47—A gas-operated assault rifle used in many Eastern Bloc and Arab countries. Cheap and easy to maintain, this rifle was used by Iraqi security forces, private contractors, and insurgents alike.

Battalion—A Marine infantry unit composed of three rifle companies, one weapons company, one headquarters company, and a small company staff. Usually around 1,200 men in total.

Call sign—The name a person uses when talking over the radio. For security reasons, the call sign is never the same as the person's real name.

Cammies—Marine slang for camouflage utility uniforms.

CO—Commanding officer.

Company—A Marine infantry unit composed of three rifle platoons and one light weapons platoon. Usually around 170 men.

Company gunnery sergeant—The enlisted Marine responsible for all of the company's training and logistical support. Called "company gunny" for short, this person is usually one of the two most senior enlisted Marines in the company.

Corporal—The lowest-ranking Marine noncommissioned officer. Usually has between three and five years of enlistment in the Marine Corps.

Enlisted—Any Marine who has not received a formal commission into the officer ranks. Usually, but not always, these Marines do not have a college degree.

EOD—Explosive Ordnance Disposal. Experts in the defusing and disposing of bombs, these men are called in every time a unit discovers an explosive device.

Fire team—A four-man unit consisting of a team leader, a SAW gunner, an assistant SAW gunner, and a grenadier armed with an M-203 attached below his M-16. Three fire teams make up a squad.

Flak—The Marine term for Kevlar vests that we wear in combat. With a pair of ceramic small-arms protective insert (SAPI) plates inside, the vest is capable of stopping AK-47 bullets. Without the plates, the vest will stop only shrapnel. Together, the plates and vest weigh almost seventeen pounds.

HQ—Headquarters.

IED—Improvised explosive device. The signature weapon of the Iraq war, the IED is a homemade bomb consisting of an explosive component—usually an old artillery shell or mortar round—and a remote detonating device, which can be anything from a length of communication wire to a cellphone receiver.

Kevlar—The Marine term for the Kevlar helmets that we wear in combat.

M-16—Short for M-16A4. The brand-new version of the assault rifle used by U.S. Marines in Iraq. Unlike the previous version, the M-16A2, the M-16A4 features a rail system that runs the length of the rifle's handgrips and upper receiver.

M-203—A tubular attachment to the M-16A4 that enables the weapon to launch 40mm grenades, which closely resemble large, fat, stubby bullets. It can be found just underneath the M-16's barrel.

M-249 SAW—Squad automatic weapon. A light machine gun carried by three Marines in every infantry squad.

NCO—Noncommissioned officer. The enlisted Marine leaders, the NCO corps is often referred to as "the backbone of the Marine Corps."

OCS—Officer Candidate School. A ten-week program that screens college students for commissioning as Marine officers.

Officer—A Marine formally commissioned into the officer ranks. All officers must pass a screening board and must have a college degree.

Platoon—A forty-three-man Marine infantry unit composed of three infantry squads, a platoon sergeant (usually a staff sergeant), and a platoon commander (usually a lieutenant).

Platoon commander—A Marine platoon's only officer and the man responsible for everything his men do or fail to do. He is the platoon's formal leader.

Platoon sergeant—A Marine platoon's senior enlisted leader and the platoon commander's right-hand man. He is usually responsible for the platoon's logistic and administrative issues, and he often advises the platoon commander before, during, and after operations.

PT—Physical training. The civilian version of the term is "workout."

ROTC—Reserve Officers' Training Corps. A program that offers college scholarships in return for military training during college and a military commitment thereafter.

RPG—Rocket-propelled grenade. The most common system is the RPG-7, a man-portable, shoulder-fired, muzzle-loaded antitank grenade launcher. A favorite of the insurgents, the RPG-7 consists of two pieces: the rocket warhead and a reusable launch tube. The warhead looks much like a half-sized American football with a finned cylinder protruding about a foot and a half out of one end.

SAPI—Small-arms protective insert. Ceramic plates inserted into specially designed pouches on the front and back of our Kevlar vests. Roughly as big as a man's chest and stomach, these plates are capable of stopping most rifle bullets.

SMAW—Shoulder-launched multipurpose assault weapon. The U.S. version of the RPG-7, this system consists of a man-portable, reloadable firing tube and the rockets themselves. Much more cumbersome to carry than the RPG-7.

Squad—A thirteen-man infantry unit. Consisting of three four-man fire teams and one leader, the squad is usually the smallest unit that is deployed independently in the USMC infantry in Iraq.

2/4—2d Battalion, 4th Marine Regiment.

USMC—United States Marine Corps.

XO—Executive officer. Usually the right-hand man of a unit's commanding officer and the person responsible for the training and logistical resupply of the company.

DONOVAN CAMPBELL is the bestselling author of *Joker One* and *The Leader's Code*. He graduated from Princeton University and Harvard Business School, finished first in his class at the Marines' Basic Officer Course, and served three combat deployments—two in Iraq and one in Afghanistan. He was awarded the Combat Action Ribbon and a Bronze Star with Valor for his time in Iraq. He presently lives in Dallas, Texas, with his wife and daughters.

DONOVAN CAMPBELL is available for select readings and lectures. To inquire about a possible appearance, please contact the Random House Speakers Bureau at 212-572-2013 or rhspeakers@randomhouse.com.

Printed in the United States
by Baker & Taylor Publisher Services